Ouida

Folle-Farine

Ouida

Folle-Farine

ISBN/EAN: 9783742852298

Manufactured in Europe, USA, Canada, Australia, Japa

Cover: Foto ©Andreas Hilbeck / pixelio.de

Manufactured and distributed by brebook publishing software (www.brebook.com)

Ouida

Folle-Farine

COLLECTION
OF
BRITISH AUTHORS

TAUCHNITZ EDITION.

VOL. 1195.

FOLLE-FARINE BY OUIDA.

IN TWO VOLUMES.

VOL. I.

"Un gazetier fumeux qui se croit un flambeau
 Dit au pauvre qu'il a noyé dans les ténèbres :
 Où donc l'aperçois-tu ce Créateur du Beau ?
 Ce Redresseur que tu célèbres ?"

BAUDELAIRE.

FOLLE-FARINE.

BY

OUIDA,

AUTHOR OF "IDALIA," "STRATHMORE," ETC.

COPYRIGHT EDITION.

IN TWO VOLUMES.

VOL. I.

LEIPZIG

BERNHARD TAUCHNITZ

1872.

The Right of Translation is reserved.

A

LA MEMOIRE

D'Ingres.

PEINTRE.—POËTE.

FOLLE-FARINE.

BOOK I.

DUST.

CHAPTER I.

Not the wheat itself; not even so much as the chaff; only the dust from the corn. The dust which no one needs or notices; the mock farina which flies out from under the two revolving circles of the grindstones; the impalpable cloud which goes forth to gleam golden in the sun a moment, and then is scattered; on the wind; into the water; up in the sunlight; down in the mud: what matters? who cares?

Only the dust: a mote in the air; a speck in the light; a black spot in the living daytime; a colourless atom in the immensity of the atmosphere, borne up one instant to gleam against the sky, dropped down the next to lie in a fetid ditch.

Only the dust: the dust that flows out from between the grindstones, grinding exceeding hard and small, as the religion which calls itself Love avers that its God does grind the world.

"It is a nothing, less than nothing. The stones turn; the dust is born; it has a puff of life; it dies. Who cares? No one. Not the good God; not any man; not even the devil. It is a thing even devil-deserted. Ah, it is very like you," said the old miller, watching the mill-stones.

Folle-Farine heard—she had heard a hundred times,—and held her peace.

Folle-Farine: the dust; only the dust.

As good a name as any other for a nameless creature. The dust;—sharp-winnowed and rejected of all, as less worthy than even the shred husks and the shattered stalks.

Folle-Farine,—she watched the dust fly in and out all day long from between the grindstones. She only wondered why, if she and the dust were thus kindred and namesakes, the wind flew away with the dust so mercifully, and yet never would fly away with her.

The dust was carried away by the breeze, and wandered wherever it listed. The dust had a sweet short summer-day life of its own ere it died. If it were worthless, it at least was free. It could lie in the curl of a green leaf, or on the white breast of a flower. It could mingle with the golden dust in a lily, and almost seem to be one with it. It could fly with the thistledown, and with the feathers of the dandelion, on every roving wind that blew.

In a vague, dreamy fashion, the child wondered why the dust was so much better dealt with than she was.

"Folle-Farine! Folle—Folle—Folle—Farine!" the other children hooted after her, echoing the name by which the grim humour of her bitter-tongued taskmaster had called her. She had got used to it, and answered to it as others to their birth-names.

It meant that she was a thing utterly useless, absolutely worthless; the very refuse of the winnowings of the flail of fate. But she accepted that too, so far as she understood it; she only sometimes wondered in a dull fierce fashion why, if she and the dust were sisters, the dust had its wings whilst she had none.

All day long the dust flew in and out and about as it liked, through the open doors, and among the tossing boughs, and through the fresh cool mists, and down the golden shafts of the sunbeams; and all day long she stayed in one place and toiled, and was first beaten and then cursed, or first cursed and then beaten,—which was all the change that her life knew. For herself, she saw no likeness betwixt her and the dust; for that escaped from the scourge and flew forth, but she abode under the flail, always.

Nevertheless, Folle-Farine was all the name she knew.

The great black wheel churned and circled in the brook water, and lichens and ferns and mosses made lovely all the dark, shadowy, silent place; the red mill roof gleamed in the sun, under a million summer leaves; the pigeons came and went all day in and out of their holes in the wall; the sweet scents of ripening fruits in many orchards filled the air; the great grindstones turned and turned and turned, and the dust floated forth to dance with the gnat and to play with the sunbeam.

Folle-Farine sat aloft, on the huge wet timbers above the wheel, and watched with her great sorrowful eyes, and wondered again, after her own fashion, why her namesake had thus liberty to fly forth whilst she had none.

Suddenly a shrill screaming voice broke the stillness savagely.

"Little devil!" cried the miller, "go fetch me those sacks, and carry them within, and pile them; neatly, do you hear? Like the piles of stone in the road."

Folle-Farine swung down from the timbers in obedience to the command, and went to the heap of sacks that lay outside the mill; small sacks, most of them; all of last year's flour.

There was an immense gladiolus growing near, in the mill-garden, where they were; a tall flower all scarlet and gold, and straight as a palm, with bees sucking into its bells, and butterflies poising on its stem. She stood a moment looking at its beauty; she was scarce any higher than its topmost bud, and was in her way beautiful, something after its fashion. She was a child of six or eight years, with limbs moulded like sculpture, and brown as the brook water; great lustrous eyes, half savage and half soft; a mouth like a red pomegranate bud, and straight dark brows—the brows of the friezes of Egypt.

Her only clothing was a little short white linen kirtle, knotted around her waist, and falling to her knees; and her skin was burned, by exposure in the sun, to a golden brown colour, though in texture it was soft as velvet, and showed all the veins like glass. Standing there in the deep grass, with the scarlet flower against her, and purple butterflies over her head, an artist would have painted her and called her by a score of names, and described for her some mystical or noble fate: as Anteros, perhaps, or as the doomed son of Procne, or as some child born to the Forsaken in the savage forests of Naxos, or conceived by Persephone, in the eternal night of hell, whilst still the earth lay black and barren and fruitless, under the ban and curse of a bereaved maternity.

But here she had only one name, Folle-Farine; and here she had only to labour drearily and stupidly, like the cattle of the field, and without their strength, and with barely so much even as their scanty fare and begrudged bed.

The sunbeams that fell on her might find out that

she had a beauty which ripened and grew rich under their warmth, like that of a red flower bud or a golden autumn fruit. But nothing else ever did. In none of the eyes that looked on her had she any sort of loveliness. She was Folle-Farine; a little wicked beast that only merited at best a whip and a cruel word, a broken crust and a malediction; a thing born of the devil, and out of which the devil needed to be scourged incessantly.

The sacks were all small; they were the property of the peasant proprietors of the district: the department of Calvados. But though small they were heavy in proportion to her age and power. She lifted one, although with effort, yet with the familiarity of an accustomed action; poised it on her back, clasped it tight with her round slender arms, and carried it slowly through the open door of the mill. That one put down upon the bricks, she came for a second,—a third,—a fourth,—a fifth,—a sixth, working doggedly, patiently and willingly, as a little donkey works.

The sacks were in all sixteen; before the seventh she paused.

It was a hot day in the late summer: she was panting and burning with the exertion; the bloom in her cheeks had deepened to scarlet; she stood a moment, resting, bathing her face in the sweet coolness of a white tall tuft of lilies.

The miller looked round where he worked, amongst his beans and cabbages, and saw.

"Little mule! Little beast!" he cried. "Would you be lazy—you!—who have no more right to live at all than an eft, or a stoat, or a toad!"

And as he spoke he came towards her. He had caught up a piece of rope with which he had been about to tie his beans to a stake, and he struck the child with it. The sharp cord bit the flesh cruelly, curling round her bare chest and shoulders, and leaving a livid mark.

She quivered a little, but she said nothing; she lifted her head and looked at him, and dropped her hands to her sides. Her eyes glowed fiercely; her red curling lips shut tight; her straight brows drew together.

"Little devil! Will you work now?" said the miller. "Do you think you are to stand in the sun and smell at flowers—you! Pouf-f-f!"

Folle-Farine did not move.

"Pick up the sacks this moment, little brute," said the miller. "If you stand still a second before they are all housed, you shall have as many stripes as there are sacks left untouched. Oh, hè: do you hear?"

She heard, but she did not move.

"Do you hear," he pursued. "As many strokes as there are sacks, little wretch. Now—I will give you three moments to choose. One!"

Folle-Farine still stood mute and immovable, her head erect, her arms crossed on her chest. A small, slender, bronze-hued, half-nude figure amongst the ruby hues of the gladioli and the pure snow-like whiteness of the lilies.

"Two!"

She stood in the same attitude, the sacks lying untouched at her feet, a purple-winged butterfly lighting on her head.

"Three!"

She was still mute; still motionless.

He seized her by the shoulder with one hand, and with the other lifted the rope.

It curled round her breast and back, again and again and again; she shuddered, but she did not utter a single cry. He struck her the ten times; with the same number of strokes as there remained sacks uncarried. He did not exert any great strength, for had he used his uttermost he would have killed her, and she was of value to him; but he scourged her with a merciless exactitude in the execution of his threat, and the rope was soon wet with drops of her bright young blood.

The noonday sun fell golden all around; the deep sweet peace of the silent country reigned everywhere; the pigeons fled to and fro in and out of their little arched homes; the millstream flowed on, singing a pleasant song; now and then a ripe apricot dropped with a low sound on the turf; close about was all the radiance of summer flowers; of heavy rich roses, of yellow lime tufts, of sheaves of old-fashioned comely phlox, and all the delicate shafts of the graceful lilies. And in the warmth the child shuddered under the scourge; against the light the black rope curled like a serpent darting to sting; among the sun-fed blossoms there fell a crimson stain.

But never a word had she uttered. She endured to the tenth stroke in silence.

He flung the cord aside amongst the grass. "Daughter of devils!—what strength the devil gives!" he muttered.

Folle-Farine said nothing. Her face was livid, her back bruised and lacerated, her eyes still glanced with undaunted scorn and untamed passion. Still she said nothing; but, as his hand released her, she darted as noiselessly as a lizard to the water's edge, set her foot on the lowest range of the woodwork, and in a second leaped aloft to the highest point, and seated herself astride on that crossbar of timber on which she had been throned when he had summoned her first, above the foam of the churning wheels, and in the deepest shadow of innumerable leaves.

Then she lifted up a voice as pure, as strong, as fresh

as the voice of a mavis in May time, and sang, with reckless indifference, a stave of song in a language unknown to any of the people of that place; a loud fierce air, with broken words of curious and most dulcet melody, which rang loud and defiant, yet melancholy, even in their rebellion, through the foliage, and above the sound of the loud mill water.

"It is a chaunt to the foul fiend," the miller muttered to himself. "Well, why does he not come and take his own; he would be welcome to it." And he went and sprinkled holy water on his rope, and said an ave or two over it to exorcise it.

Every fibre of her childish body ached and throbbed; the stripes on her shoulders burned like flame; her little brain was dizzy; her little breast was black with bruises; but still she sang on, clutching the timber with her hands to keep her from falling into the foam below, and flashing her proud eyes down through the shade of the leaves.

"Can one never cut the devil out of her?" muttered the miller, going back to his work amongst the beans.

After a while the song ceased; the pain she suffered stifled her voice despite herself; she felt giddy and sick, but she sat there still in the shadow, holding on by the jutting woodwork, and watching the water foam and eddy below.

The hours went away; the golden day died; the greyness of evening stole the glow from the gladioli and shut up the buds of the roses; the lilies gleamed but the whiter in the dimness of twilight; the vesper chimes were rung from the cathedral two leagues away over the fields.

The miller stopped the gear of the mill; the grindstones and the water-wheels were set at rest; the peace of the night came down; the pigeons flew to roost in their niches; but the sacks still lay uncarried on the grass, and a spider had found time to spin his fairy ropes about them.

The miller stood on his threshold, and looked up at her where she sat aloft in the dusky shades of the leaves.

"Come down and carry these sacks, little brute," he said. "If not—no supper for you to-night."

Folle-Farine obeyed him and came down from the huge pile, slowly, her hands crossed behind her back, her head erect, her eyes glancing like the eyes of a wild hawk.

She walked straight past the sacks, across the dew-laden turf, through the tufts of the lilies, and so silently into the house.

The entrance was a wide kitchen, paved with blue and white tiles, clean as a watercress, filled with the pungent odour of dried herbs, and furnished with brass pots and pans, with walnut presses, with pinewood tressels, and with strange little quaint pictures and images of saints. On one of the tressels were set a jug of steaming milk, some rolls of black bread, and a big dish of stewed cabbages. At the meal there was already seated a lean, brown, wrinkled, careworn old serving woman, clad in the blue kirtle and the white head gear of Normandy.

The miller stayed the child at the threshold.

"Little devil—not a bit nor drop to-night if you do not carry the sacks."

Folle-Farine said nothing, but moved on, past the food on the board, past the images of the saints, past the high lancet window, through which the moonlight had begun to stream, and out at the opposite door.

There she climbed a steep winding stairway on to which that door had opened, pushed aside a little wooden wicket, entered a loft in the roof, loosened the single garment that she wore, shook it off from her, and plunged into the fragrant mass of daisied hay and of dry orchard mosses which served her as a bed. Covered in these, and curled like a dormouse in its nest, she clasped her hands above her head, and sought to forget in sleep her hunger and her wounds. She was well used to both.

Below there was a crucifix, with a bleeding God upon it; there was a little rudely sculptured representation of the Nativity; there was a wooden figure of St. Christopher; a portrait of the Madonna, and many other symbols of the church. But the child went to her bed without a prayer on her lips, and with a curse on her head, and bruises on her body.

Sleep, for once, would not come to her. She was too hurt and sore to be able to lie without pain; the dried grasses, so soft to her usually, were like thorns beneath the skin that still swelled and smarted from the stripes of the rope. She was feverish; she tossed and turned in vain; she suffered too much to be still; she sat up and stared with her passionate wistful eyes, at the leaves that were swaying against the square casement in the wall, and the moonbeam that shone so cold and bright across her bed.

She listened, all her senses awake, to the noises of the house. They were not many: a cat's mew, a mouse's scratch, the click-clack of the old woman's step, the shrill monotony of the old man's voice, these were all. After a while even these ceased; the wooden shoes clattered up the wooden stairs, the house became quite still; there was only in the silence the endless flowing murmur of the water breaking against the motionless wheels of the mill.

Neither man nor woman had come near to bring her anything to eat or drink. She had heard them muttering their prayers before they went to rest, but no hand unlatched her door. She had no disappointment, because she had had no hope. She had rebellion, because Nature had grafted it in her; but she went no further. She did not know what it was to hope. She was only a young wild animal, well used to blows, and drilled by them, but not tamed.

As soon as the place was silent, she got out of her nest of grass, slipped on her linen skirt, and opened her casement—a small square hole in the wall, and merely closed by a loose deal shutter, with a hole cut in it, scarcely bigger than her head. A delicious sudden rush of summer air met her burning face; a cool cluster of foliage hit her a soft blow across the eyes as the wind stirred it. They were enough to allure her.

Like any other young cub of the woods, she had only two instincts—air and liberty.

She thrust herself out of the narrow window with the agility that only is born of frequent custom, and got upon the shelving thatch of a shed which sloped a foot or so below, slid down the roof, and swung herself by the jutting bricks of the outhouse wall on to the grass. The house dog, a brindled mastiff, that roamed loose all night about the mill, growled and sprang at her; then, seeing who she was, put up his gaunt head and licked her face, and turned again to resume the rounds of his vigilant patrol.

Ere he went, she caught and kissed him, closely and fervently, without a word. The mastiff was the only living thing that did not hate her; she was grateful, in a passionate, dumb, unconscious fashion. Then she took to her feet, ran, as swiftly as she could, along the margin of the water, and leaped like a squirrel into the wood, on whose edge the mill-house stood.

Once there she was content.

The silence, the shadows, the darkness where the trees stood thick, the pale quivering luminance of the moon, the mystical eërie sounds that fill a woodland by night, all which would have had terror for tamer and happier creatures of her years, had only for her a vague entranced delight. Nature had made her without one pulse of fear; and she had remained too ignorant to have been ever taught it.

It was still warm with all the balmy breath of midsummer; there were heavy dews everywhere; here and there on the surface of the water, there gleamed the white closed cups of the lotus; through the air there passed, now and then, the soft, grey, dim body of a night-bird on the wing; the wood, whose trees were pines, and limes, and maples, was full of a deep dreamy odour; the mosses that clothed many of the branches hung, film-like, in the wind in lovely coils and web-like phantasies.

Around stretched the vast country, dark and silent, as in a trance, the stillness only broken by some faint note of a sheep's bell, some distant song of a muledriver passing homeward.

The child strayed onward through the trees, insensibly soothed, and made glad, she knew not why, by all the dimness and the fragrance round her.

She stood up to her knees in the shallow freshets that every now and then broke up through the grasses; she felt the dews, shaken off the leaves above, fall deliciously upon her face and hair; she filled her hands with the night-blooming marvel-flower, and drank in its sweetness as though it were milk and honey; she crouched down and watched her own eyes look back at her from the dark gliding water of the river.

Then she threw herself on her back upon the mosses

—so cool and moist that they seemed like balm upon the bruised hot skin—and lay there looking upward at the swift mute passage of the flitting owls, at the stately flight of the broad-winged moths, at the movement of the swift brown bats, at the soft trembling of the foliage in the breeze, at the great clouds slowly sailing across the brightness of the moon. All these things were infinitely sweet to her with the sweetness of freedom, of love, of idleness, of rest, of all things which her life had never known: so dumbly may the young large-eyed antelope feel the beauty of the forest in the hot lull of tropic nights, when the speed of the pursuer has relaxed, and the aromatic breath of the panther is no more against its flank.

She lay there long, quite motionless, tracing, with a sort of voluptuous delight, all movements in the air, all changes in the clouds, all shadows in the leaves. All the immense multitude of ephemeral life which, unheard in the day, fills the earth with innumerable whispering voices after the sun has set, now stirred in every herb and under every bough around her.

The silvery ghost-like wing of an owl touched her forehead once. A little dormouse ran across her feet. Strange shapes floated across the cold white surface of the water. Quaint things, hairy, filmy-winged, swam between her and the stars. But none of these things had terror for her; they were things of the night, with which she felt vaguely the instinct of kinship.

She was only a little wild beast, they said, the offspring of darkness, and vileness, and rage and disgrace. And yet, in a vague imperfect way, the glories of the night, its mysterious and solemn beauty, its melancholy and lustrous charm, quenched the fierceness in her dauntless eyes, and filled them with dim wondering tears, and stirred the half dead soul in her to some dull pain, some nameless ecstacy, that were not merely physical.

And then, in her way, being stung by these, and moved, she knew not why, to a strange sad sense of loneliness and shame, and knowing no better she prayed.

She raised herself on her knees, and crossed her hands upon her chest, and prayed after the fashion that she had seen men and women and children pray at roadside shrines and crosses; prayed aloud, with a little beating breaking heart, like the young child she was.

"Oh Devil! if I be indeed thy daughter, stay with me; leave me not alone: lend me thy strength and power, and let me inherit of thy kingdom. Give me this, oh great Lord, and I will praise thee and love thee always."

She prayed in all earnestness, in all simplicity, in broken, faltering language; knowing no better; knowing only that she was alone on the earth and friendless, and very hungry and in sore pain, whilst this mighty unknown King of the dominion of darkness, whose child she ever heard she was, had lost her, or abandoned her; and reigned afar in some immortal world, oblivious of her misery.

The silence of the night alone gave back the echo of her own voice. She waited breathless for some answer, for some revelation, some reply; there only came the pure cold moon, sailing straight from out a cloud, and striking on the waters.

She rose sadly to her feet, and went back along the shining course of the stream, through the grasses and the mosses, and under the boughs, to her little nest under the eaves.

As she left the obscurity of the wood and passed into the fuller light, her bare feet glistening, and her shoulders wet with the showers of dew, a large dark shape flying down the wind smote her with his wings upon the eyes, lighted one moment on her head, and then swept onward lost in shade. At that moment, likewise, a radiant golden globe flashed to her sight, dropped to her footsteps, and shone an instant in the glisten from the skies.

It was but a great goshawk seeking for its prey; it was but a great meteor fading and falling at its due appointed hour; but to the heated, savage, dreamy fancy of the child it seemed an omen, an answer, a thing of prophecy, a spirit of air; nay, why not Him himself?

In legends, which had been the only lore her ears had ever heard, it had been often told he took such shapes as this.

"If he should give me his kingdom!" she thought; and her eyes flashed alight; her heart swelled; her cheeks burned. The little dim untutored brain could not hold the thought long or close enough to grasp, or sift, or measure it; but some rude rich glory, impalpable, unutterable, seemed to come to her and bathe her in its heat and colour. She was his offspring, so they all told her; why not, then, also his heir?

She felt, as felt the goatherd or the charcoal-burner in those legends she had fed on, who was suddenly called from poverty and toil, from hunger and fatigue, from a fireless hearth and a bed of leaves, to inherit some fairy empire, to ascend to some region of the gods.

Like one of these, hearing the summons to some great unknown imperial power smite all his poor pale barren life to splendour, so Folle-Farine, standing by the water's side in the light of the moon, desolate, ignorant, brute-like, felt elected to some mighty heritage unseen of men. If this were waiting for her in the future, what matter, now, were stripes or wounds or woe?

She smiled a little, dreamily, like one who beholds fair visions in his sleep, and stole back over the starlit grass, and swung herself upward by the tendrils of ivy, and crouched once more down in her nest of mosses.

And either the courage of the spirits of darkness, or the influence of instincts dumb but nascent, was with her; for she fell asleep in her little loft in the roof as though she were a thing cherished of heaven and earth, and dreamed happily all through the hours of the slowly-rising dawn: her bruised body and her languid brain and her aching heart all stilled and soothed, and her hunger and passion and pain forgotten; with the night-blooming flowers still clasped in her hands, and on her closed mouth a smile.

For she dreamed of her Father's kingdom, a kingdom which no man denies to the creature that has beauty and youth, and is poor and yet proud, and is of the sex of its mother.

CHAPTER II.

In one of the most fertile and most fair districts of northern France there was a little Norman town, very, very old and beautiful exceedingly by reason of its ancient streets, its high peaked roofs, its marvellous galleries and carvings, its exquisite greys and browns, its silence and its colour, and its rich still life.

Its centre was a great cathedral, noble as York or Chartres; a cathedral, whose spire shot to the clouds, and whose innumerable towers and pinnacles were all pierced to the day, so that the blue sky shone and the birds of the air flew all through them. A slow brown river, broad enough for market boats and for corn barges, stole through the place to the sea, lapping as it went the wooden piles of the houses, and reflecting the quaint shapes of the carvings, the hues of the signs and the draperies, the dark spaces of the dormer windows, the bright heads of some casement-cluster of carnations, the laughing face of a girl leaning out to smile on her lover.

All around it lay the deep grass unshaven, the leagues on leagues of fruitful orchards, the low blue hills tenderly interlacing one another, the fields of colza, where the white head-dress of the women workers flashed in the sun like a silvery pigeon's wing. To the west there were the deep green woods, and the wide plains golden with gorse of Arthur's and of Merlin's lands; and beyond, to the northward, was the dim stretch of the ocean breaking on a yellow shore, whither the river ran, and whither led straight shady roads, hidden with linden and with poplar trees, and marked ever and anon by a wayside wooden Christ, or by a little murmuring well crowned with a crucifix.

A beautiful, old, shadowy, ancient place: picturesque everywhere; often silent, with a sweet sad silence that was chiefly broken by the sound of bells or the chaunting of choristers. A place of the Middle Ages still. With lanterns swinging on cords from house to house as the only light; with wondrous scroll-works and quaint signs at the doors of all its traders; with monks' cowls and golden croziers and white-robed acolytes in its streets; with the subtle smoke of incense coming out from the cathedral door to mingle with the odours of the fruits and flowers in the market-place; with great flat-bottomed boats drifting down the river under the leaning eaves of its dwellings; and with the galleries of its opposing houses touching so nearly that a girl leaning in one could stretch a Provence rose or toss an Easter egg across to her neighbour in the other.

Doubtless, there were often squalor, poverty, dust, filth, and uncomeliness within these old and beautiful homes. Doubtless often the dwellers therein were housed like cattle and slept like pigs, and looked but once out to the woods and waters of the landscapes round for one hundred times that they looked at their hidden silver in an old delf jug, or at their tawdry coloured prints of St. Victorian or St. Scævola.

But yet much of the beauty and the nobility of the old, simple, restful rich-hued life of the past still abode there, and remained with them. In the straight, lithe form of their maidens, untrammelled by modern garb, and moving with the free majestic grace of forest does. In the vast, dim, sculptured chambers, where the grandam span by the wood fire and the little children played in the shadows, and the lovers whispered in the embrasured window. In the broad market-place, where the mules cropped the clover, and the tawny awnings caught the sunlight, and the white caps of the girls framed faces fitted for the pencils of missal painters, and the flush of colour from mellow wall-fruits and grape-clusters glanced amidst the shelter of deepest freshest green. In the perpetual presence of their cathedral, which through sun and storm, through frost and summer, through noon and midnight stood there amidst them, and watched the galled oxen tread their painful way, and the scourged mules droop their humble heads, and the helpless harmless flocks go forth to the slaughter, and the old weary lives of the men and women pass through hunger and cold to the grave, and the sun and the moon rise and set, and the flowers and the children blossom and fade, and the endless years come and go, bringing peace, bringing war; bringing harvest, bringing famine; bringing life, bringing death; and, beholding these, still said to the multitude in its terrible irony, "Lo! your God is Love."

This little town lay far from the great Paris highway and all greatly frequented tracks. It was but a short distance from the coast, but near no harbour of greater extent than such as some small fishing village had made in the rocks for the trawlers. Few strangers ever came to it, except some wandering painters or antiquaries. It sent its apples and eggs, its poultry and honey, its colza and corn to the use of the great cities; but it was rarely that any of its own people went thither.

Now and then some one of the oval-faced, blue-eyed, lithe-limbed maidens of its little homely households would sigh and flush and grow restless, and murmur of Paris; and would steal out in the break of a warm grey morning whilst only the birds were still waking; and would patter away in her wooden shoes over the broad, white, southern road, with a stick over her shoulder, and a bundle of all her worldly goods upon the stick. And she would look back often, often, as she went; and when all was lost in the blue haze of distance save the lofty spire which she still saw through her tears, she would say in her heart, with her lips parched and trembling, "I will come back again. I will come back again."

But none such ever did come back.

They came back no more than did the white sweet sheaves of the lilies which the women gathered and sent to be bought and sold in the city—to gleam one faint summer night in a gilded balcony, and to be flung out the next morning, withered and dead.

One amongst the few who had thus gone whither the lilies went, and of whom the people would still talk as their mules paced homewards through the lanes at twilight, had been Reine Flamma, the daughter of the miller of Yprés.

Yprés was a beechen-wooded hamlet on the northern outskirt of the town, a place of orchards and wooded tangle; through which there ran a branch of the brimming river, hastening to seek and join the sea, and caught a moment on its impetuous way, and forced to work by the grim mill-wheels that had churned the foam-bells there for centuries. The mill-house was very ancient; its timbers were carved all over into the semblance of shields and helmets, and crosses, and fleur-de-lis, and its frontage was of quaint pargetted work, black and white, except where the old blazonries had been.

It had been handed down from sire to son of the same race through many generations—a race hard, keen, unlearned, superstitious, and caustic-tongued—a race wedded to old ways, credulous of legend, chaste of life, cruel of judgment; harshly strong, yet ignorantly weak; a race holding dearer its heirloom of loveless, joyless, bigoted virtue even than those gold and silver pieces which had ever been its passion, hidden away in earthen pipkins under old apple-roots, or in the crannies of wall timber, or in secret nooks of oaken cupboards.

Claude Flamma, the last of this toilsome, God-fearing, man-begrudging, Norman stock, was true to the type and the traditions of his people.

He was too ignorant even to read; but priests do not deem this a fault. He was avaricious; but many will honour a miser quicker than a spendthrift. He was cruel; but in the market-place he always took heed to give his mare a full feed, so that if she were pinched of her hay in her stall at home none were the wiser, for she had no language but that of her wistful black eyes; and this is a speech to which men stay but little to listen. The shrewd, old, bitter-tongued, stern-living man was feared and respected with the respect that fear begets; and in truth he had a rigid virtue in his way, and was proud of it, with scorn for those who found it hard to walk less straightly and less circumspectly than himself.

He married late; his wife died in childbirth; his daughter grew into the perfection of womanhood under the cold, hard, narrow rule of his severity and his superstition. He loved her, indeed, with as much love as it was possible for him ever to feel, and was proud of her beyond all other things; saved for her, toiled for her, muttered ever that it was for her when at confession he related how his measures of flour had been falsely weighted, and how he had filched from the corn brought by the widow and the fatherless. For her he had sinned: from one to whom the good report of his neighbours and the respect of his own conscience were as the very breath of life, it was the strongest proof of love that he could give. But this love never gleamed one instant in his small sharp grey eyes, nor escaped ever by a single utterance from his lips. Reprimand, or homily, or cynical rasping sarcasm, was all she ever heard from him. She believed that he despised, and almost hated her; he held it well for women to be tutored in subjection and in trembling.

At twenty-two Reine Flamma was the most beautiful woman in Calvados, and the most wretched.

She was straight as a pine; cold as snow; graceful as a stem of wheat: lovely and silent; with a mute proud face, in which the eyes alone glowed with a strange, repressed, speechless passion and wishfulness. Her life was simple, pure, chaste, blameless, as the lives of the many women of her race who, before her, had lived and died in the shadow of that water-fed wood had always been. Her father rebuked and girded at her, continually dreaming that he could paint whiter even the spotlessness of this lily, refine even the purity of this virgin gold.

She never answered him anything, nor in anything contradicted his will; not one amongst all the youths and maidens of her birthplace had ever heard so much as a murmur of rebellion from her; and the priests said that such a life as this would be fitter for the cloister than the marriage-bed. None of them ever read the warning that these dark blue slumbering eyes would have given to any who should have had the skill to construe them right. There were none of such skill there; and so she, holding her peace, the men and women noted her ever with a curious dumb reverence, and said amongst themselves that the race of Flamma would die well and nobly in her.

"A saint!" said the good old gentle bishop of the district, as he blessed her one summer evening in her father's house, and rode his mule slowly through the pleasant poplar lanes and breeze-blown fields of colza back to his little quiet homestead, where he tended his own cabbages and garnered his own honey.

Reine Flamma bowed her tall head meekly, and took his benediction in silence.

The morning after, the miller, rising as his custom was at daybreak, and reciting his paternosters, thanked the Mother of the World that she had given him thus strength and power to rear up his motherless daughter in purity and peace. Then he dressed himself in his grey patched blouse, groped his way down the narrow stair, and went in his daily habit to undraw the bolts and unloose the chains of his dwelling.

There was no need that morning for him; the bolts were already back; the house-door stood wide open; on the threshold a brown hen perched pluming herself; there were the ticking of the clock, the cherming of the birds, the rushing of the water; these were the only sounds upon the silence.

He called his daughter's name: there was no answer. He mounted to her chamber: it had no tenant. He searched hither and thither, in the house, and the stable, and the granary: in the mill, and the garden, and the wood; he shouted, he ran, he roused his neighbours, he looked in every likely and unlikely place: there was no reply.

There was only the howl of the watch-dog, who sat with his face to the south and mourned unceasingly.

And from that day neither he nor any man living there ever heard again of Reine Flamma.

Some indeed did notice that at the same time there disappeared from the town one who had been there through all that spring and summer. One who had lived strangely, and been clad in an odd rich fashion, and had been whispered as an Eastern prince by reason of his scattered gold, his unfamiliar tongue, his black-browed, star-eyed, deep-hued, beauty, like the beauty of the passion-flower. But none had ever seen this stranger and Reine Flamma in each other's presence; and the rumour was discredited as a foulness absurd and unseemly to be said of a woman whom their bishop had called a saint. So it died out, breathed only by a few mouths, and it came to be accepted as a fact that she must have perished in the deep fast-flowing river by some false step on the mill-timber, as she went at dawn to feed her doves, or by some strange sad trance of sleep-walking, from which she had been known more than once to suffer.

Claudis Flamma said little; it was a wound that bled inwardly. He toiled, and chaffered, and drove hard bargains, and worked early and late with his hireling, and took for the household service an old Norman peasant woman more aged than himself, and told no man that he suffered. All that he ever said was, "She was a saint: God took her;" and in his martyrdom he found a hard pride and a dull consolation.

It was no mere metaphoric form of words with him. He believed in miracles and all manner of Divine interposition, and he believed likewise that she, his angel, being too pure for earth, had been taken by God's own hand up to the bosom of Mary. This honour which had befallen his first-begotten shed both sanctity and splendour on his cheerless days; and when the little children and the women saw him pass, they cleared from his way as from a prince's, and crossed themselves as they changed words with one whose daughter was the bride of Christ.

So six years passed away; and the name of Reine Flamma was almost forgotten, but embalmed in memories of religious sanctity, as the dead heart of a saint is embedded in amber and myrrh.

At the close of the sixth year there happened what many said was a thing devil-conceived and wrought out by the devil to the shame of a pure name, and to the hindrance of the people of God.

One winter's night Claudis Flamma was seated in his kitchen, having recently ridden home his mare from the market in the town.

The fire burned in ancient fashion on the hearth, and it was so bitter without that even his parsimonious habits had relaxed, and he had piled some wood, liberally mingled with dry moss, that cracked, and glowed, and shot flame up the wide black shaft of the chimney.

The day's work was over; the old woman-servant sat spinning flax on the other side of the fire; the great mastiff was stretched sleeping quietly on the brick floor; the blue pottery, the brass pans, the oaken presses that had been the riches of his race for generations, glimmered in the light; the doors were barred, the shutters closed; around the house the winds howled, and beneath its walls the fretting water hissed.

The miller, overcome with the past cold and present warmth, nodded on his wooden settle and slept, and muttered dreamily in his sleep, "A saint—a saint!—God took her."

The old woman, hearing, looked across at him, and shook her head, and went on with her spinning with lips that moved inaudibly: she had been wont to say, out of her taskmaster's hearing, that no woman who was beautiful ever was a saint as well. And some thought that this old creature, Marie Pitchou, who had used to live in a miserable hut on the other side of the wood, had known more than she had chosen to tell of the true fate of Reine Flamma.

Suddenly a blow on the panels of the door sounded through the silence. The miller, awakened in a moment, started to his feet and grasped his ash staff with one hand, and with the other the oil-lamp burning on the tressel. The watch-dog arose, but made no hostile sound.

A step crushed the dead leaves without and passed away faintly; there was stillness again; the mastiff went to the bolted door, smelt beneath it, and scratched at the panels.

On the silence there sounded a small, timid, feeble beating on the wood from without; such a slight fluttering noise as a wounded bird might make in striving to rise.

"It is nothing evil," muttered Flamma. "If it were evil the beast would not want to have the door opened. It may be some one sick or stray."

All this time he was in a manner charitable, often conquering the niggardly instincts of his character to try and save his soul by serving the wretched. He was a miser, and he loved to gain, and loathed to give; but since his daughter had been taken to the saints he had striven with all his might to do good enough to be taken likewise to that heavenly rest.

Any crust bestowed on the starveling, any bed of straw afforded to the tramp, caused him a sharp pang; but since his daughter had been taken he had tried to please God by this mortification of his own avarice and diminution of his own gains. He could not vanquish the nature that was engrained in him. He would rob the widow of an ephah of wheat, and leave his mare famished in her stall, because it was his nature to find in all such saving a sweet savour; but he would not turn away a beggar or refuse a crust to a wayfarer, lest, thus refusing, he might turn away from him an angel unawares.

The mastiff scratched still at the panels; the sound outside had ceased.

The miller, setting the lamp down on the floor, gripped more firmly the ashen stick, undrew the bolts, turned the stout key, and opened the door slowly, and with caution. A loud gust of wind blew dead leaves against his face; a blinding spray of snow scattered itself over his bent stretching form. In the darkness without, whitened from head to foot, there stood a little child.

The dog went up to her and licked her face with kindly welcome. Claudis Flamma drew her with a rough grasp across the threshold, and went out into the air to find whose footsteps had been those which had trodden heavily away after the first knock.

The snow, however, was falling fast; it was a cloudy moonless night. He did not dare to go many yards from his own portals, lest he should fall into some ambush set by robbers. The mastiff too was quiet, which indicated that there was no danger near, so the old man returned, closed the door carefully, drew the bolts into their places, and came towards the child, whom the woman Pitchou had drawn towards the fire.

She was a child of four or five years old; huddled in coarse linen and in a little red garment of fox's skin, and blanched from head to foot, for the flakes were frozen on her and on the hood that covered, gipsy-like, her curls. It was a strange, little, ice-cold, ghost-like figure, but out of this mass of icicles and whiteness there glowed great beaming frightened eyes and a mouth like a scarlet berry; the radiance and the contrast of it were like the glow of holly fruit thrust out from a pile of drifted snow.

The miller shook her by the shoulder.

"Who brought you?"

"Phratos," answered the child, with a stifled sob in her throat.

"And who is that?"

"Phratos," answered the child again.

"Is that a man or a woman?"

The child made no reply; she seemed not to comprehend his meaning. The miller shook her again, and some drops of water fell from the ice that was dissolving in the warmth.

"Why are you come here?" he asked, impatiently.

She shook her head, as though to say none knew so little of herself as she.

"You must have a name," he pursued harshly and in perplexity. "What are you called? Who are you?"

The child suddenly raised her great eyes that had been fastened on the leaping flames, and flashed them upon his in a terror of bewildered ignorance—the piteous terror of a stray dog.

"Phratos," she cried once more, and the cry now was half a sigh, half a shriek.

Something in that regard pierced him and startled him; he dropped his hand off her shoulder, and breathed quickly; the old woman gave a low cry, and staring with all her might at the child's small dark, fierce, lovely face, fell to counting her wooden beads and mumbling many prayers.

Claudis Flamma turned savagely on her as if stung by some unseen snake, and willing to wreak his vengeance on the nearest thing that was at hand.

"Fool! cease your prating!" he muttered, with a brutal oath. "Take the animal and search her. Bring me what you find."

Then he sat down on the stool by the fire, and braced his lips tightly, and locked his bony hands upon his knees. He knew what blow awaited him; he was no coward, and he had manhood enough in him to press any iron into his soul and tell none that it hurt him.

The old woman drew the stranger aside to a dusky corner of an inner chamber, and began to despoil her of her coverings. The creature did not resist; the freezing cold and long fatigue had numbed and silenced her; her eyelids were heavy with the sleep such cold produces, and she had not strength, because she had not consciousness enough, to oppose whatsoever they might choose to do to her. Only now and then her eyes opened, as they had opened on him, with a sudden lustre and fierceness, like those in a netted animal's impatient but untamed regard.

Pitchou seized and searched her eagerly, stripping her of her warm fox-skin wrap, her scarlet hood of wool, her little rough hempen shirt, which were all dripping with the water from the melted snow.

The skin of the young waif was brown, with a golden bloom on it; it had been tanned by hot suns, but it was soft as silk in texture, and transparent, showing the course of each blue vein. Her limbs were not well nourished, but they were of perfect shape and delicate bone; and the feet were the long, arched, slender feet of the southern side of the Pyrenees.

She allowed herself to be stripped and wrapped in a coarse piece of homespun linen; she was still half frozen, and in a state of stupor, either from amazement or from fear. She was quite passive, and she never spoke. Her apathy deceived the old crone, who took it for docility, and who, trusting to it, proceeded to take advantage of it, after the manner of her kind. About the small shapely head there hung a band of glittering coins; they were not gold, but the woman Pitchou thought they were, and seized them with gloating hands and ravenous eyes.

The child started from her torpor, shook herself free, and fought to guard them—fiercely, with tooth and nail, as the young fox whose skin she had worn might have fought for its dear life. The old woman on her side strove as resolutely; long curls of the child's hair were clutched out in the struggle; she did not wince or scream, but she fought—fought with all the breath and the blood that were in her tiny body.

She was no match, with all her ferocity and fury, for the sinewy grip of the old peasant; and the coins were torn off her forehead and hidden away in a hole in the wood, out of her sight, where the old peasant hoarded all her precious treasures of copper coins and other trifles that she managed to secrete from her master's all-seeing eyes.

They were little metal sequins engraved with Arabic characters, chained together after the Eastern fashion. To Pitchou they looked a diadem of gold worthy of an empress.

The child watched them thus removed in perfect silence; from the moment they had been wrenched away, and the battle had been finally lost to her, she had ceased to struggle, as though disdainful of a fruitless contest. But a great hate gathered in her eyes, and smouldered there like a half-stifled fire—it burned on and on for many a long year afterwards, unquenched.

When Pitchou brought her a cup of water and a roll of bread, she would neither eat nor drink, but turned her face to the wall,—mute.

"Those are just her father's eyes," the old woman muttered. She had seen them burn in the gloom of the evening through the orchard trees, as the stars had risen, and Reine Flamma listened to the voice that wooed her to her destruction.

She let the child be, and searched her soaked garments for any written word or any token that might be on them. Fastened roughly to the fox's skin there was a faded letter. Pitchou could not read; she took it to her master.

Claudis Flamma grasped the paper and turned its super-scription to the light of the lamp.

He could not read, but yet at sight of the characters his tough frame trembled, and his withered skin grew red with a sickly, feverish quickening of the blood.

He knew them.

Once, in a time long dead, he had been proud of

those slender letters that had been so far more legible than any that the women of her class could pen, and on beholding which the good bishop had smiled, and passed a pleasant word concerning her being almost fitted to be his own clerk and scribe.

For a moment, watching those written cyphers that had no tongue for him, and yet seemed to tell their tale so that they scorched and withered up all the fair honour and pious peace of his old age, a sudden faintness, a sudden swooning sense seized him for the first time in all his life; his limbs failed him, he sank down on his seat again, he gasped for breath; he needed not to be told anything, he knew all. He knew that the creature whom he had believed so pure that God had deemed the earth unworthy of her youth was——his throat rattled, his lips were covered with foam, his ears were filled with a rushing, hollow sound, like the roaring of his own mill-waters in a time of storm.

All at once he started to his feet, and glared at the empty space of the dim chamber, and struck his hands wildly together in the air, and cried aloud:

"She was a saint, I said—a saint! A saint in body and soul! And I thought that God begrudged her, and held her too pure for man!"

And he laughed aloud—thrice.

The child hearing, and heavy with sleep, and eagerly desiring warmth, as a little frozen beast that coils itself in snow to slumber into death, startled by that horrible mirth, came forward.

The shirt fell off her as she moved. Her little naked limbs glimmered like gold in the dusky light; her hair was as a cloud behind her; her little scarlet mouth was half open, like the mouth of a child seeking its mother's kiss; her great eyes, dazzled by the flame, flashed and burned and shone like stars. They had seen the same face ere then in Calvados.

She came straight to Claudis Flamma as though drawn by that awful and discordant laughter, and by that leaping ruddy flame upon the hearth, and she stretched out her arms and murmured a word and smiled, a little dreamily, seeking to sleep, asking to be caressed, desiring she knew not what.

He clenched his fist, and struck her to the ground. She fell without a sound. The blood flowed from her mouth.

He looked at her where she lay, and laughed once more.

"She was a saint!—a saint! And the devil begot in her *that!*"

Then he went out across the threshold and into the night, with the letter still clenched in his hand.

The snow fell, the storm raged, the earth was covered with ice and water; he took no heed, but passed through it, his head bare and his eyes blind.

The dog let him go forth alone, and waited by the child.

CHAPTER III.

ALL night long he was absent.

The old serving woman, terrified, in so far as her dull brutish nature could be roused to fear, did what she knew, what she dared. She raised the little wounded naked creature, and carried her to her own pallet bed; restored her to consciousness by such rude means as she had knowledge of, and staunched the flow of blood.

She did all this harshly, as it was her custom to do all things, and without tenderness or even pity, for the sight of this stranger was unwelcome to her, and she also had guessed the message of that unread letter.

The child had been stunned by the blow, and she had lost some blood, and was weakened and stupified and dazed; yet there seemed to her rough nurse no peril for her life, and by degrees she fell into a feverish tossing slumber, sobbing sometimes in her sleep, and crying perpetually on the unknown name of Phratos.

The old woman Pitchou stood and looked at her. She who had always known the true story of that disappearance which some had called death and some had deemed a divine interposition, had seen before that transparent brown skin, those hues in cheeks and lips like the carnation leaves, that rich, sun-fed, dusky beauty, those straight dark brows.

"She is his sure enough," she muttered. "He was the first with Reine Flamma. I wonder has he been the last."

And she went down the stairs chuckling, as the low human brute will at any evil thought.

The mastiff stayed beside the child.

She went to the fire and threw more wood on, and sat down again to her spinning-wheel, and span and dozed, and span and dozed again.

She was not curious: to her, possessing that thread to the secret of the past, which her master and her townsfolk had never held, it all seemed natural. It was an old, old story; there had been thousands like it; it was only strange because Reine Flamma had been held a saint.

The hours passed on; the lamp paled, and its flame at last died out; in the loft above, where the dog watched, there was no sound; the old woman slumbered undisturbed, unless some falling ember of the wood aroused her.

She was not curious, nor did she care how the child fared. She had led that deadening life of perpetual labour and of perpetual want in which the human animal becomes either a machine or a devil. She was a machine; put to what use she might be—to spin flax, to card wool, to wring a pigeon's throat, to bleed a calf to death, to bake or stew, to mumble a prayer or drown a kitten, it was all one to her. If she had a preference, it might be for the office that hurt some living thing; but she did not care: all she heeded was whether she had pottage enough to eat at noonday, and the leaden effigy of her Mary safe round her throat at night.

The night went on, and passed away; one gleam of dawn shone through a round hole in the shutter; she wakened with a start to find the sun arisen, and the fire dead upon the hearth.

She shook herself and stamped her chill feet upon the bricks, and tottered on her feeble way, with frozen body, to the house door. She drew it slowly open, and saw by the light of the sun that it had been for some time morning.

The earth was everywhere thick with snow; a hoar frost sparkled over all the branches; great sheets of ice were whirled down the rapid mill-stream; in one of the leafless boughs a robin sang, and beneath the bough a cat was crouched, waiting with hungry eager eyes, patient even in its famished impatience.

Dull as her sympathy was, and slow her mind, she started as she saw her master there.

Claudis Flamma was at work; the rough, hard, rude toil, which he spared to himself no more than to those who were his hirelings. He was carting wood; going to and fro with huge limbs of trees that men in youth would have found it a severe task to move; he was labouring

athlessly, giving himself no pause, and the sweat was
his brow, although he trod ankle deep in snow, and
hough his clothes were heavy with icicles.

He did not see or hear her; she went up to him and
led him by his name; he started, and raised his head
d looked at her.

Dull though she was, she was in a manner frightened
the change upon his face; it had been lean, furrowed,
ather-beaten always, but it was livid now, with blood-
ot eyes, and a bruised, broken, yet withal savage look
t terrified her. He did not speak, but gazed at her
e a man recalled from some drugged sleep back to the
eds and memories of the living world.

The old woman held her peace a few moments; then
oke out in her own blunt, dogged fashion.

"Is she to stay?"

Her mind was not awake enough for any curiosity;
e only cared to know if the child stayed: only so
uch as would concern her soup kettle, her kneaded
ugh, her spun hemp, her household labour.

He turned for a second with the gesture that a trapped
x may make, held fast, yet striving to essay a death
ip; then he checked himself, and gave a mute sign of
sent, and heaved up a fresh log of wood, and went on
th his labours, silently. She knew of old his ways too
ell to venture to ask more. She knew, too, that when
: worked like this, fasting and in silence, there had
en long and fierce warfare in his soul, and some great
il done for which he sought to make atonement.

So she left him, and passed in to the house, and built
) afresh her fire, and swept her chamber out, and
stened up her round black pot to boil, and muttered
l the while,—

"Another mouth to feed; another beast to tend."

And the thing was bitter to her; because it gave trouble and took food.

Now, what the letter had been, or who had deciphered it for him, Claudis Flamma never told to any man; and from the little strange creature no utterance could be ever got.

But the child who had come in the night and the snow tarried at Yprès from that time thenceforward.

Claudis Flamma nourished, sheltered, clothed her; but he did all these begrudgingly, harshly, scantily; and he did all these with an acrid hate and scorn, which did not cease but rather grew with time.

The blow which had been her earliest welcome was not the first that she received from him by many; and whilst she was miserable exceedingly, she showed it, not as children do, but rather like some chained and untamed animal, in tearless stupor and in sudden, sharp ferocity. And this the more because she spoke but a very few words of the language of the people amongst whom she had been brought; her own tongue was one full of round vowels and strange sounds, a tongue unknown to them.

For many weeks he said not one word to her, cast not one look at her; he let her lead the same life that was led by the beetles that crawled in the timbers, or by the pigs that couched and were kicked in the straw. The woman Pitchou gave her such poor scraps of garments or of victuals as she chose; she could crouch in the corner of the hearth where the fire warmth reached; she could sleep in the hay in the little loft under the roof; so much she could do and no more.

After that first moment in which her vague appeal for pity and for rest had been answered by the blow that struck her senseless, the child had never made a moan, nor sought for any solace.

All the winter through she lay curled up on the tiles by the fence, with her arms round the great body of the dog and his head upon her chest; they were both starved, beaten, kicked, and scourged, with brutal words oftentimes; they had the community of misfortune, and they loved one another.

The blow on her head, the coldness of the season, the scanty food that was cast to her, all united to keep her brain stupified and her body almost motionless. She was like a young bear that is motherless, wounded, frozen, famished, but which, coiled in an almost continual slumber, keeps its blood flowing and its limbs alive. And, like the bear, with the spring she awakened.

When the townsfolk and the peasants came to the mill, and first saw this creature there, with her wondrous vivid hues, and her bronzed half-naked limbs, they regarded her in amazement, and asked the miller whence she came. He set his teeth, and answered ever:

"The woman that bore her was Reine Flamma."

The avowal was a penance set to himself, but to it he never added more; and they feared his bitter temper and his caustic tongue too greatly to press it on him, or even to ask him whether his daughter were with the living or the dead.

With the unfolding of the young leaves, and the loosening of the frost-bound waters, and the unveiling of the violet and the primrose under the shadows of the wood, all budding life revives, and so did hers. For she could escape from the dead, cold, bitter atmosphere of the silent and loveless house, where her bread was begrudged, and the cudgel was her teacher, out into the freshness and the living sunshine of the young blossoming world, where the birds and the beasts and the tender blue flowers and the curling green boughs were her comrades, and where she could stretch her limbs in freedom, and coil herself among the branches, and steep her limbs in the coolness of waters, and bathe her aching feet in the moisture of rain-filled grasses.

With the spring she arose, the true forest animal she was; wild, fleet, incapable of fear, sure of foot, in unison with all the things of the earth and the air, and stirred by them to a strange, dumb, ignorant, passionate gladness.

She had been scarce seen in the winter; with the breaking of the year the people from more distant places, who rode their mules down to the mill on their various errands, stared at this child and wondered amongst themselves greatly, and at length asked Claudis Flamma whence she came.

He answered ever, setting hard his teeth:

"The woman that bore her was one accursed, whom men deemed a saint—Reine Flamma."

They dared not ask him more; for many were his debtors.

But when they went away, and gossiped amongst themselves by the wayside well or under the awnings of the market stalls, they said to one another that it was just as they had thought long ago; the creature had been no better than her kind; and they had never credited the fable that God had taken her, though they had humoured the miller because he was aged and in his dotage. Whilst one old woman, a withered and witch-like crone, who had toiled in from the fishing village with a kreel upon her back and the smell of the sea about her rags, heard, standing in the market-place, and laughed, and mocked them, these seers who were so wise after the years had gone, and when the truth was clear.

"You knew, you knew, you knew!" she echoed, with a grin upon her face. "Oh, yes! you were so wise! Who, seven years through, said that Reine Flamma was a saint, and taken by the saints into their keeping? And who hissed at me for a foul-mouthed crone when I said that the devil had more to do with her than the good God, and that the black-browed gipsy, with jewels for eyes in his head, like the toad, was the only master to whom she gave herself? Oh-hé, you were so wise!"

So she mocked them, and they were ashamed, and held their peace; well knowing that indeed no creature amongst them had ever been esteemed so pure, so chaste, and so honoured of heaven as had been the miller's daughter.

Many remembered the "gipsy with the jewelled eyes," and saw those brilliant, fathomless, midnight eyes reproduced in the small rich face of the child whom Reine Flamma, as her own father said, had borne in shame whilst they had been glorifying her apotheosis. And it came to be said, as time went on, that this unknown stranger had been the fiend himself, taking human shape for the destruction of one pure soul, and the confusion of all true children of the church.

Legend and tradition still held fast their minds in this remote, ancient, and priest-ridden place; in their belief the devil was still a living power, traversing the earth and air in search of souls, and not seldom triumphing: of metaphor or myth they were ignorant, Satan to them was a personality, terrific, and oftentimes irresistible, assuming at will shapes grotesque or awful, human or spiritual. Their forefathers had beheld him; why not they?

So the henhucksters and poulterers, the cider-makers and tanners, the fisherfolk from the sea-board, and the peasant proprietors from the country round, came at length in all seriousness to regard the young child at Yprès as a devil-born thing. "She was hell-begotten," they would mutter, when they saw her; and they would cross themselves, and avoid her if they could.

The time had gone by, unhappily, as they considered, when men had been permitted to burn such creatures as this; they knew it and were sorry for it; the world, they thought, had been better when Jews had blazed like torches, and witches had crackled like firewood; such treats were forbidden now, they knew, but many, for all that, thought within themselves that it was a pity it should be so, and that it was mistaken mercy in the age they lived in which forbade the purifying of the earth by fire of such as she.

In the winter time, when they first saw her, unusual floods swept the country, and destroyed much of their property; in the spring which followed there were mildew and sickness everywhere; in the summer there was a long drought, and by consequence there came a bad harvest, and great suffering and scarcity.

There were not a few in the district who attributed all these woes to the advent of the child of darkness, and who murmured openly in their huts and homesteads that no good would befall them so long as this offspring of hell were suffered in their midst.

Since, however, the time was past when the broad market place could have been filled with a curious, breathless, eager crowd, and the grey cathedral have grown red in the glare of flames fed by a young living body, they held their hands from doing her harm, and said these things only in their own ingle-nooks, and contented themselves with forbidding their children to consort with her, and with drawing their mules to the other side of the road when they met her. They did not mean to be cruel, they only acted in their own self-defence, and dealt with her as their fellow countrymen dealt with a cagote—"only."

Hence, when, with the reviving year the child's dulled brain awakened, and all the animal activity in her sprang into vigorous action, she found herself shunned, marked, and glanced at with averted looks of mingled dread and scorn. "A daughter of the devil!" she heard again and again muttered as they passed her; she grew to take shelter in this repute as in a fortress, and to be proud, with a savage pride, of her imputed origin.

It made her a little fierce, mute, fearless, reckless, all daring, and all enduring animal. An animal in her ferocities, her mute instincts, her supreme patience, her physical perfectness of body and of health. Perfect of shape and hue; full of force to resist; ignorant either of hope or fear; desiring only one thing, liberty; with no knowledge, but with unerring instinct.

She was at an age when happier creatures have scarce escaped from their mother's arms; but she had not even thus early a memory of her mother, and she had been shaken off to live or die, to fight or famish, as a young fox whose dam has been flung to the hounds is driven away to starve in the winter woods, or save himself, if he have strength, by slaughter.

She was a tame animal only in one thing:—she took blows uncomplainingly, and as though comprehending that they were her inevitable portion.

"The child of the devil!" they said. In a dumb, half unconscious fashion, this five-year-old creature wondered sometimes why the devil had not been good enough to give her a skin that would not feel, and veins that would not bleed.

She had always been beaten ever since her birth; she was beaten here; she thought it a law of life as other children think it such to have their mother's kiss and their daily food and nightly prayer.

Claudis Flamma did after his manner his duty by her. She was to him a thing accursed, possessed, loathsome, imbued with evil from her origin; but he did what he deemed his duty. He clothed her, if scantily; he fed her, if meagrely; he lashed her with all the caustic gibes that came naturally to his tongue; he set her hard tasks to keep her from idleness; he beat her when she did not, and not seldom when she did, them. He dashed holy water on her many times; and used a stick to her without mercy.

After this light he did his duty. That he should hate her, was to fulfil a duty also in his eyes; he had always been told that it was right to abhor the things of darkness; and to him she was a thing of utter darkness, a thing born of the black ruin of a stainless soul, begotten by the pollution and corruption of an infernal tempter.

He never questioned her as to her past—that short past, like the span of an insect's life, which yet had sufficed to gift her with passions, with instincts, with desires, even with memories,—in a word, with character:— a character he could neither change nor break; a thing formed already, for good or for evil, abidingly.

He never spoke to her except in sharp irony or in curt command. He set her hard tasks of bodily labour which she did not dispute, but accomplished so far as her small strength lay, with a mute dogged patience, half ferocity, half passiveness.

In those first winter days of her arrival he called her Folle-Farine; taking the most worthless, the most useless, most abject, the most despised thing he knew in all daily life from which to name her; and the name hered to her, and was the only one by which she was er known.

Folle-Farine!—as one may say, the Dust.

In time she grew to believe that it was really hers; en as in time she began to forget that strange, deep, h tongue in which she had babbled her first words, d to know no other tongue than the Norman-French out her.

Yet in her there existed imagination, tenderness, atitude, and a certain wild and true nobility, though e old man Flamma would never have looked for them, ver have believed in them. She was devil-born: she is of devil nature in his eyes.

Upon his mill-ditch, foul and fœtid, refuse would metimes gather, and receiving the seed of the lily, uld give birth to blossoms born stainless out of corption: but the allegory had no meaning for him. Had y one pointed it out to him he would have taken the eaker into his orchard, and said:

"Will the crab bear a fruit not bitter? Will the ghtshade give out sweetness and honey? Fool!—as e stem so the branch, as the sap so the blossom."

And this fruit of sin and shame was poison in his ght.

CHAPTER IV.

THE little dim mind of the five-year-old child was ot a blank; it was indeed filled to overflowing with ictures of a country that her tongue could not have told f, even had she spoken the language of the people midst whom she had been cast.

A land altogether unlike that in which she had been set down on that bitter night of snow and storm: a land noble and wild, and full of colour, broken into vast heights and narrow valleys, clothed with green beech-woods and with forests of oak and of walnut, filled with the noise of torrents leaping from crag to crag, and of brown mountain streams rushing, broad and angry, through wooded ravines. A land made beautiful by moss-grown water-mills, and lofty gateways of grey rock; and still shadowy pools, in which the bright fish leaped; and mules' bells that rang drowsily through leafy gorges; and limestone crags that pierced the clouds, spire-like, and fantastic in a thousand shapes; and high blue crests of snow-topped mountains, whose pinnacles glowed to the divinest flush of rose and amber with the setting of the sun.

This land she remembered vaguely, yet gloriously, as the splendours of a dream of Paradise rest on the brain of some young sleeper wakening in squalor, cold, and pain. But the people of the place she had been brought to could not comprehend her few, shy, sullen words, and her strange imperfect trills of song; and she could not tell them that this land had been no realm enchanted of fairy or of fiend, but only the forest region of the Liébana.

Thither, one rich autumn day, a tribe of Spanish gypsies had made their camp. They were a score in all; they held themselves one of the noblest branches of their wide family; they were people with pure Eastern blood in them, and all the grace and the gravity of the Oriental in their forms and postures.

They stole horses and sheep; they harried cattle; they stopped the mules in the passes, and lightened their load of wine-skins: they entered the posada, when they eigned to enter one at all, with neither civil question or show of purse, but with a gleam of the teeth, like a threatening dog, and the flash of the knife, half drawn out of the girdle. They were low thieves and mean liars; wild daredevils and loose livers; loathers of labour and lovers of idle days and plundering nights; yet they were beautiful, with the noble, calm, scornful beauty of the east, and they wore their rags with an air that was in self an empire.

They could play, too, in heavenly fashion, on their old three-stringed viols; and when their women danced on the sward by moonlight, under the broken shadows of some Moorish ruin, clanging high their tambourines above their graceful heads, and tossing the shining sequins that bound their heavy hair, the muleteer or the herdsman, seeing them from afar, shook with fear, and thought of the tales told him in his childhood by his grandam of the spirits of the dead Moors that rose to revelry, at midnight, in the haunts of their old lost kingdom.

Amongst them was a man yet more handsome than the rest, taller and lither still; wondrous at leaping and wrestling, and all athletic things; surest of any to win a woman, to tame a horse, to strike down a bull at a blow, to silence an angry group at a wineshop with a single glance of his terrible eyes.

His name was Taric.

He had left them often to wander by himself into many countries, and at times when, by talent or by terrorism, he had netted gold enough to play the fool to his fancy, he had gone to some strange city, where credulity and luxury prevailed, and there had lived like a prince, as his own phrase ran, and gamed and intrigued, and feasted, and roystered right royally whilst his gains lasted.

Those spent, he would always return awhile, and lead the common, roving, thieving life of his friends and brethren, till the fit of ambition or the run of luck were again on him. Then his people would afresh lose sight of him to light on him, velvet-clad, and wine-bibbing, in some painter's den in some foreign town, or welcome him ragged, famished, and footweary, on their own sunburnt sierras.

And the mystery of his ways endeared him to them; and they made him welcome whenever he returned, and never quarrelled with him for his faithlessness; but if there were anything wilder or wickeder, bolder or keener, on hand than was usual, his tribe would always say—"Let Taric lead."

One day their camp was made in a gorge under the great shadows of the Picos da Europa, a place that they loved much, and settled in often, finding the chesnut woods and the cliff caverns fair for shelter, the heather abounding in grouse, and the pools full of trout, fair for feeding. That day Taric returned from a year-long absence, suddenly standing, dark and mighty, between them and the light, as they lay around their soup kettle, awaiting their evening meal.

"There is a woman in labour, a league back; by the great cork-tree, against the bridge," he said to them. "Go to her some of you."

And, with a look to the women which singled out two for the errand, he stretched himself in the warmth of the fire, and helped himself to the soup, and lay quiet, vouchsafing them never a word, but playing meaningly with the knife handle thrust into his shirt; for he saw that some of the men were about to oppose his share of a common meal which he had not earned by a common right.

It was Taric—a name of some terror came to their fierce souls.

Taric, the strongest and fleetest and most well-favoured of them all; Taric, who had slain the bull that all the matadors had failed to daunt; Taric, who had torn up the young elm, when they needed a bridge over a flood, as easily as a child plucks up a reed; Taric, who had stopped the fiercest contrabandista in all those parts, and cut the man's throat with no more ado than a butcher slits a lamb's.

So they were silent, and let him take his portion of the fire and of the broth, and of the thin red wine.

Meanwhile the two gypsies, Quità and Zarâ, went on their quest, and found things as he had said.

Under the great cork-tree, where the grass was long and damp, and the wood grew thickly, and an old rude bridge of unhewn blocks of rock spanned, with one arch, the river as it rushed downward from its limestone bed aloft, they found a woman just dead, and a child just born.

Quità looked the woman all over hastily, to see if, by any chance, any gold or jewels might be on her; there were none. There was only an ivory cross on her chest, which Quità drew off and hid. Quità covered her with a few boughs and left her.

Zarâ wrapped the child in a bit of her woollen skirt, and held it warm in her breast, and hastened to the camp with it.

"She is dead, Taric," said Quità, meaning the woman she had left.

He nodded his handsome head.

"This is yours, Taric?" said Zarâ, meaning the child she held.

He nodded again, and drank another drop of wine, and stretched himself.

"What shall we do with her?" asked Quità.

"Let her lie there," he answered her.

"What shall we do with it?" asked Zarâ.

He laughed, and drew his knife against his own brown throat in a significant gesture.

Zarâ said no word to him, but she went away with the child under some branches, on which was hung a tattered piece of awning, orange striped, that marked her own especial resting place.

Out of the group about the fire, one man, rising, advanced, and looked Taric full in the eyes.

"Has the woman died by foul means?"

Taric, who never let any living soul molest or menace him, answered him without offence, and with a savage candour.

"No—that I swear. I used no foul play against her. Go look at her if you like. I loved her well enough while she lived. But what does that matter? She is dead. So best. Women are as many as the mulberries."

"You loved her, and you will let the wolves eat her body?"

Taric laughed.

"There are few wolves in the Liébana. Go and bury her if you choose, Phratos."

"I will," the other answered him; and he took his way to the cork-tree by the bridge.

The man who spoke was called Phratos.

He was not like his tribe in anything: except in a mutual love for a life that wandered always, and was to no man responsible, and needed no roof-tree, and wanted no settled habitation, but preferred to dwell wild with the roe and the coney, and to be hungry and unclad, rather than to eat the good things of the earth in submission and in durance.

He had not their physical perfection: an accident at his birth had made his spine misshapen, and his gait halting. His features would have been grotesque in their ugliness, except for the sweet pathos of the eyes and the gay archness of the mouth.

Amongst a race noted for its singular beauty of face and form, Phratos alone was deformed and unlovely; and yet both deformity and unloveliness were in a way poetic and uncommon; and in his rough sheepskin garments, knotted to his waist with a leathern thong, and with his thick tangled hair falling down on his shoulders, they were rather the deformity of the brake-haunting faun, the unloveliness of the moon-dancing satyr, than those of a man and a vagrant. With the likeness he had the temper of the old dead gods of the forests and rivers; he loved music, and could make it, in all its innumerable sighs and songs, give a voice to all creatures and things of the world, of the waters and the woodlands; and for many things he was sorrowful continually, and for other things he for ever laughed and was glad.

Though he was misshapen, and even, as some said, not altogether straight in his wits, yet his kin honoured him.

For he could draw music from the rude strings of his old viol that surpassed their own melodies as far as the shining of the sun on the summits of the Europa surpassed the trembling of the little lamps under the painted road-side Calvaries.

He was only a gypsy; he only played as the fancy moved him, by a bright fountain at a noonday halt, under the ruined arches of a Saracenic temple; before the tawny gleam of a vast dim plain at sunrise; in a cool shadowy court, where the vines shut out all light; beneath a balcony at night, when the moonbeams gleamed on some fair unknown face, thrust for a moment from the darkness through the white magnolia flowers. Yet he played in suchwise as makes women weep, and holds children and dogs still to listen, and moves grown men to shade their eyes with their hands, and think of old dead times, when they played and prayed at their mothers' knees.

And his music had so spoken to himself that, although true to his tribe and all their traditions, loving the vagrant life in the open air, and being incapable of pursuing any other, he yet neither stole nor slew, neither tricked nor lied, but found his way vaguely to honesty and candour, and, having found them, clove to them, so that none could turn him: living on such scant gains as were thrown to him for his music from balconies and posada windows and winehouse doors in the hamlets and towns through which he passed, and making a handful of pulse and a slice of melon, a couch of leaves and a draught of water, suffice to him for his few and simple wants.

His people reproached him, indeed, with demeaning their race by taking payment in lieu of making thefts; and they mocked him often, and taunted him, though in a manner they all loved him,—the reckless and bloodstained Taric most, perhaps, of all. But he would never quarrel with them, neither would he give over his strange ways which so incensed them, and with time they saw that Phratos was a gifted fool, who, like other mad simple creatures, had best be left to go on his own way unmolested and without contradiction.

If, too, they had driven him from their midst, they

would have missed his music sorely; that music which awoke them at break of day soaring up through their roof of chesnut leaves like a lark's song piercing the skies.

Phratos came now to the dead woman, and drew off the boughs, and looked at her. She was quite dead. She had died where she had first sunk down, unable to reach her promised resting place. It was a damp green nook on the edge of the bright mountain river, at the entrance of that narrow gorge in which the encampment had been made.

The face, which was white and young, lay upward, with the shadows of the flickering foliage on it; and the eyes, which Quità had not closed, were large and blue; her hair, which was long and brown, was loose, and had got wet amongst the grass, and had little buds of flowers and stray golden leaves twisted in it.

Phratos felt sorrow for her as he looked.

He could imagine her history.

Taric, whom many women had loved, had besought many a one thus to share his fierce free life for a little space, and then drift away out of it by chance, or be driven away from it by his fickle passions, or be taken away like this woman by death.

In her bosom, slipped in her clothes, was a letter. It was written in a tongue he did not know. He held it awhile, thinking, then he folded it up and put it in his girdle,—it might be of use, who could tell? There was the child, there, that might live; unless the camp broke up, and Zarâ left it under a walnut tree to die, with the last butterflies of the fading summer, which was in all likelihood all she would do.

Nevertheless he kept the letter, and when he had looked long enough at the dead creature, he turned to the tools he had brought with him, and set patiently to make her grave.

He could only work slowly, for he was weak of body, and his infirmity made all manual toil painful to him. His task was hard, even though the earth was so soft from recent heavy rains.

The sun set whilst he was still engaged on it; and it was quite nightfall before he had fully accomplished it. When the grave was ready he filled it carefully with the golden leaves that had fallen, and the thick many-coloured mosses that covered the ground like a carpet.

Then he laid the body tenderly down within that forest shroud, and, with the moss like a winding-sheet between it and the earth which had to fall on it, he committed the dead woman to her resting-place.

It did not seem strange to him, or awful, to leave her there.

He was a gypsy, and to him a grave under a forest tree and by a mountain stream seemed the most natural rest at last that any creature could desire or claim. No rites seemed needful to him, and no sense of any neglect, cruel or unfitting, jarred on him in thus leaving her in her loneliness, with only the cry of the bittern or the bell of the wild roe as a requiem.

Yet a certain sorrow for this unknown and lost life was on him, bohemian though he was, as he took up his mattock and turned away, and went backward down the gorge, and left her to lie there for ever, through rain and sunshine, through wind and storm, through the calm of the summer and the flush of the autumn, and the wildness of the winter, when the swollen stream should sweep above her tomb, and the famished beasts of the hills would lift up their voices around it.

When he reached the camp, he gave the letter to Taric.

Taric, knowing the tongue it was written in, and being able to understand the character, looked at it, and read it through by the light of the flaming wood. When he had done so he tossed it behind, in among the boughs, in scorn.

"The poor fool's prayer to the brute that she hated!" he said, with a scoff.

Phratos lifted up the letter and kept it.

In a later time he found some one who could decipher it for him.

It was the letter of Reine Flamma to the miller at Yprès, telling him the brief story of her fatal passion, and imploring from him mercy to her unborn child should it survive her and be ever taken to him.

Remorse and absence had softened to her the harshness and the meanness of her father's character; she only remembered that he had loved her, and had deemed her pure and faithful as the saints of God. There was no word in the appeal by which it could have been inferred that Claudis Flamma had been other than a man much wronged and loving much, patient of heart, and without blame in his simple life.

Phratos took the letter and cherished it. He thought it might some day serve her offspring. This old man's vengeance could not, he thought, be so cruel to the child as might be the curse and the knife of Taric.

"She must have been beautiful?" said Phratos to him, after a while, that night; "and you care no more for her than that."

Taric stretched his mighty limbs in the warmth of the flame and made his answer:

"There will be as good grapes on the vines next

year as any we gathered this. What does it signify?—she was only a woman.

"She loved me; she thought me a god, a devil, a prince, a chief,—all manner of things;—the people thought so too. She was sick of her life. She was sick of the priests and the beads, and the mill and the market. She was fair to look at, and the fools called her a saint. When a woman is young and has beauty, it is dull to be worshipped—in that way.

"I met her in the wood one summer night. The sun was setting. I do not know why I cared for her—I did. She was like a tall white lily; these women of ours are only great tawny sunflowers.

"She was pure and straight of life; she believed in heaven and hell; she was innocent as a child unborn; it was tempting to kill all that. It is so easy to kill it when a woman loves you. I taught her what passion and freedom and pleasure and torment all meant. She came with me,—after a struggle, a hard one. I kept her loyally while the gold lasted; that I swear. I took her to many cities. I let her have jewels and music, and silk dresses, and fine linen. I was good to her; that I swear.

"But after a bit she pined, and grew dull again, and wept in secret, and at times I caught her praying to the white cross which she wore on her breast. That made me mad. I cursed her and beat her. She never said anything; she seemed only to love me more, and that made me more mad.

"Then I got poor again, and I had to sell her things one by one. Not that she minded that, she would have sold her soul for me. We wandered north and south; and I made money sometimes by the dice, or by breaking a horse, or by fooling a woman, or by snatching a jewel off one of their churches; and I wanted to get rid of her, and I could not tell how. I had not the heart to kill her outright.

"But she never said a rough word, you know, and that makes a man mad. Maddalena or Kara or Rachel —any of them,—would have flown and struck a knife at me, and hissed like a snake, and there would have been blows and furious words and bloodshed; and then we should have kissed, and been lovers again, fast and fierce. But a woman who is quiet, and only looks at you with great, sad, soft eyes, when you strike her,—what is one to do?

"We were horribly poor at last: we slept in barns and haylofts; we ate berries and drank the brook water. She grew weak, and could hardly walk. Many a time I have been tempted to let her lie and die in the hedgeway or on the plains, and I did not,—one is so foolish sometimes for sake of a woman. She knew she was a burden and curse to me—I may have said so, perhaps; I do not remember.

"At last I heard of you in the Liébana, from a tribe we fell in with on the other side of the mountains, and so we travelled here on foot. I thought she would have got to the women before her hour arrived. But she fell down there, and could not stir: and so the end came. It is best as it is. She was wretched, and what could I do with a woman like that, who would never hearken to another lover, nor give up her dead God on his cross, nor take so much as a broken crust if it were stolen, nor even show her beauty to a sculptor to be carved in stone —for I tried to make her do that, and she would not. It is best as it is. If she had lived we could have done nothing with her. And yet I see her sometimes as I saw her that night, so white and so calm, in the little green wood, as the sun set——"

His voice ceased, and he took up a horn full of vino clarete; and drained it, and was very still, stretching his limbs to bask in the heat of the fire. The wine had loosened his tongue, and he had spoken from his heart, —truthfully.

Phratos, his only hearer, was silent.

He was thinking of the great blue sightless eyes that he had closed, and of the loose brown hair on which he had flung the wet leaves and the earth-clogged mosses.

"The child lives?" he said at length.

Taric, who was sinking to sleep after the long fatigues of a heavy tramp through mountain passes, stirred sullenly with an oath.

"Let it go to hell," he made answer.

And these were the only words of baptism that were spoken over the nameless daughter of Taric the gypsy and of Reine Flamma.

That night Phratos called out to him in the moonlight the woman Zarâ, who came from under her tent, and stood under the glistening leaves, strong and handsome, with shining eyes and snowy teeth.

"The child lives still?" he asked.

Zarâ nodded her head.

"You will try and keep it alive?" he pursued.

She shrugged her shoulders.

"What is the use? Taric would rather it were dead."

"What matter what Taric wishes. Living or dead, it will not hinder him. A child more or less with us, what is it? Only a draught of goat's milk or a handful of meal. So little; it cannot be felt. You have a child of your own, Zarâ; you cared for it?"

"Yes," she answered, with a sudden softening gleam of her bright savage eyes.

She had a brown, strong, year-old boy, who kicked his naked limbs on the sward with joy at Phratos' music.

"Then have pity on this motherless creature," said Phratos, wooingly. "I buried that dead woman; and her eyes, though there was no sight in them, still seemed to pray to mine—and to pray for her child. Be merciful, Zarâ. Let the child have the warmth of your arms and the defence of your strength. Be merciful, Zarâ; and your seed shall multiply and increase tenfold, and shall be stately, and strong, and shall spread as the branches of the plane-trees, on which the storm spends its fury in vain, and beneath which all things of the earth can find refuge. For never was a woman's pity fruitless, nor the fair deeds of her days without recompense."

Zarâ listened quietly, as the dreamy, poetic, persuasive words stole on her ear like music. Like the rest of her people, she half believed in him as a seer and prophet; her teeth shone out in a soft sudden smile.

"You are always a fool, Phratos," she said; "but it shall be as you fancy."

And she went in out of the moonlit leaves and the clear cool, autumn night into the little dark stifling tent, where the new-born child had been laid away in a corner upon a rough-and-ready bed of gathered dusky fir-needles.

"It is a little cub, not worth the saving; and its dam was not of our people," she said to herself, as she lifted the wailing and alien creature to her bosom.

"It is for you, my angel, that I do it," she murmured, looking at the sleeping face of her own son.

Outside the tent the sweet strains of Phratos' music rose sighing and soft; and mingling, as sounds mingle in a dream, with the murmurs of the forest leaves and the rushing of the mountain river. He gave her the only payment in his power.

Zarâ, hushing the strange child at her breast, listened, and was half-touched half-angered.

"Why should he play for this little stray thing, when he never played once for you, my glory?" she said to her son, as she put the dead woman's child roughly away, and took him up in its stead, to beat together in play his rosy hands and cover his mouth with kisses.

For even from these, the world's outcasts, this new life of a few hours' span was rejected as unworthy and despised.

Nevertheless, the music played on through the still forest night; and nevertheless, the child grew and throve.

The tribe of Taric abode in the Liébana or in the adjacent country along the banks of the Deva during the space of four years and more, scarcely losing in that time the sight, either from near or far, of the rosy peaks of the Europa.

He did not abide with them; he quarrelled with them violently concerning some division of a capture of wine-skins, and went on his own way to distant provinces and cities; to the gambling and the roystering, the woman-fooling and the bull-fighting, that his soul lusted after always.

His daughter he left to dwell in the tent of Zarâ, and under the defence of Phratos.

Once or twice, in sojourns of a night or two amongst his own people, as the young creature grew in stature and strength, Taric had glanced at her, and called her to him, and felt the litheness of her limbs and the weight of her hair, and laughed as he thrust her from him, thinking that, in time to come, she—who would know nothing of her mother's dead God on the cross, and of her mother's idle, weak scruples,—might bring him a fair provision in his years of age, when his hand should have lost its weight against men and his form its goodliness in the sight of women.

Once or twice he had given her a kick of his foot, or blow with his leathern whip, when she crawled in the grass too near his path, or lay asleep in the sun as he chanced to pass by her.

Otherwise he had nought to do with her, absent or present; otherwise he left her to chance and the devil, who were, as he said, according to the Christians, the natural patrons and sponsors of all love children. Chance and the devil, however, had not wholly their way in the Liébana; for beside them there was Phratos.

Phratos never abandoned her.

Under the wolfskin and pineboughs of Zarâ's tent there was misery very often.

Zarâ had a fresh son born to her with each succeeding year; and having a besotted love for her own offspring, had little but indifference and blows for the stranger who shared their bed and food. Her children, brown and curly, naked and strong, fought one another like panther cubs, and rode in a cluster like red mountain-ash berries in the sheep-skin round her waist, and drank by turns out of the pitcher of broth, and slept all together on dry ferns and mosses, rolled in warm balls one in another like young bears.

But the child who had no affinity with them, who was not even wholly of their tribe, but had in her what they deemed the taint of gentile blood, was not allowed to gnaw her bare bone or her ripe fig in peace if they wished for it; was never carried with them in the sheepskin nest, but left to totter after in the dust or mud as best she might; was forced to wait for the leavings in the pitcher, or go without if leavings there were none; and was kicked away by the sturdy limbs of these young males when she tried to creep for warmth's sake in amongst them on their fern bed. But she minded all this little; since in the Liébana there was Phratos.

Phratos was always good to her. The prayer which those piteous dead eyes had made he always answered. He had always pity for the child.

Many a time, but for his remembrance, she would have starved outright or died of cold in those wild winters, when the tribe huddled together in the caverns of the limestone, and the snow-drifts were driven up by northern winds and blocked them there for many days. Many a time but for his aid she would have dropped on their march and been left to perish as she might on the long sunburnt roads, in the arid mid-summers, when the gypsies plodded on their dusty way through the sinuous windings of hill-side paths and along the rough stones of dried-up water courses, in gorges and passages known alone to them and the wild deer.

When her throat was parched with the torment of long thirst, it was he who raised her to drink from the rill in the rock, high above, to which the mothers lifted their eager children leaving her to gasp and gaze unpitied. When she was driven away from the noonday meal by the hungry and clamorous youngsters, who would admit no share of their partridge broth and stewed lentils, it was he who bruised the maize between stones for her eating, and gathered for her the wild fruit of the quince and the mulberry.

When the sons of Zarâ had kicked and bruised and spurned her from the tent, he would lead her away to some shadowy place where the leaves grew thickly, and play to her such glad and buoyant tunes that the laughter seemed to bubble from the listening brooks and ripple amongst the swinging boughs, and make the wild hare skip with joy, and draw the timid lizard from his hole to frolic. And when the way was long, and the stony paths cruel to her little bare feet, he would carry her aloft on his misshapen shoulders, where his old viol always travelled; and would beguile the steep way with a thousand quaint, soft, grotesque conceits of all the flowers and leaves and birds and animals: talking rather to himself than her, yet talking with a tender fancifulness, half humour and half pathos, that soothed her tired senses like a lullaby. Hence it came to pass that the sole creature whom she loved and who had pity for her was the uncouth, crippled, gay, sad, gentle, dauntless creature whom his tribe had always held half-wittol and half-seer.

Thus the life in the hills of the Liébana went on till the child of Taric had entered her sixth year.

She had both beauty and grace; she had the old Moresco loveliness in its higher type; she was fleet as the roe, strong as the young izard, wild as the woodpartridge on the wing; she had grace of limb from the postures and dances with which she taught herself to keep time to the sweet, fantastic music of the viol; she was shy and sullen, and fierce and savage, to all save himself, for the hand of every other was against her; but to him, she was docile as the dove to the hand that feeds it. He had given her a string of bright sequins to hang on her hair, and when the peasants of the mountains and valleys saw her by the edge of some green woodland pool, whirling by moonlight to the sound of his melodies, they took her to be some unearthly spirit, and told wonderful things over their garlic of the elf crowned with stars they had seen dancing on a round lotus leaf in the hush of the night.

In the Liébana she was beaten often, hungry almost always, cursed fiercely, driven away by the mothers, mocked and flouted by the children; and this taught her silence and ferocity. Yet in the Liébana she was happy, for one creature loved her, and she was free—free to lie in the long grass, to bathe in the still pools, to watch the wild things of the woods, to wander ankle deep in forest blossoms, to sleep under the rocking of pines, to run against the sweet force of the wind, to climb the trees and swing cradled in leaves, and to look far away at the snow on the mountains, and to dream, and to love, and to be content in dreaming and loving, their mystical glory that awoke with the sun.

One day in the red autumn, Taric came; he had been wholly absent more than two years.

He was superb to the sight still, with matchless splendour of face and form, but his carriage was more reckless and disordered than ever, and in his gem-like and night-black eyes, there was a look of cunning and of subtle ferocity new to them.

His life had gone hardly with him, and to the indolence, the passions, the rapacity, the slothful sensuality of the gypsy—who had retained all the vices of his race whilst losing their virtues of simplicity in living, and of endurance under hardship—the gall of a sharp poverty had become unendurable: and to live without dice, and women, and wine, and boastful brawling, seemed to him to be worse than any death.

The day he returned, they were still camped in the Liébana; in one of its narrow gorges, overhung with a thick growth of trees, and coursed through by a headlong hill-stream, that spread itself into darkling breadths and leafy pools, in which the fish were astir under great snowy lilies and a tangled web of water plants.

He strode into the midst of them, as they sat round their camp-fire lit beneath a shelf of rock, as his wont was; and was welcomed and fed and plied with such as they had, with that mixture of sullen respect and incurable attachment which his tribe preserved, through all their quarrels, for this, the finest and the fiercest, the most fickle and the most faithless of them all.

He gorged himself, and drank, and said little.

When the meal was done, the young of the tribe scattered themselves in the red evening light under the great walnuts; some at feud, some at play.

"Which is mine?" he asked, surveying the children. They showed her to him. The sequins were round her head; she swung on a bough of ash; the pool beneath mirrored her; she was singing as children sing, without words, yet musically and gladly, catching at the fireflies that danced above her in the leaves.

"Can she dance?" he asked lazily of them.

"In her own fashion,—as a flower in the wind," Phratos answered him, with a smile; and willing to woo for her the good graces of her father, he slung his viol off his shoulders and tuned it, and beckoned the child.

She came, knowing nothing who Taric was; he was only to her a fierce-eyed man like the rest, who would beat her, most likely, if she stood between him and the sun, or overturned by mischance his horn of liquor.

Phratos played, and all the gypsy children, as their wont was, danced.

But she danced all alone, and with a grace and a fire that surpassed theirs. She was only a baby still; she had only her quick ear to guide her, and her only teacher was such inborn instinct as makes the birds sing and the young kids gambol.

Yet she danced with a wondrous subtlety and intensity of ardour beyond her years; her small brown limbs glancing like bronze in the fire-glow, the sequins flashing in her flying hair, and her form flung high in air, like a bird on the wing, or a leaf on the wind; never still, never ceasing to dart, and to leap, and to whirl, and to sway, yet always with a sweet dreamy indolence, even in her fiery unrest.

Taric watched her under his bent brow until the music ceased, and she dropped on the grass spent and panting like a swallow after a long ocean flight.

"She will do," he muttered.

"What is it you mean with the child?" some women asked.

Taric laughed.

"The little vermin is good for a gold piece or two," he answered.

Phratos said nothing, but he heard.

After awhile the camp was still; the gypsies slept. Two or three of their men went out to try and harry cattle by the light of the moon if they should be in luck; two others went forth to set snares for the wood partridges and rabbits; the rest slumbered soundly, the dogs curled to a watching sleep of vigilant guard in their midst.

Taric alone sat by the dying fire. When all was very quiet, and the stars were clear in midnight skies, the woman Zarâ stole out of her tent to him.

"You signed to me," she said to him in a low voice. "You want the child killed?"

Taric showed his white teeth like a wolf.

"Not I; what should I gain?"

"What is it you want, then, with her?"

"I mean to take her, that is all. See here—a month ago, on the other side of the mountains, I met a fantoccini player. It was at a wine-shop, hard by Luzarches. He had a woman-child with him who danced to his music, and whom the people praised for her beauty, and who anticked like a dancing dog, and who made a great deal of silver. We got friends, he and I. At the week's end the brat died: some sickness of the throat, they said. Her master tore his hair and raved; the little wretch was worth handfuls of coin to him. For such another he would give twelve gold pieces. He shall have her. She will dance for him and me; there is plenty to be made in that way. The women are fools over a handsome child; they open their larders and their purses. I shall take her away before sunrise; he says he teaches them in seven days, by starving and giving the stick. She will dance while she is a child. Later on—there are the theatres; she will be strong and handsome, and in the great cities, now, a woman's comeliness is as a mine of gold ore. I shall take her away by sunrise."

"To sell her?"

The hard fierce heart of Zarâ rebelled against him; she had no tenderness save for her own offspring, and she had maltreated the stray child many a time; yet the proud liberty and the savage chastity of her race were roused against him by his words.

Taric laughed again.

"Surely; why not? I will make a dancing dog of her for the peasants' pastime; and in time she will make dancing dogs of the nobles and the princes for her own sport. It is a brave life—none better."

The gypsy woman stood, astonished and irresolute. If he had flung his child in the river, or thrown her off a rock, he would have less offended the instincts and prejudices of her clan.

"What will Phratos say?" she asked at length.

"Phratos? A rotten fig for Phratos! What can he say—or do? The little beast is mine; I can wring its neck if I choose, and if it refuse to pipe when we play for it, I will."

The woman sought in vain to dissuade him; he was inflexible. She left him at last, telling herself that it was no business of hers. He had a right to do what he chose with his own. So went and lay down amongst her brown-faced boys, and was indifferent, and slept.

Taric likewise slept, upon a pile of moss under the ledge of the rock, lulled by the heat of the fire, which, ere lying down, he had fed with fresh boughs of resinous wood.

When all was quite still, and his deep quiet breathing told that his slumber was one not easily broken, a man softly rose from the ground and threw off a mass of dead leaves that had covered him, and stood erect, a dark, strange, misshapen figure, in the moonlight: it was Phratos.

He had heard, and understood all that Taric meant for the present and the future of the child: and he knew that when Taric vowed to do a thing for his own gain, it were easier to uproot the chain of the Europa than to turn him aside from his purpose.

"It was my doing!" said Phratos to himself bitterly, as he stood there, and his heart was sick and sore in him, as with self-reproach for a crime.

He thought awhile, standing still in the hush of the midnight; then he went softly, with a footfall that did not waken a dog, and lifted up the skins of Zarâ's tent as they hung over the fir-poles. The moonbeams slanting through the foliage strayed in, and showed him the woman, sleeping among her rosy robust children, like a mastiff with her litter of tawny pups; and away from them, on the bare ground closer to the entrance, the slumbering form of the young daughter of Taric.

She woke as he touched her, opening bright bewildered eyes.

"Hush! it is I, Phratos," he murmured over her, and the stifled cry died on her lips.

He lifted her up in his arms and left the tent with her, and dropped the curtain of sheepskin, and went out into the clear, crisp, autumn night. Her eyes had closed again, and her head had sunk on his shoulder heavy with sleep; she had not tried to keep awake one moment after knowing that it was Phratos who had come for her; she loved him, and in his hold feared nothing.

Taric lay on the ledge of the rock, deaf with the torpor of a half-drunken slumber, dreaming gloomily; his hand playing in his dreams with the knife that was thrust in his waist-band.

Phratos stepped gently past him, and through the outstretched forms of the dogs and men, and across the died-out embers of the fire, over which the emptied soup-kettle still swung, as the night-breeze blew to and fro its chain. No one heard him.

He went out from their circle and down the path of the gorge in silence, carrying the child. She was folded in a piece of sheepskin, and in her hair there were still the sequins. They glittered in the white light as he went; as the wind blew, it touched the chords of the viol on his shoulder, and struck a faint musical sighing sound from them.

"Is it morning?" the child murmured, half asleep.

"No, dear; it is night," he answered her, and she

was content and slept again—the strings of the viol sending a soft whisper in her drowsy ear, each time that the breeze arose and swept across them.

When the morning came it found him far on his road, leaving behind him the Liébana.

There followed a bright month of autumn weather. The child was happy as she had never been.

They moved on continually through the plains and the fields, the hills and the woods, the hamlets and the cities; but she and the viol were never weary. They rode aloft whilst he toiled on. Yet neither was he weary, for the viol murmured in the wind, and the child laughed in the sunshine.

It was late in the year.

The earth and sky were a blaze of russet and purple, and scarlet and gold. The air was keen and swift, and strong like wine. A summer fragrance blended with a winter frost. The grape harvest had been gathered in, and had been plentiful, and the people were liberal and of good humour.

Sometimes before a wine-shop or beneath a balcony, or in a broad market-square at evening, Phratos played; and the silver and copper coins were dropped fast to him. When he had enough by him to get a crust for himself, and milk and fruit for her, he did not pause to play, but moved on resolutely all the day, resting at night only.

He bought her a little garment of red foxes' furs; her head and her feet were bare. She bathed in clear running waters, and slept in a nest of hay. She saw vast towers, and wondrous spires, and strange piles of wood and stone, and rivers spanned by arches, and great forests half leafless, and plains red in stormy sunset light, and towns that lay hid in soft gold mists of vapour; and saw all these as in a dream, herself borne high in air, wrapped warm in fur, and lulled by the sweet familiar fraternity of the old viol. She asked no questions, she was content, like a mole or a dormouse; she was not beaten or mocked, she was never hungry nor cold; no one cursed her, and she was with Phratos.

It takes time to go on foot across a great country, and Phratos was nearly always on foot.

Now and then he gave a coin or two, or a tune or two, for a lift on some straw-laden waggon, or some mule-cart full of pottery or of vegetables, that was crawling on its slow way through the plains of the marshy lands, or the poplar-lined leagues of the public highways. But as a rule he plodded on by himself, shunning the people of his own race, and shunned in return by the ordinary populace of the places through which he travelled. For they knew him to be a Spanish gypsy by his skin and his garb and his language, and by the starry-eyed Arab-faced child who ran by his side in her red fur and her flashing sequins.

"There is a curse written against all honest folk on every one of those shaking coins," the peasants muttered as she passed them.

She did not comprehend their sayings, for she knew none but her gypsy tongue, and that only very imperfectly; but she knew by their glance that they meant that she was something evil; and she gripped tighter Phratos' hand—half-terrified, half-triumphant.

The weather grew colder and the ground harder. The golden and scarlet glories of the south and of the west, their red leafage and purple flowers, gorgeous sunsets and leaping waters, gave place to the level pastures, pale skies, leafless woods, and dim grey tints of the northerly lands.

The frosts became sharp, and mists that came from unseen seas enveloped them. There were marvellous old towns; cathedral spires that arose, ethereal as vapour; still dusky cities, aged with many centuries, that seemed to sleep eternally in the watery halo of the fog; green cultivated hills, from whose smooth brows the earth-touching clouds seemed never to lift themselves; straight sluggish streams, that flowed with leisurely laziness through broad flat meadow lands, white with snow and obscure with vapour. For these they had exchanged the pomp of dying foliage, the glory of crimson fruits, the fierce rush of the mistral, the odours of the noël-born violets, the fantastic shapes of the aloes and olives raising their dark spears and their silvery network against the amber fires of a winter dawn in the rich south-west.

The child was chilled, oppressed, vaguely awe-struck, and disquieted; but she said nothing; Phratos was there and the viol.

She missed the red forests and the leaping torrents, and the prickly fruits, and the smell of the violets and the vineyards, and the wild shapes of the cactus, and the old myrtles that were hoary and contorted with age. But she did not complain nor ask any questions; she had supreme faith in Phratos.

One night, at the close of a black day in mid-winter, the sharpest and hardest in cold that they had ever encountered, they passed through a little town whose roadways were mostly canals, and whose spires and roofs and pinnacles and turrets and towers were all beautiful with the poetry and the majesty of a long perished age.

The day had been bitter; there was snow everywhere; great blocks of ice choked up the water; the belfry chimes rang shrilly through the rarified air; the few folks that were astir were wrapped in wool or sheepskin; through the casements there glowed the ruddy flush of burning logs; and the muffled watchmen passing to and fro in antique custom on their rounds called out, under the closed houses, that it was eight of the night in a heavy snow-storm.

Phratos paused in the town at an old hostelry to give the child a hot drink of milk and a roll of rye bread. There he asked the way to the wood and the mill of Yprès.

They told it him sullenly and suspiciously: since for a wild gypsy of Spain the shrewd, thrifty, plain people of the north had no liking.

He thanked them, and went on his way, out of the barriers of the little town along a road by the river towards the country.

"Art thou cold, dear?" he asked her, with more tenderness than common in his voice.

The child shivered under her little fur skin, which would not keep out the searching of the hurricane and the driving of the snowflakes; but she drew her breath quickly, and answered him, "No."

They came to a little wood, leafless and black in the gloomy night; a dead crow swung in their faces on a swaying pear-tree; the roar of the mill-stream loudly filled what otherwise would have been an intense silence.

He made his way in by a little wicket through an orchard and through a garden, and so to the front of the mill-house. The shutters were not closed; through the driving of the snow he could see within. It looked to him—a houseless wanderer from his youth up—strangely warm and safe and still.

An old man sat on one side of the wide hearth; an old woman, who span, on the other; the spinning-wheel turned, the thread flew, the logs smoked and flamed, the red glow played on the blue and white tiles of the chimney-place, and danced on the pewter and brass on the shelves; from the rafters there hung smoked meats and dried herbs and strings of onions; there was a crucifix, and below it a little Nativity, in wax and carved wood.

He could not tell that the goodly stores were only gathered there to be sold later at famine prices to a starving peasantry; he could not tell that the wooden god was only worshipped in a blind, bigoted, brutal selfishness, that desired to save its own soul, and to leave all other souls in eternal damnation.

He could not tell; he only saw old age and warmth, and comfort; and what the people who hooted him as a heathen called the religion of Love.

"They will surely be good to her?" he thought. "Old people, and prosperous, and alone by their fireside."

It seemed that they must be so.

Any way, there was no other means to save her from Taric.

His heart was sore within him, for he had grown to love the child; and to the vagrant instincts of his race the life of the house and of the hearth seemed like the life of the cage for the bird. Yet Phratos, who was not altogether as his own people were, but had thought much and often in his own wild way, knew that such a life was the best for a woman child,—and, above all, for a woman child who had such a sire as Taric.

To keep her with himself was impossible. He had always dwelt with his tribe, having no life apart from theirs; and even if he had left them, wherever he had wandered, there would Taric have followed, and found him, and claimed the child by his right of blood. There was no other way to secure her from present misery and future shame, save only this; to place her with her mother's people.

She stood beside him, still and silent, gazing through the snowflakes at the warmth of the mill-kitchen within.

He stooped over her, and pushed between her fur garment and her skin the letter he had found on the breast of the dead woman in the Liébana.

"Thou wilt go in there to the old man yonder, and sleep by that pleasant fire to-night," he murmured to her. "And thou wilt be good and gentle, and even as thou art to me always; and to-morrow at noontide I will come and see how it fares with thee."

Her small hands tightened upon his.

"I will not go without thee," she muttered in the broken tongue of the gipsy children.

There were food and milk, fire and shelter, safety from the night and the storm there, she saw; but these were nought to her without Phratos. She struggled against her fate as the young bird struggles against being thrust into the cage,—not knowing what captivity means, and yet afraid of it and rebelling by instinct.

He took her up in his arms, and pressed her close to him, and for the first time kissed her. For Phratos, though tender to her, had no woman's foolishness, but had taught her to be hardy and strong, and to look for neither caresses nor compassion—knowing well that to the love child of Taric in her future years the first could only mean shame, and the last could only mean alms, which would be shame likewise.

"Go, dear," he said softly to her; and then he struck with his staff on the wooden door, and lifting its latch, unclosed it; and thrust the child forward, ere she could resist, into the darkness of the low entrance place.

Then he turned and went swiftly himself through the

orchard and wood into the gloom and the storm of the night.

He knew that to show himself to a northern householder were to do her evil and hurt; for between the wanderer of the Spanish forests and the peasant of the Norman pastures there could be only defiance, mistrust, and disdain.

"I will see how it is with her to-morrow," he said to himself as he faced again the wind and the sleet. "If it be well with her—let it be well. If not, she must come forth with me, and we must seek some lair where her wolf-sire shall not prowl and discover her. But it will be hard to find; for the vengeance of Taric is swift of foot and has a far-stretching hand and eyes that are sleepless."

And his heart was heavy in him as he went. He had done what seemed to him just and due to the child and her mother; he had been true to the vow he had made answering the mute prayer of the sightless dead eyes; he had saved the flesh of the child from the whip of the trainer, and the future of the child from the shame of the brothel; he had done thus much in saving her from her father, and he had done it in the only way that was possible to him.

Yet his heart was heavy as he went; and it seemed to him even as though he had thrust some mountain bird with pinions that would cleave the clouds, and eyes that would seek the sun, and a song that would rise with the dawn, and a courage that would breast the thunder, down into the darkness of a trap, to be shorn and crippled and silenced for evermore.

"I will see her to-morrow," he told himself; restless with a vague remorse, as though the good he had done had been evil.

But when the morrow dawned there had happened that to Phratos which forbade him to see whether it were well with her that day or any day in all the many years that came.

For Phratos that night, being blinded and shrouded in the storm of snow, lost such slender knowledge as he had of that northern country, and wandered far afield, not knowing where he was in the wide white desert, on which no single star-ray shone.

The violence of the storm grew with the hours. The land was a sheet of snow. The plains were dim and trackless as a desert. Sheep were frozen in their folds, and cattle drowned amidst the ice in the darkness. All lights were out, and the warning peals of the bells were drowned in the tempest of the winds.

The land was strange to him, and he lost all knowledge where he was. Above, beneath, around, were the dense rolling clouds of snow. Now and then through the tumult of the hurricane there was blown a strange harsh burst of jangled chimes that wailed a moment loudly on the silence and then died again.

At many doors he knocked: the doors of little lonely places standing in the great colourless waste.

But each door, being opened cautiously, was with haste shut in his face again.

"It is a gypsy," the people muttered, and were afraid; and they drew their bars closer and huddled together in their beds, and thanked their saints that they were safe beneath a roof.

He wrapped his sheepskin closer round him and set his face against the blast.

A hundred times he strove to set his steps backwards to the town, and a hundred times he failed; and moved only round and round vainly, never escaping the maze of the endless white fields.

Now the night was long, and he was weakly.

In the midst of the fields there was a cross, and at the head of the cross hung a lantern. The wind tossed the light to and fro. It flickered on the head of a woman. She lay in the snow, and her hand grasped his foot as he passed her.

"I am dead," she said to him: "dead of hunger. But the lad lives—save him."

And as she spoke, her lips closed together and her throat rattled, and she died.

The boy slept at her feet, and babbled in his sleep, delirious.

Phratos stooped down and raised him. He was a child of eight years, and worn with famine and fever, and his gaunt eyes stared hideously up at the driving snow.

Phratos folded him in his arms, and went on with him: the snow had nearly covered the body of his mother.

All around were the fields. There was no light, except from the lantern on the cross. A few sheep huddled near without a shepherd. The stillness was intense. The bells had ceased to ring or he had wandered far from the sound of them.

The lad was senseless; he muttered drearily foolish words of fever; his limbs hung in a dead weight; his teeth chattered. Phratos, bearing him, struggled on: the snow was deep and drifted heavily; every now and then he stumbled and plunged to his knees in a rift of earth or in a shallow pool of ice.

At last his strength, feeble at all times, failed him; his arms could bear their burden no longer; he let the young boy slip from his hold upon the ground; and stood, breathless and broken, with the snowflakes beating on him.

"The woman trusted me," he thought; she was a stranger, she was a beggar, she was dead. She had no bond upon him, neither could she ever bear witness against him. Yet he was loyal to her.

He unwound the sheepskin that he wore, and stripped himself of it and folded it about the sick child, and with a slow laborious effort drew the little body away under the frail shelter of a knot of furze, and wrapped it closely round, and left it there.

It was all that he could do.

Then, with no defence between him and the driving cold, he strove once more to find his road.

It was quite dark; quite still.

The snow fell ceaselessly; the white wide land was pathless as the sea.

He stumbled on as a mule may that being blind and bruised yet holds its way from the sheer instinct of its sad dumb patience.

His veins were frozen; his beard was ice; the wind cut his flesh like a scourge; a sickly dreamy sleepiness stole on him.

He knew well what it meant.

He tried to rouse himself; he was young, and his life had its sweetness; and there were faces he would fain have seen again, and voices whose laughter he would fain have heard.

He drew the viol round and touched its strings; but his frozen fingers had lost their cunning, and the soul of the music was chilled and dumb: it only sighed in answer.

He kissed it softly as he would have kissed a woman's

lips, and put it in his bosom. It had all his youth in it.

Then he stumbled onward yet again, feebly, being a cripple and cold to the bone, and pierced with a million thorns of pain.

There was no light anywhere.

The endless wilderness of the ploughed lands stretched all around him; where the little hamlets clustered the storm hid them; no light could penetrate the denseness of that changeless gloom; and the only sound that rose upon the ghastly silence was the moaning of some perishing flock locked in a flood of ice, and deserted by its shepherd.

But what he saw and what he heard were not these; going barefoot and blindfold to his death, the things of his own land were with him; the golden glories of sunsets of paradise; the scarlet blaze of a wilderness of flowers; the sound of the fountains at midnight; the glancing of the swift feet in the dances; the sweetness of songs sad as death sung in the desolate courts of old palaces; the deep dreamy hush of white moons shining through lines of palms straight on a silvery sea. These arose and drifted before him, and he ceased to suffer or to know, and sleep conquered him; and he dropped down on the earth noiselessly and powerlessly as a leaf sinks; and the snow fell and covered him.

When the morning broke a peasant, going to his labour in the fields while the stormy winter sun rose red over the whitened world, found both his body and the child's.

The boy was warm and living still beneath the shelter of the sheepskin: Phratos was dead.

The people succoured the child, and nursed and fed

him so that his life was saved; but to Phratos they only gave such burial as the corby gives the stricken deer.

"It is only a gypsy; let him lie," they said; and they left him there, and the snow kept him.

His viol they robbed him of, and cast it as a plaything to their children. But the children could make no melody from its dumb strings.

For the viol was faithful; and its music was dead too.

And his own land and his own people knew him never again; and never again at evening was the voice of his viol heard in the stillness; and never again did the young men and maidens dance to his bidding, and the tears and the laughter rise and fall at his will, and the beasts and the birds frisk and sing at his coming, and the children in his footsteps cry:—"Lo, it is summer, since Phratos is here!"

BOOK II.

"Yo contra todos, y todos contra yo."

CHAPTER I.

THE hottest sun of a hot summer shone on a straight dusty road. An old man was breaking stones by the wayside; he was very old, very bent, very lean, worn by ninety years if he had been worn by one; but he struck yet with a will, and the flints flew in a thousand pieces under his hammer, as though the youth and the force of nineteen years instead of ninety were at work on them.

When the noon bell rang from a little odd straight steeple, with a slanting roof, that peered out of the trees to the westward, he laid his hammer aside, threw off his brass-plated cap, wiped his forehead of its heat and dust, sat down on his pile of stones, and took out a hard black crust and munched it with teeth that were still strong and white.

The noontide was very quiet; the heat was intense, for there had been no rainfall for several weeks; there was one lark singing high up in the air, with its little breast lifted to the sun; but all the other birds were mute and invisible, doubtless hidden safely in some delicious shadow, swinging drowsily on tufts of linden bloom, or underneath the roofing of broad chestnut leaves.

The road on either side was lined by the straight forms of endless poplars, standing side by side as sentinels. The fields were all ablaze on every acre with the gold of ripening corn or mustard, and the scarlet flame of innumerable poppies. Here and there they were broken by some little house, white or black, or painted in bright colours, which lifted up amongst its leaves a little tower like a sugar-loaf, or a carved gable, and a pointed arch beneath it. Now and then they were divided by rows of trees standing breathless in the heat, or breadths of apple orchards, some with early fruits already ripe, some with fruits as yet green as their foliage.

Through it all the river ran, silver in the light; with shallow fords, where the deep-flanked bullocks drank; and ever and anon an ancient picturesque bridge of wood, time-bronzed and moss-embedded.

The old man did not look round once; he had been on these roads a score of years; the place had to him the monotony and colourlessness which all long familiar scenes wear to the eyes that are weary of them.

He was ninety-five; he had to labour for his living; he ate black bread; he had no living kith or kin; no friend save in the mighty legion of the dead; and he sat in the scorch of the sun; he hated the earth and the sky, the air and the landscape: why not? They had no loveliness for him; he only knew that the flies stung him, and that the red ants could crawl through the holes in his shoes, and bite him sharply with their little piercing teeth.

He sat in such shade as the tall lean poplar gave, munching his hard crusts; he had a fine keen profile and a long white beard that were thrown out as sharply as sculpture against the golden sunlight, in which the gnats were dancing. His eyes were fastened on the dust as he ate; blue piercing eyes that had still something of the fire of their youth; and his lips under the white hair moved a little now and then, half audibly.

His thoughts were with the long dead years of an unforgotten time—a time that will be remembered as long as the earth shall circle round the sun.

With the present he had nothing to do; he worked to satisfy the lingering cravings of a body that age seemed to have lost all power to kill; he worked because he was too much of a man still to beg, and because suicide looked to his fancy like a weakness, but life for all that was over with him; life in the years of his boyhood had been a thing so splendid, so terrible, so drunken, so divine, so tragic, so intense, that the world seemed now to him to have grown pale and grey and pulseless, with no sap in its veins, no hue in its suns, no blood in its humanity.

For his memory held the days of 'Thermidor; the weeks of the White Terror; the winter dawn, when the drums rolled out a King's threnody; the summer nights, when all the throats of Paris cried "Marengo!"

He had lived in the wondrous awe of that abundant time when every hour was an agony or a victory; when every woman was a martyr or a bacchanal; when the same scythe that had severed the flowering grasses served also to cleave the fair breasts of the mother, the tender throat of the child; when the ground was purple with the blue blood of men as with the juices of out-trodden grapes, and when the waters were white with the bodies of virgins as with the moon-fed lilies of summer. And now he sat here by the wayside, in the dust and the sun, only feeling the sting of the fly and the bite of the ant; and the world seemed dead to him, because so long ago, though his body still lived on, his soul had cursed God and died.

Through the golden motes of the dancing air and of the quivering sunbeams, whilst high above the lark sang on, there came along the road a girl.

She was bare-footed and bare-throated, lithe of movement, and straight and supple, as one who passed her life on the open lands and was abroad in all changes of the weather.

She walked with the free and fearless measure of the country women of Rome or the desert-born women of Nubia; she had barely entered her sixteenth year, but her bosom and limbs were full and firm, and moulded with almost all the luxuriant splendour of maturity; her head was not covered after the fashion of the country, but had a scarlet kerchief wound about, and on it she bore a great flat basket, filled high with fruits and herbs and flowers; a mass of colour and of blossom, through whose leaves and tendrils her dark level brows and her great eyes, blue black as a tempestuous night, looked out, set straight against the sun.

She came on, treading down the dust with her long and slender feet, that were such feet as a sculptor would give to his Cleopatra or his Phryne. Her face was grave, shadowed, even fierce; and her mouth, though scarlet as a berry and full and curled, had its lips pressed close on one another, like the lips of one who has long kept silence, and may keep it—until death.

As she saw the old man her eyes changed and lightened with a smile which for the moment banished all the gloom and savage patience from her eyes, and made them mellow and lustrous as a southern sun.

She paused before him, and spoke, showing her

beautiful white teeth, small and even, like rows of cowrie shells.

"You are well, Marcellin?"

The old man started, and looked up with a certain gladness on his own keen visage, which had lost all expression save such as an intense and absorbed retrospection will lend.

"Fool!" he made answer, harshly yet not unkindly. "When will you know that so long as an old man lives so long it cannot be 'well' with him?"

"Need one be a man, or old, to answer so?"

She spoke in the accent and the language of the province, but with a voice rich and pure and cold; not the voice of the north, or of any peasantry. She put her basket down from off her head, and leaned against the trunk of the poplar beside him, crossing her arms upon her bare chest.

"To the young everything is possible; to the old nothing," he said curtly.

Her eyes gleamed with a fierce thirsty longing; she made him no reply.

He broke off half his dry bread and tendered it to her. She shook her head and motioned it away; yet she was as hungered as any hawk that has hunted all through the night and the woods, and has killed nothing. The growing life, the superb strength, the lofty stature of her made her need constant nourishment, as young trees need it; and she was fed as scantily as a blind beggar's dog, and less willingly than a galley slave.

The kindly air had fed her richly, strongly, continually; that was all.

"Possible!" she said slowly, after awhile. "What is possible? I do not understand."

The old man, Marcellin, smiled grimly.

"You see that lark? It soars there, and sings there. It is possible that a fowler may hide in the grasses; it is possible that it may be shot as it sings; it is possible that it may have the honour to die in agony to grace a rich man's table. You see?"

She mused a moment; her brain was rapid in intuitive perception, but barren of all culture; it took her many moments to follow the filmy track of a metaphorical utterance. But by degrees she saw his meaning, and the shadow settled over her face again.

"The possible, then, is only—the worse?" she said slowly.

The old man smiled still grimly.

"Nay; our friends the priests say there is a 'possible' which will give—one day—the fowler who kills the lark the wings of the lark, and the lark's power to sing *Laus Deo* in heaven. *I* do not say—they do."

"The priests!"

All the scorn of which her curved lips were capable curled on them, and a deep hate gathered in her eyes—a hate that was unfathomable and mute.

"Then there is no 'possible' for me," she said bitterly, "if so be that priests hold the gifts of it?"

Marcellin looked up at her from under his bushy white eyebrows; a glance fleet and keen as the gleam of blue steel.

"Yes, there is," he said curtly. "You are a woman child, and have beauty: the devil will give you one."

"Always the devil!" she muttered. There was impatience in her echo of the words, and yet there was an awe also as of one who uses a name that is mighty and full of majesty, although familiar.

"Always the devil!" repeated Marcellin. "For the world is always of men."

His meaning this time lay too deep for her, and passed her; she stood leaning against the poplar, with her head bent and her form motionless in the sunlight like a statue of bronze.

"If men be devils they are my brethren," she said suddenly; "why do they then so hate me?"

The old man stroked his beard.

"Because Fraternity is Hate. Cain said so; but God would not believe him."

She mused over the saying; silent still.

The lark dropped down from heaven, suddenly falling through the air, mute. It had been struck by a sparrow-hawk, which flashed black against the azure of the skies and the white haze of the atmosphere; and which flew down in the track of the lark and seized it ere it gained the shelter of the grass and bore it away within his talons.

Marcellin pointed to it with his pipe-stem.

"You see there are many forms of the 'possible'"—

"When it means Death," she added.

The old man took his pipe back and smoked.

"Of course, Death is the key-note of creation."

Again she did not comprehend; a puzzled pain clouded the lustre of her eyes.

"But the lark praised God—why should it be so dealt with?"

Marcellin smiled grimly.

"Abel was praising God; but that did not turn aside the steel."

She was silent yet again; he had told her that old story of the sons born of Eve, and the one whom, hearing it, she had understood and pitied had been Cain.

At that moment, through the roadway that wound across the meadows and through the corn lands and the trees, there came in sight a gleam of scarlet that was not from the poppies, a flash of silver that was not from the river, a column of smoke that was not from the weeds that burned on the hillside.

There came a cloud, with a melodious murmur softly rising from it; a cloud that moved between the high flowering hedges, the tall amber wheat, the slender poplars, and the fruitful orchards; a cloud that grew larger and clearer as it drew more near to them, and left the green water meadows and the winding field paths for the great high road.

It was a procession of the Church.

It drew closer and closer by slow imperceptible degrees, until it approached them; the old man sat upright, not taking his cap from his head nor his pipe from his mouth; the young girl ceased to lean for rest against the tree, and stood with her arms crossed on her breast.

The Church passed them; the great gilt crucifix held aloft, the scarlet and the white of the floating robes catching the sunlight; the silver chains and silver censers gleaming; the fresh young voices of the singing children cleaving the air like a rush of wind; the dark shorn faces of the priests bowed over open books, the tender sound of little bells ringing across the low deep monotony of prayer.

The Church passed them; the dust of the parched road rose up in a choking mass; the heavy mist of the incense hung darkly on the sunlit air; the tramp of the many feet startled the birds from their rest, and pierced through the noonday silence.

It passed them, and left them behind it; but the fresh leaves were choked and whitened; the birds were fluttered and affrightened; the old man coughed, the girl strove to brush the dust motes from her smarting eyelids.

"That is the Church!" said the stone-breaker, with a smile. "Dust—terror—a choked voice—and blinded eyes."

Now she understood; and her beautiful curled lips laughed mutely.

The old man rammed some more tobacco into the bowl of his pipe.

"That is the Church!" he said. "To burn incense and pray for rain, and to fell the forests that were the rain-makers."

The procession passed away out of sight, going along the highway and winding by the course of the river, calling to the bright blue heavens for rain; whilst the little bells rang and the incense curled and the priests prayed themselves hoarse, and the peasants toiled footsore, and the eager steps of the choral children trod the tiny gnat dead in the grasses and the bright butterfly dead in the dust.

The priests had cast a severer look from out their down-dropped eyelids; the children had huddled together, with their voices faltering a little; and the boy choristers had shot out their lips in gestures of defiance and opprobrium as they had passed these twain beneath the wayside trees. For the two were both outcasts.

"Didst thou see the man that killed the king?" whispered to another one fair and curly-headed baby, who was holding in the sun her little, white, silver-fringed banner, and catching the rise and fall of the sonorous chaunt as well as she could with her little, lisping tones.

"Didst thou see the daughter of the devil?" muttered to another a handsome golden brown boy, who had left his herd untended in the meadow to don his scarlet robes and swing about the censer of his village chapel.

And they all sang louder, and tossed more incense on high, and marched more closely together under the rays of the gleaming crucifix as they went; feeling that they had been beneath the shadow of the powers of darkness, and that they were purer and holier and more exalted, because they had thus passed by in scorn what was accursed with psalms on their lips, with the cross as their symbol.

So they went their way through the peaceful country with a glory of sunbeams about them—through the corn, past the orchards, by the river, into the heart of the old brown, quiet town, and about the foot of the great cathedral, where they kneeled down in the dust and prayed, then rose and sang the "Angelus."

Then, the tall dark-visaged priest, who had led them all thither under the standard of the golden crucifix, lifted his voice alone and implored God, and exhorted man; implored for rain and all the blessings of harvest, exhorted to patience and the imitation of God.

The people were moved and saddened, and listened, smiting their breasts; and after a while rising from their knees, many of them in tears, dispersed and went their ways, muttering to one another:—"We have had no such harvests as those of old since the man that slew a saint came to dwell here;" and answering to one another: —"We had never such droughts as these in the sweet cool weather of old, before the offspring of hell was amongst us."

For the priests had not said to them, "Lo! your mercy is parched as the earth, and your hearts as the heavens are brazen."

CHAPTER II.

In the days of his youngest youth, in the old drunken days that were dead, this old stone-breaker Marcellin had known such life as it is given to few men to know —a life of the soul and the senses; a life of storm and delight; a life mad with blood and with wine; a life of divinest dreams; a life when women kissed them, and bade them slay; a life when mothers blessed them and bade them die; a life, strong, awful, splendid, unutterable; a life seized at its fullest and fiercest and fairest, out of an air that was death, off an earth that was hell.

When his cheeks had had a boy's bloom and his curls a boy's gold he had seen a nation in delirium; he had been one of the elect of a people; he had uttered the words that burn, and wrought the acts that live; he had been of the Thousand of Marsala, and he had been of the avengers in Thermidor: he had raised his flute-like voice from the tribune, and he had cast in his vote for the death of a king; passions had been his playthings, and he had toyed with life as a child with a match; he had beheld the despised enthroned in power, and desolation left within kings' palaces; he too had been fierce, and glad, and cruel, and gay, and drunken, and proud, as the whole land was; he had seen the white beauty of royal women bare in the hands of the mob, and the throats that princes had caressed kissed by the broad steel knife; he had had his youth in a wondrous time, when all men had been gods or devils, and all women martyrs or furies.

And now,—he broke stones to get daily bread, and those who passed him by cursed him, saying:

"This man slew a king."

For he had outlived his time, and the life that had been golden and red at its dawn was now grey and pale as the ashes of a fire grown cold; for in all the list of the world's weary errors there is no mistake so deadly as age.

Years before, in such hot summer weather as this against which the Church had prayed, the old man, going homewards to his little cabin amidst the fields, had met a little child coming straight towards him in the full crimson glow of the setting sun, and with the flame of the poppies all around her.

He hardly knew why he looked at her, but when he had once looked his eyes rested there.

She had the hues of his youth about her; in that blood-red light, amongst the blood-red flowers, she made him think of women's forms that he had seen in all their grace and their voluptuous loveliness clothed in the red garment of death, and standing on the dusky red of the scaffold as the burning mornings of the summers of slaughter had risen over the land.

The child was all alone before him in that intense glow as of fire; above her there was a tawny sky, flushed here and there with purple; around here stretched the solitary level of the fields burnt yellow as gold by the long months of heat. There were stripes on her shoulders blue and black from the marks of a thong.

He looked at her, and stopped her, why he hardly knew, except that a look about her, beaten but yet unsubdued, attracted him. He had seen the look of yore in the years of his youth, on the faces of the nobles he hated.

"Have you been hurt?" he asked her in his harsh, strong voice. She put her heavy load of faggots down and stared at him.

"Hurt?" She echoed the word stupidly. No one ever thought she could be hurt; what was done to her was punishment and justice.

"Yes. Those stripes—they must be painful?"

She gave a gesture of assent with her head, but she did not answer.

"Who beat you?" he pursued.

A cloud of passion swept over her bent face.

"Flamma."

"You were wicked?"

"They said so."

"And what do you do when you are beaten?"

"I shut my mouth."

"For what?"

"For fear they should know it hurt me—and be glad."

Marcellin leaned on his elm stick, and fastened on her his keen passionless eyes with a look which, for him who shunned and was shunned by all his kind, was almost sympathy.

"Come to my hut," he said to her. "I know a herb that will take the fret and the ache out of your bruises."

The child followed him passively, half stupidly; he was the first creature that had ever bidden her go with him, and this rough pity of his was sweet to her, with an amazing incredible balm in it which only those can know who see raised against them every man's hand, and hear on their ears the mockery of all the voices of their world.

Under reviling, and contempt, and constant rejection, she had become savage as a trapped hawk, wild as an escaped panther; but to him she was obedient and passive, because he had spoken to her without a taunt and without a curse, which until now had been the sole two forms of human speech that she had heard.

His little hut was in the midst of those spreading cornfields, set where two pathways crossed each other, and stretched down the gentle slope of the cultured lands to join the great highway—a hut of stones and plaited rushes, with a roof of thatch, where the old republican, hardy of frame and born of a toiling race, dwelt in solitude, and broke his scanty bitter bread without lament, if without content.

He took some leaves of a simple herb that he knew, soaked them with water, and bound them on her shoulders, not ungently, though his hand was so rough with labour, and, as men said, had been so often red with carnage.

Then he gave her a draught of goat's milk, sweet and fresh, from a wooden bowl; shared with her the dry black crusts that formed his only evening meal; bestowed on her a gift of a rare old scarlet scarf of woven wools and eastern broideries, one of the few relics of his buried life; lifted the faggots on her back, so that she could carry them with greater ease; and set her on her homeward way.

"Come to me again," he said, briefly, as she went across the threshold.

The child bent her head in silence, and kissed his hand quickly and timidly, like a grateful dog that is amazed to have a caress, and not a blow.

"After a forty years' vow I have broken it; I have pitied a human thing," the old man muttered as he stood in his doorway looking after her shadow as it passed small and dark across the scarlet light of the poppies.

"They call him vile, and they say that he slew men,"

thought the child, who had long known his face, though he never had noted hers; and it seemed to her that all mercy lay in her father's kingdom—which they called the kingdom of evil. The cool moist herbs slaked the heat of her bruises; and the draught of milk had slaked the thirst of her throat.

"Is evil good?" she asked in her heart as she went through the tall red poppies.

And from that evening thenceforward Folle-Farine and Marcellin cleaved to one another, being outcasts from all others.

CHAPTER III.

As the religious gathering broke up and split in divers streams to divers ways, the little town returned to its accustomed stillness—a stillness that seemed to have in it the calm of a thousand sleeping years, and the legends and the dreams of half a score of old dead centuries.

On market-days and saint-days, days of high feast or of perpetual chaffering, the town was full of colour, movement, noise, and population.

The country people crowded in, filling it with the jingling of mule-bells; the fisher people came, bringing in with them the crisp salt smell of the sea and the blue of the sea on their garments; its own tanners and ivory carvers, and fruiterers, and lacemakers turned out by the hundred in all the quaint variety of costumes which their forefathers had bequeathed to them, and to which they were still wise enough to adhere. But at other times when the fishers were in their hamlets, and the peasantry on their lands and in their orchards, and the townsfolk at their labours in the old rich renaissance mansions which they had turned into tanneries, and granaries, and wool-sheds, and work-shops, the place was profoundly still; scarcely a child at play in the streets, scarcely a dog asleep in the sun.

When the crowds had gone the priests laid aside their vestments, and donned the black serge of their daily habit, and went to their daily avocations in their humble dwellings.

The crosses and the censers were put back upon their altars, and hung up upon their pillars.

The boy choristers and the little children put their white linen and their scarlet robes back in cupboards and presses, with heads of lavender and sprigs of rosemary to keep the moth and the devil away, and went to their fields, to their homes, to their herds, to their paper kites, to their daisy chains, to the poor rabbits they pent in a hutch, to the poor flies they killed in the sun.

The town became quite still, the market-place quite empty; the drowsy silence of a burning, cloudless afternoon was over all the quiet places about the cathedral walls, where of old the bishops and the canons dwelt; grey shady courts; dim open cloisters; houses covered with oaken carvings, and shadowed with the spreading branches of chestnuts and of lime-trees that were as aged as themselves.

Under the shelter of one of the lindens, after the populace had gone, there was seated on a broad stone bench the girl who had stood by the wayside erect and unbending as the procession had moved before her.

She had flung herself down in dreamy restfulness. She had delivered her burden of vegetables and fruit at a shop near by, whose awning stretched out into the street like a toadstool yellow with the sun. The heat was intense; she had been on foot all day; she sat to rest a moment, and put her burning hands under a little rill of water that spouted into a basin in a niche in the wall. An ancient well, with a stone image of the Madonna sculptured above, and a wreath of vineleaves in stone running around, in the lavish ornamentation of an age when men loved loveliness for its own sake, and begrudged neither time nor labour in its service.

She leaned over the fountain, kept so cool by the roofing of the thick green leaves; there was a metal cup attached to the basin by a chain, and she filled it at the running thread of water, and stooped her lips to it again and again thirstily.

The day was sultry; the ways were long and white with powdered limestone; her throat was still parched with the dust raised by the many feet of the multitude; and although she had borne in the great basket which now stood empty at her side, cherries, peaches, mulberries, melons, full of juice and lusciousness, this daughter of the devil had not taken even one to freshen her dry mouth.

Folle-Farine stooped to the water and played with it, and drank it, and steeped her lips and her arms in it; lying there on the stone bench, with her bare feet curled one in another, and her slender round limbs full of the voluptuous repose of a resting panther. The coolness, the murmur, the clearness, the peace, the soft flowing movement of water, possess an ineffable charm for natures that are passion-tossed, feverish, and full of storm.

There was a dreamy peace about the place, too, which had charms likewise for her; in the dusky arch of the long cloisters, in the grey lichen-grown walls, in the broad pamments of the paven court, in the clusters of strange delicate carvings beneath and below; in the sculptured friezes where little nests that the birds had made in the spring still rested, and in the dense brooding thickness of the boughs which brought the sweetness and the shadows of the woods into the heart of the peopled town.

She stayed there, loath to move; loath to return where a jeer, a bruise, a lifted stick, a muttered curse, were all her greeting and her guerdon.

As she lay thus, one of the doors in the old houses in the cloisters opened; the head of an old woman was thrust out, crowned with the high fanshaped comb, and the towering white linen cap, that are the female note of that especial town.

The old woman was the mother of the sacristan, and she, looking out, shrieked shrilly to her son:

"Georges, Georges! come hither. The devil's daughter is drinking the blest water!"

The sacristan was hoeing amongst his cabbages in the garden behind his house, surrounded with clipt yew, and damp from the deep shade of the cathedral, that overshadowed it.

He ran out at his mother's call, hoe in hand, himself an old man, though stout and strong.

The well in the wall was his especial charge and pride; immeasurable sanctity attached to it.

According to tradition, the water had spouted from the stone itself, at the touch of a branch of blossoming pear, held in the hand of St. Jerome, who had returned to earth in the middle of the fourteenth century, and dwelt for a while near the cathedral, working at the honourable trade of a cordwainer, and accomplishing mighty miracles throughout the district. It was said that some of his miraculous power still remained in the fountain, and that even yet, those who drank on St. Jerome's day, in full faith and with believing hearts, were, oftentimes, cleansed of sin, and purified of bodily disease.

Wherefore on that day, throngs of peasantry flocked in from all sides, and crowded round it, and drank; to the benefit of the sacristan in charge, if not to that of their souls and bodies.

Summoned by his mother, he flew to the rescue of the sanctified spring.

"Get you gone!" he shouted. "Get you gone, you child of hell! How durst you touch the blessed basin? Do you think that God struck water from the stone for such as you?"

Folle-Farine lifted her head and looked him in the face with her audacious eyes, and laughed; then tossed her head again, and plunged it into the bright living water, till her lips, and her cheeks, and all the rippling hair about her temples sparkled with its silvery drops.

The sacristan, infuriated at once by the impiety and the defiance, shrieked aloud.

"Insolent animal! Daughter of Satan! I will teach you to taint the gift of a saint with lips of the devil!"

And he seized her roughly with one hand upon her shoulder, and with the other raised the hoe and brandished the wooden staff of it above her head in threat to strike her; whilst his old mother, still thrusting her lofty headgear and her wrinkled face from out the door, screamed to him to show he was a man, and have no mercy.

As his grasp touched her, and the staff cast its shadow across her, Folle-Farine sprang up, defiance and fury breathing from all her beautiful fierce face.

She seized the staff in her right hand, wrenched it with a swift movement from his hold, and catching his head under her left arm, rained blows on him from his own weapon, with a sudden gust of breathless rage which blinded him, and lent to her slender muscular limbs, the strength and the force of man. Then, as rapidly as she had seized and struck him, she flung him from her with such violence that he fell prostrate on the pavement of the court; caught up the metal pail which stood by ready filled, dashed the water over him where he lay, and turning from him without a word, walked across the courtyard slowly, and with a haughty grace in all the carriage of her bare limbs, and the folds of her ragged garments; bearing the empty osier basket on her head, deaf as the stones around to the screams of the sacristan and his mother.

In these secluded cloisters, and in the high noontide, when all were sleeping or eating in the cool shelter of their darkened houses, the old woman's voice remained unheard.

The saints heard, no doubt, but they were too lazy to stir from their niches in that sultry noontide; except the baying of a chained dog aroused, there was no answer to the outcry, and Folle-Farine passed out into the market place unarrested, and not meeting another living creature.

As she turned into one of the squares that led to the open country, she saw in the distance one of the guardians of the peace of the town moving quickly towards the cloisters, with his glittering lace shining in the sun, and his long scabbard clattering upon the stones. She laughed a little as she saw.

"They will not come after *me*," she said to herself. "They are too afraid of the devil."

She judged rightly; they did not come.

She crossed all the wide scorching square, whose white stones blazed in the glare of the sun.

There was nothing in sight except a stray cat prowling

in a corner, and three sparrows quarrelling over a foul-smelling heap of refuse.

The quaint old houses round seemed all asleep, with the shutters closed like tired eyelids over their little, dim, aged, orbs of windows. The gilded vanes on their twisted chimneys, and carved parapets, pointed motionless to the warm south. There was not a sound, except the cawing of some rooks, who built their nests high aloft in the fretted pinnacles of the cathedral.

Undisturbed she crossed the square, and took her way down the crooked street that led her homeward to the outlying country. It was an old, twisting, dusky place, with the water flowing through its centre as its only roadway; and in it there were the oldest houses of the town, all of timber, black with age, and carved with the wonderful florid fancies and grotesque conceits of the years when a house was to its master a thing beloved and beautiful, a bulwark, an altar, a heritage, an heirloom to be dwelt in all the days of a long life, and bequeathed in all honour and honesty to a noble offspring.

The street was very silent, the ripple of the water was the chief sound that filled it. Its tenants were very poor, and in many of its antique mansions the beggars shared shelter with the rats and the owls. In one of these dwellings, however, there were still some warmth and colour.

The orange and scarlet flowers of a nasturtium curled up its twisted pilasters; the big, fair clusters of hydrangea filled up its narrow casements; a breadth of many-coloured saxifrage, with leaves of green and rose, and blossoms of purple and white, hung over the balcony rail, which five centuries earlier had been draped with cloth of gold; and a little yellow song bird made music in the empty niche from which the sculptured flower-de-luce had been so long torn down.

From that window a woman looked, leaning with folded arms above the rose-tipped saxifrage, and beneath the green-leaved vine.

She was a fair woman, white as the lilies, and she had silver pins in her amber hair, and a mouth that laughed sweetly. She called to Folle-Farine,

"You brown thing; why do you stare at me?"

Folle-Farine started and withdrew the fixed gaze of her lustrous eyes.

"Because you are beautiful," she answered curtly.

All beautiful things had a fascination for her. This woman above was very fair to see, and she looked at her as she looked at the purple butterflies in the sun; at the stars shining down through the leaves; at the vast, dim, gorgeous figures in the cathedral windows; at the happy children running to their mothers with their hands full of primroses, as she saw them in the woods at spring-time; at the laughing groups round the wood-fires in the new year time when she passed a lattice pane that the snow-drift had not blocked; at all the things that were so often in her sight, and yet with which her life had no part or likeness.

She stood there on the rough flints, in the darkness cast from the jutting beams of the house; and the other happier creature leaned above there in the light, white and rose-hued, and with the silver bells of the pins shaking in her yellow tresses.

"You are old Flamma's grand-daughter," cried the other, from her leafy nest above. "You work for him all day long at the mill?"

"Yes."

"And your feet are bare, and your clothes are rags,

and you go to and fro like a packhorse, and the people hate you? You must be a fool. Your father was the devil, they say: why do you not make him give you good things?"

"He will not hear," the child muttered wearily; had she not besought him endlessly with breathless prayer.

"Will he not? Wait a year—wait a year."

"What then?" asked Folle-Farine, with a quick startled breath.

"In a year you will be a woman, and he always hears women, they say."

"He hears you?"

The fair woman above laughed:

"Perhaps; in his fashion. But he pays me ill as yet," and she plucked one of the silver pins from her hair, and stabbed the rosy foam of the saxifrage through and through with it; for she was but a gardener's wife, and was restless and full of discontent.

"Get you gone," she added quickly, "or I will throw a stone at you, you witch; you have the evil eye, they say, and you may strike me blind if you stare so."

Folle-Farine went on her way over the sharp stones with a heavy heart. That picture in the casement had made that passage bright to her many a time; and when at last that picture had moved and spoken, it had only mocked her and reviled her as the rest did.

The street was dark for her like all the others now.

The gardener's wife, leaning there, with the green and gold of the vineleaves brushing her hair, looked after her down the crooked way.

"That young wretch will be more beautiful than I," she thought; and the thought was bitter to her, as such a one is to a fair woman.

Folle-Farine went slowly and sadly through the street,

with her head dropped, and the large osier basket trailing behind her over the stones.

She was well used to be pelted with words hard as hailstones, and usually heeded them little, or gave them back with sullen, fierce defiance. But from this woman they had wounded her; from that bright bower of golden leaves and scarlet flowers she had faintly fancied some stray beam of light might wander even to her.

She was soon outside the gates of the town, and beyond the old walls, where the bramble and the lichen grew over the huge stones of ramparts and fortifications, useless and decayed from age.

The country roads and paths, the silver streams and the wooden bridges, the lanes through which the market mules picked their careful way, the fields in which the white-capped peasant women and the brindled oxen were at work, stretched all before her in a radiant air, sweet with the scent of ripening fruits from many orchards.

Here and there a wayside crucifix rose dark against the sun; here and there a chapel bell sounded from under some little peaked red roof. The cattle dozed beside meadow ditches that were choked with wild flowers; the dogs lay down beside their sheep and slept.

At the first cottage which she passed, the housewife sat out under a spreading chestnut tree, weaving lace upon her knee.

Folle-Farine looked wistfully at the woman, who was young and pretty, and who darted her swift skilled hand in and out and around the bobbins, keeping time meanwhile with a mirthful burden that she sang.

The woman looked up and frowned as the girl passed by her.

A little way farther on there was a winehouse by the

roadside, built of wood, vine-wreathed, and half hidden in the tall flowering briars of its garden.

Out of the lattice there was leaning a maiden with the silver cross on her bosom shining in the sun, and her meek blue eyes smiling down from under the tower of her high white cap. She was reaching a carnation to a student who stood below, with long fair locks and ruddy cheeks, and a beard yellow with the amber down of twenty years; and who kissed her white wrist as he caught the red flower.

Folle-Farine glanced at the pretty picture with a dull wonder and a nameless pain: what could it mean to be happy like that?

Half a league onward she passed another cottage shadowed by a sycamore-tree, and with the swallows whirling around its tall twisted stone chimneys, and a beurré pear covering with branch and bloom its old grey walls. An aged woman sat sipping coffee in the sun, and a young one was sweeping the blue and white tiles with a broom, singing gaily as she swept.

"Art thou well placed, my mother?" she asked, pausing to look tenderly at the withered brown face, on which the shadows of the sycamore leaves were playing.

The old mother smiled, steeping her bread in the coffee-bowl.

"Surely, child; I can feel the sun and hear you sing."

She was happy though she was blind.

Folle-Farine stood a moment and looked at them across a hedge of honeysuckle.

"How odd it must be to have anyone to care to hear your voice like that!" she thought; and she went on her way through the poppies and the corn, half softened, half enraged.

Was she lower than they because she could find no one to care for her or take gladness in her life? or was she greater than they because all human delights were to her as the dead letters of an unknown tongue?

Down a pathway fronting her which ran midway between the yellowing seas of wheat and a belt of lilac clover, and over which a swarm of bees was murmuring, there came a countrywoman, crushing the herbage under her heavy shoes, ragged, picturesque, sunbrowned, swinging deep brass pails as she went to the herds on the hillside. She carried a child twisted into the folds of her dress; a boy, half asleep, with his curly head against her breast.

As she passed, the woman drew her kerchief over her bosom and over the brown rosy face of the child.

"She shall not look at thee, my darling," she muttered. "Her look withered Rémy's little limb." And she covered the child jealously, and turned aside, so that she should tread a separate pathway through the clover, and needed not to brush the garments of the one she was compelled to pass.

Folle-Farine heard, and laughed aloud.

She knew of what the woman was thinking.

In the summer of the previous year, as she had passed the tanyard on the western bank of the river, the tanner's little son, rushing out in haste, had curled his mouth in insult at her, and clapping his hands, hissed in a child's love of cruelty the mocking words which he had heard his elders use of her. In answer, she had only turned her head and looked down at him with calm eyes of scorn.

But the child, running out fast, and startled by that regard, had slipped upon a shred of leather and had fallen heavily, breaking his left leg at the knee.

The limb, unskilfully dealt with, and enfeebled by a tendency to disease, had never been restored, but hung limp, crooked, useless, withered from below the knee. Through all the country side the little cripple, Rémy, creeping out into the sun upon his crutches, was pointed out in a passionate pity as the object of her sorcery, the victim of her vengeance.

When she had heard what they said she had laughed as she laughed now, drawing together her straight brows and showing her glistening teeth.

All the momentary softness died in her now as the peasant covered the boy's face and turned aside into the clover. She laughed aloud, and swept on through the half-ripe corn with that swift, harmonious, majestic movement which was inborn in her, as it is inborn in the deer or the antelope; singing again as she went those strange wild airs, like the sigh of the wind, which were all the language which lingered in her memory from the land that had seen her birth.

To such aversion as this she was too well used for it to be a matter of even notice to her. She knew that she was marked and shunned by the community amidst which her lot was cast; and she accepted proscription without wonder and without resistance.

Folle-Farine: the Dust. What lower thing did earth hold?

In this old-world district, amidst the pastures and corn-lands of Normandy, superstition had taken a hold with the passage of centuries and the advent of revolution had done very little to lessen.

Few of the people could read and fewer still could write. They knew nothing but what their priests and their politicians told them to believe. They went to their beds with the poultry, and rose as the cock crew:

they went to mass, as their ducks to the osier and weed ponds; and to the conscription as their lambs to the slaughter.

They understood that there was a world beyond them, but they remembered it only as the best market for their fruit, their fowls, their lace, their skins. Their brains were as dim as were their oil-lit streets at night; though their lives were content and mirthful, and for the most part pious. They went out into the summer meadows chaunting aves, in seasons of drought to pray for rain on their parching orchards, in the same credulity with which they groped through the winter fog, bearing torches and chaunting dirges to gain a blessing at seed time on their bleak black fallows.

The beauty and the faith of the old Mediæval life were with them still; and with its beauty and its faith were its bigotry and its cruelty likewise.

They led simple and contented lives; for the most part honest, and amongst themselves cheerful and kindly; preserving much grace of colour, of costume, of idiosyncracy, because apart from the hueless communism and characterless monotony of modern cities.

But they believed in sorcery and in devilry; they were brutal to their beasts, and could be as brutal to their foes; they were steeped in legend and tradition from their cradles; and all the darkest superstitions of dead ages still found home and treasury in their hearts and at their hearths.

Therefore, believing her a creature of evil, they were inexorable against her; and thought that in being so they did their duty.

They had always been a religious people in this birth country of the Flamma race; the strong poetic reverence of their forefathers, which had symbolised itself in the carving of every lintel, corbel, or buttress in their streets, and in the fashion of every spire on which a weather-vane could gleam against the sun, was still in their blood; the poetry had departed, but the bigotry remained.

Their ancestors had burned wizards and witches by the score in the open square of the cathedral place, and their grandsires and granddams had in brave, dumb, ignorant peasant fashion held fast to the lily and the cross, and gone by hundreds to the salutation of the axe and the baptism of the sword in the red days of revolution.

They were the same people still; industrious, frugal, peaceful, loyal, wedded to old ways and to old relics, content on little, and serene of heart; yet, withal, where they feared or where they hated, brutal with the brutality begotten of abject ignorance. And they had been so to this outcast whom they all called Folle-Farine.

When she had first come amidst them, a little desolate foreign child, mute with the dumbness of an unknown tongue, and cast adrift amongst strange people, unfamiliar ways, and chill blank glances, she had shyly tried in a child's vague instincts of appeal and trust to make friends with the other children that she saw, and to share a little in the mothers' smiles and the babies' pastimes that were all around her in the glad green world of summer.

But she had been denied and rejected with hard words and harder blows; at her coming the smiles had changed to frowns, and the pastime into terror.

She was proud, she was shy, she was savage; she felt rather than understood that she was suspected and reviled; she ceased to seek her own kind, and only went for companionship and sympathy to the creatures of the fields and the woods, to the things of the earth and the sky and the water.

"Thou art the devil's daughter!" half in sport hissed the youths in the market-place against her as the little child went amongst them, carrying a load for her grandsire, heavier than her arms knew how to bear.

"Thou wert plague-spotted from thy birth," said the old man himself, as she strained her small limbs to and fro the floors of his storehouses, carrying wood or flour or tiles or rushes, or whatever there chanced to need such convoy.

"Get thee away, we are not to touch thee!" hissed the six-year-old infants at play by the river when she waded in amidst them to reach with her lither arms the far off water-flower which they were too timorous to pluck, and tendered it to the one who had desired it.

"The devil begot thee, and my cow fell ill yester-night after thou hadst laid hands on her!" muttered the old women, lifting a stick as she went near to their cattle in the meadows to brush off with a broad dockleaf the flies that were teasing the poor, meek, patient beasts.

So, cursed when she did her duty and driven away when she tried to do good, her young soul had hardened itself and grown fierce, mute, callous, isolated.

There were only the four-footed things, so wise, so silent, so tender of heart, so bruised of body, so innocent, and so agonised, that had compassion for her, and saved her from utter desolation. In the mild sad gaze of the cow, in the lustrous suffering eyes of the horse, in the noble frank faith of the dog, in the soft bounding glee of the lamb, in the unwearied toil of the ass, in the tender industry of the bird, she had sympathy and she had example.

She loved them and they loved her.

She saw that they were sinless, diligent, faithful, devoted, loyal servers of base masters; loving greatly, and for their love goaded, beaten, overtasked, slaughtered.

She took the lesson to heart; and hated men and women with a bitter hatred.

So she had grown up for ten years, caring for no human thing, except in a manner for the old man Marcellin, who was, like her, proscribed.

The priests had striven to turn her soul what they had termed heavenward; but their weapons had been wrath and intimidation. She would have none of them. No efforts that they or her grandsire made had availed; she would be starved, thrashed, cursed, maltreated as they would; she could not understand their meaning, or would not submit herself to their religion.

As years went on they had found the contest hopeless, so had abandoned her to the devil, who had made her; and the daughter of one whom the whole province had called saint had never passed within church-doors or known the touch of holy water save when they had cast it on her as an exorcism. And when she met a priest in the open roads or on the byepaths of the fields, she always sang in loud defiance her wildest melodies.

Where had she learnt these?

They had been sung to her by Phratos, and taught by him.

Who had he been?

Her old life was obscure to her memory, and yet glorious even in that dimness.

She did not know who those people had been with whom she had wandered, nor in what land they had dwelt.

But that wondrous free life remained on her remembrance as a thing never to be forgotten or to be known again; a life odorous with bursting fruits and budding flowers; full of strangest and of sweetest music; spent for ever under green leaves and suns that had no setting; for ever beside fathomless waters and winding forests; for ever rhymed to melody and soothed to the measure of deep winds and drifting clouds.

For she had forgotten all except its liberty and its loveliness; and the old gipsy life of the Liébana remained with her only as some stray fragment of an existence passed in another world from which she was now an exile, and revived in her only in the fierce passion of her nature, in her bitter, vague rebellion, in her longing to be free, in her anguish of vain desires for richer hues and bluer skies and wilder winds than those amidst which she toiled.

At times she remembered likewise the songs and the melodies of Phratos; remembered them when the moon rays swept across the white breadth of water lilies, or the breath of the spring stole through the awakening woods; and when she remembered them she wept—wept bitterly, where none could look on her.

She never thought of Phratos as a man; as of one who had lived in a human form, and was now lying dead in an earthly grave. Her memory of him was as of some nameless creature half divine, whose footsteps brought laughter and music, with eyes bright as a bird's, yet sad as a dog's, and a voice for ever singing; clad in goat's hair, gigantic and gay; a creature that had spoken tenderly to her, that had bidden her laugh and rejoice, that had carried her when she was weary; that had taught her to sleep under the dewy leaves, and to greet the things of the night as soft sisters, and to fear nothing in the whole living world, in the earth, or the air, or the sky, and to tell the truth though a falsehood were to save the bare feet from flintstones, and naked shoulders from the stick, and an empty body from hunger and thirst. A creature that seemed to her in her memories even as the faun seemed to the fancies of the children of the Piræus; a creature half man and half animal, glad and grotesque, full of mirth and of music, belonging to the forest, to the brook, to the stars, to the leaves, wandering like the wind, and, like the wind, homeless.

This was all her memory; but she cherished it; in the face of the priests she bent her straight black brows and curled her scornful scarlet lips, but for the sake of Phratos she held one religion; though she hated men she told them never a lie, and asked of them never alms.

She went now along the white level roads, the empty basket balanced on her head, her form moving with the free harmonious grace of desert women, and she sang as she went the old sweet songs of the broken viol.

She was friendless and desolate; she was ill-fed, she was heavily tasked; she toiled without thanks; she was ignorant of even so much knowledge as the peasants about her had; she was without a past or a future, and her present had in it but daily toil and bitter words; hunger, and thirst, and chastisement.

Yet for all that she sang;—sang because the vitality in her made her dauntless of all evil; because the abundant life opening in her made her glad in despite of fate; because the youth, and the strength, and the soul that were in her could not utterly be brutalised, could not wholly cease from feeling the gladness of the sun, the coursing of the breeze, the liberty of nature, the sweet quick sense of living.

Before long she reached the spot where the old man Marcellin was breaking his stones.

His pile was raised much higher; he sat astride on a log of timber and hammered the flints on and on, on and on, without looking up; the dust, where the tramp of the people had raised it, was still thick on the leaves and the herbage; and the prayers and the chants had failed as yet to bring the slightest cloud, the faintest rain mist across the hot unbroken azure of the skies.

Marcellin was her only friend; the proscribed always adhere to one another; when they are few they can only brood and suffer, harmlessly; when they are many they rise as with one foot and strike as with one hand. Therefore, it is always perilous to make the lists of any proscription over long.

The child, who was also an outcast, went to him and paused; in a curious, lifeless, bitter way they cared for one another; this girl who had grown to believe herself born of hell, and this man who had grown to believe that he had served hell.

With the bastard Folle-Farine and with the regicide Marcellin the people had no association, and for them no pity; therefore they had found each other by the kinship of proscription; and in a way there was love between them.

"You are glad, since you sing!" said the old man to her as she passed him again on her homeward way, and paused again beside him.

"The birds in cages sing," she answered him. "But, think you they are glad?"

"Are they not?"

She sat down a moment beside him, on the bank which was soft with moss, and odorous with wild flowers curling up the stems of the poplars and straying over into the corn beyond.

"Are they? Look. Yesterday I passed a cottage, it

is on the great south road; far away from here. The house was empty; the people, no doubt, were gone to labour in the fields; there was a wicker cage hanging to the wall, and in the cage there was a blackbird. The sun beat on his head; his square of sod was a dry clod of bare earth; the heat had dried every drop of water in his pan; and yet the bird was singing. Singing how? In torment, beating his breast against the bars till the blood started, crying to the skies to have mercy on him and to let rain fall. His song was shrill; it had a scream in it; still he sang. Do you say the merle was glad?"

"What did you do?" asked the old man, still breaking his stones with a monotonous rise and fall of his hammer.

"I took the cage down and opened the door."

"And he?"

"He shot up in the air first, then dropped down amidst the grasses, where a little brook which the drought had not dried, was still running; and he bathed and drank and bathed again, seeming mad with the joy of the water. When I lost him from sight he was swaying among the leaves on a bough over the river; but then he was silent."

"And what do you mean by that?"

Her eyes clouded; she was mute. She vaguely knew the meaning it bore to herself, but it was beyond her to express it. All things of nature had voices and parables for her, because her fancy was vivid and her mind was dreamy; but that mind was still too dark, and too profoundly ignorant, for her to be able to shape her thoughts into metaphor or deduction.

The bird had spoken to her; by his silence as by his song; but what he had uttered she could not well utter again. Save, indeed, that song was not gladness, and neither was silence pain.

Marcellin, although he had asked her, had asked needlessly; for he also knew.

"And what, think you, the people said when they went back and found the cage empty?" he pursued, still echoing his words and hers by the ringing sound of the falling hammer.

A smile curled her lips.

"That was no thought of mine," she said carelessly. "They had done wickedly to cage him; to set him free I would have pulled down their thatch, or stove in their door, had need been."

"Good!" said the old man briefly, with a gleam of light over his harsh lean face.

He looked up at her as he worked, the shivered flints flying right and left.

"It was a pity to make you a woman," he muttered, as his keen gaze swept over her.

"A woman!" She echoed the words dully and half wonderingly; she could not understand it in connection with herself.

A woman; that was a woman who sat in the sun under the fig tree, working her lace on a frame; that was a woman who leaned out of her lattice tossing a red carnation to her lover; that was a woman who swept the open porch of her house, singing as she cleared the dust away; that was a woman who strode on her blithe way through the clover, carrying her child at her breast.

She seemed to have no likeness to them, no kindred with them; she, a beast of burden, a creature soulless and homeless; an animal made to fetch and carry, to be cursed and beaten, to know neither love nor hope, neither past nor future, but only a certain dull patience and furious hate, a certain dim pleasure in labour and indifference to pain.

"It was a pity to make you a woman," said the old man once more. "You might be a man worth something; but a woman!—a thing that has no medium; no haven between hell and heaven; no option save to sit by the hearth to watch the pot boil and suckle the children, or to go out into the streets and the taverns to mock at men and to murder them. Which will you do in the future?"

"What?"

She scarcely knew the meaning of the word. She saw that the female creatures round her were of all shades of age, from the young girls with their peach-like cheeks to the old crones brown and withered as last year's nuts; she knew that if she lived on she would be old likewise; but of a future she had no conception, no ideal. She had been left too ignorant to have visions of any other world hereafter than this one which the low-lying green hills and the arc of the pale blue sky shut in upon her.

She had one desire, indeed—a desire vague yet fierce—the desire for liberty. But it was such desire as the bird which she had freed had known; the desire of instinct, the desire of existence, only; her mind was powerless to conceive a future, because a future is a hope, and of hope she knew nothing.

The old man glanced at her, and saw that she had not comprehended. He smiled with a certain bitter pity.

"I spoke idly," he said to himself; "slaves cannot have a future. But yet—"

Yet he saw that the creature who was so ignorant of her own powers, of her own splendours, of her own possibilities, had even now a beauty as great as that of a lustrous eastern-eyed passion flower; and he knew that to a woman who has such beauty as this the world holds out in its hand the tender of at least one future—one election, one kingdom, one destiny.

"Women are loved," she said, suddenly; "will any one love me?"

Marcellin smiled bitterly.

"Many will love you, doubtless—as the wasp loves the peach that he kisses with his sting, and leaves rotten to drop from the stem!"

She was silent again, revolving his meaning; it lay beyond her, both in the peril which it embodied from others, and the beauty in herself which it implied. She could reach no conception of herself, save as what she now was, a body servant of toil, a beast of burden like a young mule.

"But all shun me, as even the wasp shuns the bitter oak apple," she said, slowly and dreamily; "who should love me, even as the wasp loves the peach?"

Marcellin smiled his grim and shadowy smile. He made answer—

"Wait!"

She sat mute once more, revolving this strange, brief word in her thoughts—strange to her, with a promise as vague, as splendid, and as incomprehensible as the prophecy of empire to a slave.

"The future?" she said, at last. "That means something that one has not, and that is to come—is it so?"

"Something that one never has, and that never comes," muttered the old man, wearily cracking the flints in two; "something that one possesses in one's sleep, and that is farther off each time that one awakes; and yet a thing that one sees always—sees even when one lies a-dying, they say—for men are fools."

Folle-Farine listened, musing, with her hands clasped on the handle of her empty basket, and her chin resting upon them, and her eyes watching a maimed butterfly drag its wings of emerald and diamond through the hot, pale, sickly dust.

"I dream!" she said, suddenly, as she stooped and lifted the wounded insect gently on to the edge of a leaf. "But I dream wide awake."

Marcellin smiled.

"Never say so. They will think you mad. That is only what foolish things, called poets, do."

"What is a poet?"

"A foolish thing, I tell you—mad enough to believe that men will care to strain their eyes, as he strains his, to see the face of a God who never looks and never listens."

"Ah!"

She was so accustomed to be told, that all she did was unlike to others, and was either wicked or was senseless, that she saw nothing except the simple statement of a fact in the rebuke which he had given her. She sat quiet, gazing down into the thick white dust of the road, bestirred by the many feet of mules and men that had trodden through it since the dawn.

"I dream beautiful things," she pursued, slowly. "In the moonlight most often. I seem to remember, when I dream—so much! so much!"

"Remember—what should you remember? You were but a baby when they brought you hither."

"So they say. But I might live before, in my father's kingdom. In the devil's kingdom? Why not?"

"Why not, indeed! Perhaps we all lived there once; and that is why we all, through all our lives, hanker to get back to it!"

"I ask him so often to take me back, but he does not seem ever to hear."

"Chut! He will hear in his own good time. The devil never passes by a woman."

"A woman!" she repeated. The word seemed to have no likeness and no fitness with herself.

A woman—she!—a creature made to be beaten, and sworn at, and shunned, and loaded like a mule, and driven like a bullock!

"Look you," said the old man, resting his hammer for a moment, and wiping the sweat from his brow. "I have lived in this vile place forty years. I remember the woman that they say bore you—Reine Flamma. She was a beautiful woman, and pure as snow, and noble, and innocent. She wearied God incessantly. I have seen her stretched for hours at the foot of that cross. She was wretched; and she entreated her God to take away her monotonous misery, and to give her some life new and fair. But God never answered. He left her to herself. It was the devil that heard—and replied."

"Then, is the devil juster than their God?"

Marcellin leaned his hammer on his knee, and his voice rose clear and strong; as it had rung of yore from the Tribune.

"He looks so, at the least. It is his wisdom, and that is why his following is so large. Nay, I say, when God is deaf the devil listens.

"That is his wisdom, see you.

"So often the poor little weak human soul, striving to find the right way, cries feebly for help, and none answer.

"The poor little weak soul is blind and astray in the busy streets of the world.

"It lifts its voice, but its voice is so young and so

feeble, like the pipe of a newly-born bird in the dawn, that it is drowned in the shouts and the manifold sounds of those hard, crowded, cruel streets, where every one is for himself, and no man has ears for his neighbour. It is hungered, it is athirst, it is sorrowful, it is blinded, it is perplexed, it is afraid.

"It cries often, but God and man leave it to itself.

"Then the devil, who hearkens always, and who, though all the trumpets blowing their brazen music in the streets bray in his honour, yet is too wise to lose even the slightest sound of any in distress—since of such are the largest sheaves of his harvest—comes to the little soul, and teaches it with tenderness, and guides it towards the paths of gladness, and fills its lips with the bread of sweet passions, and its nostrils with the savour of fair vanities, and blows in its ear the empty breath of men's lungs, till that sickly wind seems divinest music.

"Then is the little soul dazzled and captured, and made the devil's for evermore; half through its innocence, half through its weakness; but chiefly of all because God and man would not hear its cries whilst yet it was sinless and only astray."

He ceased, and the strokes of his hammer rang again on the sharp flint stones.

She had listened with her lips parted breathlessly, and her night-like eyes dilated. In the years of his youth the old man had possessed that rare power which can tip words with fire, and send them burning and keen into the coldest heart; and the power was still there, when it woke up from the stupor of a life of toil, and the silence of a harsh old age. In the far distant time, when he had been amidst the world of men, he had known how to utter the words that charmed to stillness a raging multitude. He had not altogether lost this eloquence at such rare times as he still cared to break his silence, and to unfold the unforgotten memories of a life long dead.

He would speak thus to her, but to no other.

Folle-Farine listened, mute and breathless, her eyes uplifted to the sun, where it was sinking westward through a pomp of golden and of purple cloud. He was the only creature who ever spoke to her as though she likewise were human; and she followed his words with dumb unquestioning faith, as a dog its master's footsteps.

"The soul! What is the soul?" she muttered, at length.

He caught in his hand the beautiful diamond-winged butterfly, which now, freed of the dust and drinking in the sunlight, was poised on a fox-glove in the hedge growing near him, and held it against the light.

"What is it that moves this creature's wings, and glances in its eyes, and gives it delight in the summer's warmth, in the orchid's honey, and in the lime-tree's leaves?

"I do not know; but I know that I can kill it—with one grind of my heel.

"So much we know of the soul—no more."

She freed it from his hand.

"Whoever made it, then, was cruel. If he could give it so much power, why not have given it a little more, so that it could escape you always?"

"You ask what men have asked ten times ten thousand years—since the world began—without an answer. Because the law of all creation is cruelty, I suppose; because the dust of death is always the breath of life. The great man, dead, changes to a million worms, and lives again in the juices of the grass above his grave. It matters little. The worms destroy; the grasses nourish. Few great men do more than the first, or as much as the last."

"But get you homeward," he continued, breaking off his parable; "it is two hours past noon, and if you be late on the way you pay for it with your body. Begone."

She nodded her head, and went; he seldom used gentle words to her, and yet she knew, in a way, that he cared for her; moreover, she rejoiced in that bitter, caustic contempt in which he, the oldest man amidst them, held all men.

His words were the only thing that had aroused her dulled brain to its natural faculties; in a manner, from him she had caught something of knowledge—something, too, of intellect; he alone prevented her from sinking to that absolute unquestioning despair which surely ends in idiotcy or in self-murder.

She pursued her way in silence across the fields, and along the straight white road, and across a wooden bridge that spanned the river, to her home.

There was a gentler lustre in her eyes, and her mouth had the faint light of a half smile upon it; she did not know what hope meant; it never seemed possible to her that her fate could be other than it was, since so long the messengers and emissaries of her father's empire had been silent and leaden-footed to her call.

Yet, in a manner, she was comforted, for had not two mouths that day bidden her "wait"?

She entered at length the little wood of Yprés, and heard that rush and music of the deep mill water, which was the sole thing she had learned to love in all the place.

Beyond it were the apple orchards and fruit gardens

which rendered Claudis Flamma back full recompense for all the toil they cost him—recompense so large, indeed, that many disbelieved in that poverty which he was wont to aver weighed so hardly and so tightly on him. Both were now rich in all their mature abundance, since the stream which rushed through them had saved them from the evil effects of the long drought so severely felt in other districts. The cherry trees were scarlet with their latest fruit; the great pumpkins glowed amongst their leaves in tawny orange heaps; little russet-breasted bullfinches beat their wings vainly at the fine network that enshrouded the paler gold of the wall apricots; a grey cat was stealing amongst the delicate yellows of the pear-shaped marrows; where a round green wrinkled melon lay a-ripening in the sun, a gorgeous dragon-fly was hovering, and a mother-mavis, in her simple coif of brown and white and grey, was singing with all the gladness of her sunny summer joys.

Beyond a hedge of prickly thorn the narrower flower garden stretched, spanned by low stone walls, made venerable by the silvery beards of lichens; and the whole earth was full of colour from the crimson and the golden gladioli; from the carmine-hued carnations; from the deep-blue lupins, and the Gloire de Dijon roses; from the green slender stems, and the pure white cups, of the virginal lilies; and from the gorgeous beetles, with their purple tunics and their shields of bronze, like Grecian hoplites in battle array. While everywhere, above this sweet glad garden world, the butterflies, purple and jewelled, the redstarts in their ruby coats, the dainty azure-winged blue-warblers, the golden-girdled wasp with his pinions light as mist, and the velvet-coated bee with his pleasant harvest song, flew ever in the sunlight, murmuring, poising, praising, rejoicing.

The place was beautiful in its own simple, quiet way; lying in a hollow, where the river tumbled down in two or three short breaks and leaps which broke its habitual smooth and sluggish form, and brought it in a sheet of dark water and with a million foam-bells against the walls of the mill-house and under the ponderous wheels.

The wooden house itself also was picturesque, in the old fashion common when men built their dwellings slowly and for love; with all its countless carvings black by age, its jutting beams shapen into grotesque human likeness and tragic masks; its parquetted work run over by the green cups of stoneworts, and its high roof with deep shelving eaves bright with diapered tiles of blue and white and rose, and alive all day with curling swallows, with pluming pigeons, with cooing doves.

It was beautiful; and the heart of Reine Flamma's young daughter doubtless would have clung to it, with all a child's instinct of love and loyalty to its home, had it not been to her only a prison-house wherein three bitter gaolers for ever ruled her with a rod of iron—bigotry and penury and cruelty.

She flung herself down a moment in the garden, on the long grass under a mulberry tree, ere she went in to give her account of the fruit sold and the monies brought by her.

She had been on foot since four o'clock in the dawn of that sultry day; her only meal had been a bowl of cold milk and a hunch of dry bread crushed in her strong small teeth. She always toiled hard at such bodily labour as was set to her; to domestic work, to the work of the distaff and spindle, of the stove and the needle, they had never been able to break her; they had found that she would be beaten black and blue ere she would be bound to it; but against open air exertion she had never rebelled, and she had in her all the strength and the swiftness of the nomadic race of the Liébana, and had nought of their indolence and their dishonesty.

She was very hungry, she was again thirsty; yet she did not break off a fruit from any bough about her; she did not steep her hot lips in any one of the cool juicy apricots which studded the stones of the wall beyond her.

No one had ever taught her honesty, except indeed in that dim dead time when Phratos had closed her small hands in his whenever they had stretched out to some forbidden thing, and had said, "Take the goods the gods give thee, but steal not from men." And yet honest she was, by reason of the fierce proud savage independence in her, and her dim memories of that sole friend loved and lost.

She wanted many a thing, many a time;—nay, nearly every hour that she lived, she wanted those sheer necessaries which make life endurable; but she had taught herself to do without them rather than owe them by prayer or by plunder to that human race which she hated, and to which she always doubted her own kinship.

Buried in the grass, she now abandoned herself to the bodily delights of rest, of shade, of coolness, of sweet odours: the scent of the fruits and flowers was heavy on the air; the fall of the water made a familiar tempestuous music on her ear; and her fancy, poetic still, though deadened by a life of ignorance and toil, was stirred by the tender tones of the numberless birds that sang about her.

"The earth and the air are good," she thought, as she lay there watching the dark leaves sway in the foam and the wind, and the bright-bosomed birds float from blossom to blossom.

For there was latent in her, all untaught, that old pantheistic instinct of the divine age, when the world was young, to behold a sentient consciousness in every leaf unfolded to the light; to see a soul in every created thing the day shines on; to feel the presence of an eternal life in every breeze that moves, in every grass that grows; in every flame that lifts itself to heaven; in every bell that vibrates on the air; in every moth that soars to reach the stars.

Pantheism in the religion of the poet; and nature had made her a poet, though man as yet had but made of her an outcast, a slave, and a beast of burden.

"The earth and the air are good," she thought, watching the sun-rays pierce the purple heart of a passion-flower, the shadows move across the deep brown water, the radiant butterfly alight upon a lily, the scarlet-throated birds dart in and out, through the yellow feathery blossoms of the limes.

All birds were her friends.

Phratos had taught her in her infancy many notes of their various songs, and many ways and means of luring them to come and rest upon her shoulder and peck the berries in her hand. She had lived so much in the open fields and amongst the woods that she had made her chief companions of them. She could emulate so deftly all their voices, from the call of the wood dove to the chant of the blackbird, and from the trill of the nightingale to the twitter of the titmouse, that she could summon them all to her at will, and have dozens of them fluttering around her head and swaying their pretty bodies on her wrist.

It was one of her ways that seemed to the peasantry

so weird and magical; and they would come home from their fields on a spring day-break and tell their wives in horror how they had seen the devil's daughter in the red flush of the sunrise, ankle-deep in violets, and covered with birds from head to foot, hearing their whispers, and giving them her messages to carry in return.

One meek-eyed woman had dared once to say that St. Francis had done as much, and it had been accredited to him as a fair action and virtuous knowledge; but she was frowned down and chattered down by her louder neighbours, who told her that she might look for some sharp judgment of heaven for daring to couple together the blessed name of the holy saint and the accursed name of this foul spirit.

But all they could say could not break the charmed communion between Folle-Farine and her feathered comrades.

She loved them and they her. In the hard winter she had always saved some of her scanty meal for them, and in the springtime and the summer they always rewarded her with floods of songs and soft caresses from their nestling wings.

There were no rare birds, no birds of moor and mountain, in that cultivated and populous district; but to her all the little home-bred things of pasture and orchard were full of poetry and of character.

The robins, with that pretty air of boldness with which they veil their real shyness and timidity; the strong and saucy sparrows, powerful by the strength of all mediocrities and majorities; all the dainty families of finches in their gay apparellings; the plain brown bird that filled the night with music; the gorgeous oriole ruffling in gold, the gilded princeling of them all; the little blue warblers, the violets of the air; the kingfishers who had hovered so long over the forget-me-nots upon the rivers that they had caught the colours of the flowers on their wings; the bright black-caps green as the leaves, with their yellow waistcoats and velvet hoods, the innocent freebooters of the woodland liberties: all these were her friends and lovers, various as any human crowds of court or city.

She loved them; they and the fourfooted beasts were the sole things that did not flee from her; and the woeful and mad slaughter of them by the peasants was to her a grief passionate in its despair. She did not reason on what she felt; but to her a bird slain was a trust betrayed, an innocence defiled, a creature of heaven struck to earth.

Suddenly on the silence of the garden there was a little shrill sound of pain; the birds flew high in air, screaming and startled; the leaves of a bough of ivy shook as with a struggle.

She rose and looked; a line of twine was trembling against the foliage; in its noosed end the throat of the mavis had been caught; it hung trembling and clutching at the air convulsively with its little drawn up feet. It had flown into the trap as it had ended its joyous song and soared up to join its brethren.

There were a score of such traps set in the miller's garden.

She unloosed the cord from about its tiny neck, set it free, and laid it down upon the ivy: the succour came too late; the little gentle body was already without breath; the feet had ceased to beat the air; the small soft head had drooped feebly on one side; the lifeless eyes had started from their sockets; the throat was without song for evermore.

"The earth would be good but for men," she thought, as she stood with the little dead bird in her hand.

Its mate, which was poised on a rose bough, flew straight to it, and curled round and round about the small slain body, and piteously bewailed its fate, and mourned, refusing to be comforted, agitating the air with trembling wings, and giving out vain cries of grief.

Vain; for the little joyous life was gone; the life that asked only of God and Man a home in the green leaves; a drop of dew from the cup of a rose; a bough to swing on in the sunlight; a summer day to celebrate in song.

All the winter through, it had borne cold and hunger and pain without lament; it had saved the soil from destroying larvæ, and purified the trees from all foul germs; it had built its little home unaided, and had fed its nestlings without alms; it had given its sweet song lavishly to the winds, to the blossoms, to the empty air, to the deaf ears of men; and now it lay dead in its innocence; trapped and slain because a human greed begrudged it a berry worth the thousandth part of a copper coin.

Out from the porch of the mill-house Claudis Flamma came, with a knife in his hand and a basket, to cut lilies for one of the choristers of the cathedral, since the morrow would be the religious feast of the Visitation of Mary.

He saw the dead thrush in her hand, and chuckled to himself as he went by.

"The tenth bird trapped since sunrise," he said, thinking how shrewd and how sure in their make were these traps of twine that he set in the grass and the leaves.

She said nothing; but the darkness of disgust swept over her face, as he came in sight in the distance.

She knelt down and scraped a hole in the earth; and laid moss in it and put the mavis softly on its green and fragrant bier, and covered it with handsful of fallen rose leaves and with a sprig or two of thyme.

Around her head the widowed thrush flew ceaselessly, uttering sad cries;—who now should wander with him through the sunlight?—who now should rove with him above the blossoming fields?—who now should sit with him beneath the boughs hearing the sweet rain fall between the leaves?—who now should wake with him whilst yet the world was dark, to feel the dawn break, ere the east were red, and sing a welcome to the unborn day?

CHAPTER IV.

MEANWHILE Claudis Flamma cut the lilies for the cathedral altars, muttering many holy prayers as he gathered the flowers of Mary.

When the white lily sheaves had been borne away, kept fresh in wet moss, by the young chorister who had been sent for them, the miller turned to her.

"Where is the money?"

She, standing beside the buried bird, undid the leathern thong about her waist, opened the pouch, and counted out the coins, one by one, on the flat stone of a water tank amongst the lilies and the ivy.

There were a few silver pieces of slight value and some dozens of copper ones. The fruit had been left at various stalls and houses in small portions, for it was the custom to supply it fresh each day.

He caught them up with avidity, bit and tested each, counted them again and again, and yet again; after the third enumeration he turned sharply on her:

"There are two pieces too little: what have you done with them?"

"There are two sous short," she answered him curtly. "Twelve of the figs for the tanner Florian were rotten."

"Rotten!—they were but over ripe."

"It is the same thing."

"You dare to answer me?—animal! I say they had only tasted a little too much of the sun. It only made them the sweeter."

"They were rotten."

"They were not. You dare to speak! If they had been rotten, they lay under the others; he could not have seen——"

"I saw."

"You saw! Who are you?—a beggar—a beast—a foul offspring of sin. You dared to show them to him, I will warrant?"

"I showed him that they were not good."

"And gave him back the two sous?"

"I took seven sous for what were good. I took nothing for the rotten ones."

"Wretch! you dare to tell me that!"

A smile careless and sarcastic curled her mouth; her eyes looked at him with all their boldest, fiercest lustre.

"I never steal—not even from you, good Flamma."

"You have stolen now!" he shrieked, his thin and feeble voice rising in fury at his lost coins and his discovered treachery. "It is a lie that the figs were rotten; it is a lie that you took but seven sous. You stole the two sous to buy you bread and honey in the streets, or to get a drink at the wine shops. I know you; I know you; it is a devil's device to please your gluttonous appetite. The figs rotten!—not so rotten as is your soul would they be though they were black as night and though they stank as river mud! Go back to Denis Florian and bring me the two sous, or I will thrash you as a thief."

She laughed a hard, scornful, reckless laughter.

"You can thrash me; you cannot make me a thief."

"You will not go back to Florian?"

"I will not ask him to pay for what was bad."

"You will not confess that you stole the money?"

"I should lie if I did."

"Then strip."

She set her teeth in silence; and without a moment's hesitation unloosened the woollen sash knotted round her waist, and pushed down the coarse linen tunic from about her throat.

The white folds fell from off the perfect curves of her brown arms, and left bare her shining shoulders, beautiful as any sculptured Psyche's.

She was not conscious of degradation in her punishment; she had been bidden to bow her head and endure the lash from the earliest years she could remember. According to the only creed she knew, silence and fortitude and strength were the greatest of all the virtues.

She stood now in the cross lights among the lilies as she had stood when a little child, erect, unquailing, and ready to suffer; insensible of humiliation because unconscious of sin; and so tutored by severity and exposure that she had as yet none of the shy shame and the fugitive shrinking of her sex. She had only the boldness to bear, the courage to be silent, which she had had when she had stood amongst the same tall lilies, in the same summer radiance, in the years of her helpless infancy.

She uncovered herself to the lash as a brave hound

crouches to it; not from inborn cowardice, but simply from the habit of obedience and of endurance.

He had used her as the Greeks the Helots; he always beat her, when she was in fault, to teach her to be faultless; and, when without offence, beat her to remind her that she was the offspring of humiliation, and a slave.

He took, as he had taken in an earlier time, a thick rope which lay coiled upon the turf ready for the binding of some straying boughs; and struck her with it, slowly. His arm had lost somewhat of its strength, and his power was unequal to his will. Still rage for the loss of his copper pieces, and the sense that she had discovered the fraudulent intention of his small knavery, lent force to his feebleness; as the scourge whistled through the air and descended on her shoulders it left bruised swollen marks to stamp its passage, and curling, adder-like, bit and drew blood.

Yet to the end she stood mute and motionless, as she had stood in her childhood; not a nerve quivered, not a limb flinched; the colour rushed over her bent face and her bare chest, but she never made a movement; she never gave a sound.

When his arm dropped from sheer exhaustion, she still said not one word; she drew tight once more the sash about her waist, and fastened afresh the linen of her bodice.

The bruised and wounded flesh smarted and ached and throbbed; but she was used to such pain, and bore it as their wounds were borne by the women of the Spartan games.

"Your two sous have brought you bitterness," he muttered with a smile. "You will scarce find my fruit rotten again in haste. There are bread and beans within; go get a meal; I want the mule to take flour to Barbizène."

She did not go within to eat; the bruises and the burning of her skin made her feel sick and weak. She went away and cast herself at full length in the shade of the long grasses of the orchard; resting her chin upon her hands, cooling her aching breast against the soft damp moss; thinking, thinking, thinking, of what she hardly knew, except indeed that she wished that she were dead, like the bird she had covered with the rose leaves.

He did not leave her long to even so much peace as this; his shrill voice soon called her from her rest; he bade her get ready the mule and go.

She obeyed.

The animal was saddled with his wooden pack; as many sacks as he could carry were piled upon the framework; she put her hand upon his bridle, and set out to walk to Barbizène, which was two leagues away.

"Work is the only thing to drive the devil that begat her out of her," muttered the miller, as he watched the old mule pace down the narrow tree-shadowed road that led across the fields: and he believed that he did rightly in this treatment of her.

It gratified the sharp hard cruelty of temper in him, indeed, but he did not think that in such self-indulgence he ever erred. He was a bitter, cunning, miserly old man, whose solitary tenderness of feeling and honesty of pride had been rooted out for ever when he had learned the dishonour of the woman whom he had deemed a saint. In the ten years of time which had passed since first the little brown large-eyed child had been sent to seek asylum with him, he had grown harder and keener and more severe with each day that rose.

Her presence was abhorrent to him, though he kept her, partly from a savage sense of duty, partly from the persuasion that she had the power in her to make the strongest and the cheapest slave he had ever owned. For the rest, he sincerely and devoutly believed that the devil, in some witchery of human guise, had polluted his daughter's body and soul, and that it was by the foul fiend and by no earthly lover that she had conceived and borne the creature who now abode with him.

Perhaps, also, as was but natural, he sometimes felt more furious against this offspring of hell because ever and again some gleam of fantastic inborn honour, some strange savage instinct of honesty, would awake in her and oppose him, and make him ashamed of those small and secret sins of chicanery wherein his soul delighted, and for which he compounded with his gods.

He had left her mind a blank, because he thought the body laboured hardest when the brain was still asleep, which is true; she could not read; she could not write; she knew absolutely nothing.

Yet there was a soul awake in her; there were innumerable thoughts and dreams brooding in her fathomless eyes; there was a desire in her, fierce and unslaked, for some other life than this life of the packhorse and of the day labourer which alone she knew.

He had done his best to degrade and to brutalise her, and in much he had succeeded; but he had not succeeded wholly. There was a liberty in her that escaped his thraldom; there was a soul in her that resisted the deadening influence of her existence.

She had none of the shame of her sex; she had none of the timorous instincts of womanhood. She had a savage stubborn courage, and she was insensible of the daily outrages of her life. She would strip bare to his word obediently, feeling only that it would be feeble and worthless to dread the pain of the lash. She would bathe in the woodland pool, remembering no more that she might be watched by human eyes than does the young tigress that has never beheld the face of man.

In all this she was brutalised and degraded by her tyrant's bondage: in other things she was far higher than he, and escaped him.

Stupified as her mind might be by the exhaustion of severe physical labour, it had still irony and it had still imagination; and under the hottest heats of temptation there were two things which by sheer instinct she resisted, and resisted so that neither of them had ever been forced on her—they were falsehood and fear.

"It is the infamous strength of the devil!" said Claudis Flamma, when he found that he could not force her to deviate from the truth.

The world says the same of those who will not feed it with lies.

CHAPTER V.

THAT long dry summer was followed by an autumn of drought and scarcity.

The prayers of the priests and peoples failed to bring down rain. The wooden Christs gazed all day long on parching lands and panting cattle. Even the broad deep rivers shrank and left their banks to bake and stink in the long drought.

The orchards sickened for lack of moisture, and the peasants went about with feverish faces, ague-stricken limbs, and trembling hearts. The corn yielded ill in the hard scorched ground, and when the winter came it was a time of dire scarcity and distress.

Claudis Flamma and a few others like him alone prospered.

The mill-house at Yprès served many purposes. It was a granary, a market, a baker's shop, an usurer's den, all in one.

It looked a simple and innocent place. In the summer time it was peaceful and lovely, green and dark and still, with the blue sky above it, and the songs of birds all around; with its old black timbers, and its many-coloured orchards, and its pretty leafy gardens, and its grey walls washed by the hurrying stream. But in the winter it was very dreary, utterly lonely. The water roared, and the leafless trees groaned in the wind, and the great leaden clouds of rain or fog enveloped it duskily.

To the starving, wet, and woe-begone peasants who would go to it with aching bones and aching hearts, it seemed desolate and terrible. They dreaded with a great dread the sharp voice of its master—the hardest and the shrewdest and the closest fisted Norman of them all.

For they were most of them his debtors, and so were in a bitter subjugation to him, and had to pay those debts as best they might with their labour or their suffering; with the best of all their wool, or oil, or fruit; often with the last bit of silver that had been an heirloom for five centuries, or with the last bit of money buried away in an old pitcher under their apple tree to be the nest egg of their little pet daughter's dowry.

And yet Claudis Flamma was respected among them; for he could outwit them, and was believed to be very wealthy, and was a man who stood well with the good saints and with holy Church:—a wise man, in a word, with whom these northern folks had the kinship of mutual industry and avarice.

For the most part the population around Yprès was

thrifty and thriving in a cautious, patient, certain way of well-doing; and, by this portion of it, the silent old miser was much honoured as a man laborious and penurious, who chose to live on a leek and a rye loaf, but who must have, it was well known, put by large gains in the thatch of his roof or under the bricks of his kitchen.

By the smaller section of it—poor, unthrifty, loose-handed fools—who belied the province of their birth so far as to be quick to spend and slow to save, and who therefore fell into want and famine and had to borrow of others their children's bread, the old miller was hated with a hate deeper and stronger because forced to be mute, and to submit, to cringe, and to be trod upon, in the miserable servitude of the hopeless debtor.

In the hard winter which followed on that sickly autumn these and their like fell farther in the mire of poverty than ever, and had to come and beg of Flamma loans of the commonest necessaries of their bare living. They knew that they would have to pay a hundredfold in horrible extortion when the spring and summer should bring them work, and give them fruit on their trees and crops on their little fields; but they could do no better.

It had been for many years the custom to go to Flamma in such need; and being never quit of his hold, his debtors never could try for aid elsewhere.

The weather towards the season of Noel became frightfully severe; the mill stream never stopped, but all around it was frozen, and the swamped pastures were sheets of ice. The birds died by thousands in the open country, and several of the sheep perished in snow storms on the higher lands.

There was dire want in many of the hovels and homesteads, and the bare harvests of a district, usually so opulent in the riches of the soil, brought trouble and dearth in their train.

'Sickness prevailed because the old people and the children in their hunger ate berries and roots unfit for human food; the waters swelled, the ice melted, and many homes were flooded, and some even swept away.

Old Pitchou and Claudis Flamma alone were content; the mill wheel never stopped work, and famine prices could be asked in this extremity.

Folle-Farine worked all that winter, day after day, month after month, with scarcely a word being spoken to her, or scarcely an hour being left her that she could claim as her own.

She looked against the snow as strangely as a scarlet rose blossoming in frost, there could have done; but the people that came to and fro, even the young men amongst them, were too used to that dark vivid silent face of hers, and those lithe brown limbs that had the supple play and the golden glow of the East in them, to notice them as any loveliness: and if they did note them on some rare time, thought of them only as the marks of a vagrant and accursed race.

She was so unlike to themselves that the northern peasantry never dreamed of seeing beauty in her; they turned their heads away when she went by, striding after her mule or bearing her pitcher from the well with the free and vigorous grace of a mountain or desert-born creature.

The sheepskin girt about her loins, the red kerchief knotted to her head, the loose lithe movements of her beautiful limbs, the sullen fire and fierce dreams in her musing eyes—all these were so unlike themselves that they saw nothing in them except what was awful or unlovely.

Half the winter went by without a kind word to her from any one except such as in that time of suffering and scarcity Marcellin spoke to her. So had every winter gone since she had come there—a time so long ago that the memory of Phratos had become so dim to her that she often doubted if he also were not a mere shadow of a dream like all the rest.

Half the winter she fared hardly and ate sparingly, and did the work of the mule and the bullocks: indifferent and knowing no better, and only staring at the stars when they throbbed in the black skies on a frosty night, and wondering if she would ever go to them, or if they would ever come to her—those splendid and familiar yet unknown things that looked on all the misery of the earth, and shone on tranquilly and did not seem to care.

Time came close on to the new year, and the distress and the cold were together at their height. The weather was terrible; and the poor suffered immeasurably.

A score of times a-day she heard them ask bread at the mill, and a score of times saw them given a stone; she saw them come in the raw fog, pinched and shivering, and sick with ague, and she saw her grandsire deny them with a grating sarcasm or two, or take from them fifty times its value for some niggard grant of food.

"Why should I think of it, why should I care?" she said to herself; and yet she did both, and could not help it.

There was among the sufferers one old and poor, who lived not far from the mill, by name Manon Dax.

She was a little old hardy brown woman, shrivelled and bent, yet strong, with bright eyes like a robin's and a tough frame, eighty years old.

She had been southern born, and the wife of a stone

cutter; he had been dead fifty years, and she had seen all her sons and daughters and their offspring die too; and had now, left on her hand to rear, four young great-grandchildren, almost infants, who were always crying to her for food as new-born birds cry in their nests.

She washed a little, when she could get any linen to wash, and she span, and she picked up the acorns and the nuts, and she tilled a small plot of ground that belonged to her hut, and she grew cabbages and potatoes and herbs on it, and so kept a roof over her head, and fed her four nestlings, and trotted to and fro in her wooden shoes all day long, and worked in hail and rain, in drought and tempest, and never complained, but said that God was good to her.

She was anxious about the children, knowing she could not live long—that was all. But then she felt sure that the Mother of God would take care of them, and so was cheerful; and did what the day brought her to do, and was content.

Now on Manon Dax, as on thousands of others, the unusual severity of the winter fell like a knife.

She was only one amongst thousands. Nobody noticed her; still it was hard.

All the springs near her dwelling were frozen for many weeks; there was no well nearer than half a league; and half a league out and half a league back every day over ground sharp and slippery with ice, with two heavy pails to carry, is not a little when one is over eighty, and has only a wisp of woollen serge between the wind and one's withered limbs.

The acorns and horse-chestnuts had all been disputed with her fiercely by boys rough and swift, who foresaw a time coming in which their pigs would be ill-fed. The roots in her little garden plot were all black and killed by the cold. The nettles had been all gathered and stewed and eaten.

The snow drove in through a big hole in her roof. The woods were ransacked for every bramble and broken bough by reivers younger and more agile than herself; she had nothing to eat, nothing to burn.

The children lay in their little beds of hay and cried all day long for food, and she had none to give them.

"If it were only myself!" she thought, stopping her ears not to hear them; if it had been only herself it would have been so easy to creep away into the corner among the dry grass, and to lie still till the cold froze the pains of hunger and made them quiet; and to feel numb and tired, and yet glad that it was all over, and to murmur that God was good, and so to let death come —content.

But it was not only herself.

The poor are seldom so fortunate—they themselves would say so unhappy—as to be alone in their homes.

There were the four small lives left to her by the poor dead foolish things she had loved,—small lives that had been rosy even on so much hunger, and blithe even amidst so much cold; that had been mirthful even at the flooding of the snowdrift, and happy even over a meal of mouldy crusts, or of hips and haws from the hedges. Had been—until now, when even so much as this could not be got, and when their beds of hay were soaked through with snow-water; now—when they were quite silent, except when they sobbed out a cry for bread.

"I am eighty-two years old, and I have never since I was born asked man or woman for help, or owed man or woman a copper coin," she thought, sitting by her black hearth, across which the howling wind drove, and stopping her ears to shut out the children's cries.

She had often known severe winters, scanty food, bitter living,—she had scores of times in her long years been as famished as this, and as cold, and her house had been as desolate.

Yet she had borne it all and never asked for an alms, being strong and ignorant, and being also in fear of the world, and holding a debt a great shame.

But now she knew that she must do it, or let those children perish; being herself old and past work, and having seen all her sons die out in their strength before her.

The struggle was long and hard with her.

She would have to die soon, she knew, and she had striven all her lifetime so to live that she might die saying, "I have asked nothing of any man."

This perhaps, she thought sadly, had been only a pride after all; a feeling foolish and wicked, that the good God sought now to chasten.

Any way she knew that she must yield it up and go and ask for something; or else those four small things, that were like a cluster of red berries on a leafless tree, must suffer and must perish.

"It is bitter, but I must do it," she thought. "Sure it is strange that the good God cares to take any of us to himself through so sharp a way as hunger. It seems, if I saw His face now, I should say, 'Not heaven for me, Monseigneur: only bread and a little wood.'"

And she rose up on her bent stiff limbs, and went to the pile of hay on which the children were lying, pale and thin, but trying to smile, all of them, because they saw the tears on her cheeks.

"Be still, my treasures," she said to them, striving to

speak cheerily, and laying her hands on the curls of the eldest born; "I go away for a little while to try and get you food. Be good, Bernardou, and take care of them till I come back."

Bernardou promised, being four years old himself; and she crept out of the little black door of the hut into the white road and the rushing winds.

"I will go to Flamma," she said to herself.

It was three in the afternoon, nearly dark at the season of midwinter. The business of the day was done.

The people had come and gone, favoured or denied, according to such sureties as they could offer.

The great wheel worked on in the seething water; the master of the mill sat against the casement to catch the falling light, adding up the sums in his ledger——crooked little signs such as he had taught himself to understand, though he could form neither numerals nor letters with his pen.

All around him in the storehouses there were corn, wood, wool, stores of every sort of food. All around him, in the room he lived in, there were hung the salt meats, the sweet herbs, and the dried fruits, that he had saved from the profusion of other and healthier years. It pleased him to know that he held all that, and also withheld it.

It moved him with a certain saturnine glee to see the hungry wistful eyes of the peasants stare longingly at all those riches, whilst their white lips faltered out an entreaty—which he denied. It was what he liked; to sit there and count his gains after his fashion, and look at his stores and listen to the howling wind and driving hail, and chuckle to think how lean and cold and sick they were outside—those fools who had mocked him because his saint had been a gipsy's leman.

To be prayed to for bread, and give the stone of a bitter denial; to be implored with tears of supplication, and to answer with a grim jest; to see a woman come with children dying for food, and to point out to her the big brass pans full of milk, and say to her "All that makes butter for Paris," and then to see her go away wailing and moaning that her child would die, and tottering feebly through the snow—all this was sweet to him.

Before his daughter had gone from him, he had been, though a hard man, yet honest, and had been, though severe, not cruel; but since he had been aware of the shame of the creature whom he had believed in as an angel, every fibre in him had been embittered and salted sharp with the poignancy of an acrid hate towards all living things. To hurt and to wound, and to see what he thus struck bleed and suffer, was the only pleasure life had left for him. He had all his manhood walked justly, according to his light, and trusted in the God to whom he prayed; and his God and his trust had denied and betrayed him, and his heart had turned to gall.

The old woman toiled slowly through the roads which lay between her hut and the water-mill.

They were roads which passed through meadows and along corn-fields, beside streamlets, and amongst little belts of woodland, lanes and paths green and pleasant in the summer, but now a slough of frozen mud, and whistled through by north-east winds. She held on her way steadily, stumbling often, and often slipping and going slowly, for she was very feeble from long lack of food, and the intensity of the cold drove through and through her frame.

Still she held on, bravely, in the teeth of the rough winds and of the coming darkness, though the weather was so wild that the poplar trees were bent to the earth, and the little light in the Calvary lamp by the river blew to and fro, and at last died out. Still she held on, a little dark tottering figure, with a prayer on her lips and a hope in her heart.

The snow was falling, the clouds were driving, the waters were roaring, in the twilight: she was only a little black speck in the vast grey waste of the earth and the sky, and the furious air tossed her at times to and fro like a withered leaf. But she would not let it beat her; she groped her way with infinite difficulty, grasping a bough for strength, or waiting under a tree for breath a moment, and thus at last reached the mill-house.

Such light as there was left showed her the kitchen within, the stores of wood, the strings of food; it looked to her as it had looked to Phratos, a place of comfort and of plenty; a strong safe shelter from the inclement night.

She lifted the latch and crept in, and went straight to Claudis Flamma, who was still busy beneath the window with those rude signs which represented to him his earthly wealth.

She stood before him white from the falling snow, with her brown face working with a strong emotion, her eyes clear and honest, and full of an intense anxiety of appeal.

"Flamma," she said simply to him, "we have been neighbours fifty years and more—thou and I, and many have borrowed of thee to their hurt and shame, but I never. I am eighty-two, and I never in my days asked anything of man or woman or child. But I come to-night to ask bread of you,—bread for the four little children at home. I have heard them cry three days, and have had nothing to give them save a berry or two off the trees. I cannot bear it any more. So I have come to you."

He shut his ledger, and looked at her. They had been neighbours, as she had said, half a century and more; and had often knelt down before the same altar, side by side.

"What dost want?" he asked simply.

"Food," she made answer; "food and fuel. They are so cold—the little ones."

"What canst pay for them?" he asked.

"Nothing—nothing now. There is not a thing in the house except the last hay the children sleep on. But if thou wilt let me have a little—just a little—while the weather is so hard, I will find means to pay when the weather breaks. There is my garden; and I can wash and spin. I will pay faithfully. Thou knowest I never owed a brass coin to any man. But I am so old, and the children are so young——"

Claudis Flamma got up and walked to the other side of the kitchen. Her eyes followed him with wistful, hungry longing.

Where he went there stood pans of new milk, baskets of eggs, rolls of bread, piles of faggots. Her feeble heart beat thickly with eager hope, her dim eyes glowed with pleasure and with thankfulness.

He came back and brought to her a few sharp rods, plucked from a thorn tree.

"Give these to thy children's children," he said, with a dark smile. "For these—and for no more—will they recompense thee when they shall grow to maturity."

She looked at him startled and disquieted, yet thinking that he meant but a stern jest.

"Good Flamma, you mock me," she murmured, trembling; "the babes are little, and good. Ah, give me food quickly, for God's sake! A jest is well in season, but to an empty body and a bitter heart it is like a stripe."

He smiled, and answered her in his harsh grating voice,

"I give thee the only thing given without payment in this world—advice. Take it or leave it."

She reeled a little as if he had struck her a blow with his fist, and her face changed terribly, whilst her eyes stared without light or sense in them.

"You jest, Flamma! You only jest!" she muttered. "The little children starve, I tell you. You will give me bread for them? Just a little bread? I will pay as soon as the weather breaks."

"I can give nothing. I am poor, very poor," he answered her, with the habitual lie of the miser; and he opened his ledger again, and went on counting up the dots and crosses by which he kept his books.

His servant Pitchou sat spinning by the hearth: she did not cease her work, nor intercede by a word.

The poor can be better to the poor than any princes; but the poor can also be more cruel to the poor than any slave drivers.

The old woman's head dropped on her breast, she turned feebly, and felt her way, as though she were blind, out of the house and into the air.

It was already dark with the darkness of descending night.

The snow was falling fast. Her hope was gone: all was cold—cold as death.

She shivered and gasped, and strove to totter on: the children were alone. The winds blew and drove the snow flakes in a white cloud against her face; the bending trees creaked and groaned as though in pain; the roar of the millwater filled the air.

There was now no light: the day was gone, and the moon was hidden; beneath her feet the frozen earth cracked and slipped and gave way.

She fell down; being so old and so weakly she could not rise again, but lay still with one limb broken under her, and the winds and the storm beating together upon her.

"The children! the children!" she moaned feebly, and then was still: she was so cold, and the snow fell so fast; she could not lift herself nor see what was around her; she thought that she was in her bed at home, and felt as though she would soon sleep.

Through the dense gloom around her there came a swiftly moving shape, that flew as silently and as quickly as a night bird, and paused as though on wings beside her.

A voice that was at once timid and fierce, tender and savage, spoke to her through the clouds of driven snow spray.

"Hush, it is I! I—Folle-Farine. I have brought you my food. It is not much—they never give me much. Still it will help a little. I heard what you said—I was in the loft. Flamma must not know; he might make you pay. But it is all mine, truly mine, take it."

"Food—for the children!"

The blessed word aroused her from her lethargy; she raised herself a little on one arm, and tried to see whence the voice came that spoke to her. But the effort exhausted her; she fell again to the ground with a groan —her limb was broken.

Folle-Farine stood above her; her dark eyes gleaming like a hawk's through the gloom, and full of a curious, startled pity.

"You cannot get up; you are old," she said, abruptly.

"See—let me carry you home. The children! yes, the children can have it. It is not much; but it will serve."

She spoke hastily and roughly; she was ashamed of her own compassion. What was it to her, whether any of these people lived or died? They had always mocked and hated her.

"If I did right, I should let them rot, and spit on their corpses," she thought, with the ferocity of vengeance that ran in her oriental blood.

Yet she had come out in the storm, and had brought away her food for strangers, though she had been at work all day long, and was chilled to the bone, and was devoured with a ravenous hunger.

Why did she do it?

She did not know. She scorned herself. But she was sorry for this woman, so poor and so brave, with her eighty-two years, and so bitterly denied in her extremity.

Manon Dax dimly caught the muttered words, and feebly strove to answer them, whilst the winds roared and the snow beat upon her fallen body.

"I cannot rise," she murmured; "my leg is broken, I think. But it is no matter. Go you to the little ones; whoever you are, you are good, and have pity. Go to them, go. It is no matter for me. I have lived my life —any way. It will soon be over. I am not in pain— indeed."

Folle-Farine stood in silence a moment, then she stooped and lifted the old creature in her strong young arms, and with that heavy burden set out on her way in the teeth of the storm.

She had known the woman, and the little ones, by sight and name long and well.

Once or twice when she had passed by them, the

grandam, tender of heart, but narrow of brain, and believing all the tales of her neighbours, had drawn the children closer to her, under the wing of her serge cloak, lest the evil eye that had bewitched the tanner's youngest born, should fall on them, and harm them in like manner.

Nevertheless the evil eyes gleamed on her with a wistful sorrow, as Folle-Farine bore her with easy strength and a sure step, through the frozen woodland ways, as she would have borne the load of wood, or the sack of corn, which she was so well used to carry to and fro like a pack-horse.

Manon Dax did not stir, she did not even strive to speak again; she was vaguely sensible of a slow, buoyant, painless movement, of a close soft pressure that sheltered her from the force of the winds, of a subtle warmth that stole through her emaciated aching frame, and made her drowsy and forgetful, and content to be still.

She could do no more. Her day for struggle and for work was done.

Once she moved a little. Her bearer paused and stopped and listened.

"Did you speak?"

Manon Dax gave a soft troubled sigh.

"God is good," she muttered, like one speaking in a dream.

Folle-Farine held on her way, as before her Phratos had once held on his: fiercely blown, blinded by the snow, pierced by the blasts of the hurricane, but sure of foot on the ice as a reindeer, and sure of eye in the dark as a night-hawk.

"Are you in pain?" she asked once of the burden she carried.

There was no answer.

"She is asleep," she thought; and went onward.

The distance of the road was nothing to her, fleet and firm of step, and inured to all hardships of the weather; yet it cost her an hour to travel it, heavily weighted as she was, soaked with snow-water, blown back continually by the opposing winds, and forced to stagger and to pause by the fury of the storm.

At last she reached the hut.

The wind had driven open the door. The wailing cries of the children echoed sorrowfully on the stillness, answered by the bleating of sheep, cold and hungry in their distant folds. The snow had drifted in unchecked; all was quite dark.

She felt her way within over the heaps of the snow, and being used by long custom to see in the gloom, as the night-haunting beasts and birds can see, she found the bed of hay, and laid her burden gently down on it.

The children ceased their wailing; the two eldest ones crept up close to their grandmother; and pressed their cheeks to hers, and whispered to her eagerly, with their little famished lips:

"Where is the food, where is the food?"

But there was still no answer.

The clouds drifted a little from the moon which had been so long obscured; it shone for a moment through the vapour of the heavy sky; the whitened ground threw back the rays increased tenfold; the pale gleam reached the old still face of Manon Dax.

There was a feeble smile upon it—the smile with which her last words had been spoken in the darkness; "God is good!"

She was quite dead.

CHAPTER VI.

ALL that night Folle-Farine tarried with the children.

The youngest had been suffocated whilst they had been alone, by the snow that had fallen through the roof, from which its elders had been too small and weakly to be able to drag it out, unaided. She laid it, stiff already in the cold of the night, beside the body of its old grandam, who had perished in endeavouring to save it; they lay together, the year-old child and the aged woman, the broken bud and the leafless bough. They had died of hunger, as the birds die on the moors and plains; it is a common fate.

She stayed beside the children, who were frightened and bewildered and quite mute. She divided such food as she had brought between them, not taking any herself. She took off the sheepskin which she wore in winter tied round her loins as her out-door garment, and made a little nest of it for the three, and covered them with it. She could not close the door, from the height of the drifted snow, and the wind poured in all night long, though in an hour the snow ceased to fall.

Now and then the clouds parting a little, let a ray of the moon stray in; and then she could see the quiet faces of the old dead woman and the child.

"They die of famine—and they die saying their 'God is good,'" she thought; 'and she pondered on it deeply, with the bitter and melancholy irony which life had already taught her.

The hours of the night dragged slowly on; the winds howled above the trembling hovel; the children sobbed themselves to sleep at last, lulled by the warmth of the sheepskin, in which they crept together like young birds in a nest.

She sat there patiently; frozen and ravenous; yet not drawing a corner of the sheepskin to her own use, nor regretting a crumb of the bread she had surrendered.

She hated the human race, whose hand was always against her. She had no single good deed to thank them for, nor any single gentle word. Yet she was sorry for that old creature, who had been so bitterly dealt with all her years through, who had died saying "God was good." She was sorry for those little helpless, unconscious starving animals, who had lost the only life that could labour for theirs.

She forgave—because she forgot—that in other winters this door had been shut against her as against an accursed thing, and these babes had mocked her in their first imperfect speech.

The dawn broke; the sharp grey winter's day came; the storm had lulled; but the whole earth was frost-bound and white with snow, the air was piercing, the sky dark and overcast.

She had to leave them; she was bound to her daily labour at the mill; she knew that if when the sun rose she were found absent, she and they too would surely suffer. What to do for them she could not tell. She had no friend save Marcellin, who himself was as poor as these. She never spoke to any living thing, except a sheep-dog, or a calf bleating for its mother, or a toil-worn bullock staggering over the ploughed clods.

Between her, and all those around her, there were perpetual enmity and mistrust, and scarcely so much of a common bond as lies in a common humanity. For in her title to a common humanity with them they disbelieved; while she in her scorn rejected all claim to it.

At daybreak there passed by the open door in the mist, a peasant going to his cattle in the fields beyond,

amidst the fields, a few huts, a stone crucifix, some barns and stacks, and a single wineshop made up a little village, celebrated in the district for its wide spreading orchards and their excellence of fruits.

Even so early the little hamlet was awake; the shutters were opened; the people were astir; men were brushing the snow from their thresholds; women were going out to their field-work; behind the narrow lattices the sleepy eyes and curly heads of children peered, while their fingers played with the fanciful encrustations of the frost.

The keeper of the tavern was unbarring his house door; a girl broke the ice in a pool for her ducks to get at the water; a few famished robins flew to and fro songless.

His own wife was on her doorstep; to her he darted.

"Manon Dax is dead!" he shouted.

"What of that?" said his wife, shouldering her broom; a great many had died that winter, and they were so poor and sharp-set with famine themselves, that they had neither bread nor pity to spare.

"This of that!" cried the old man, doggedly, and full of the excitement of his own terrors. "The young devil of Yprès has killed her, that I am sure. She is there in the hut in the dark, with her eyes glaring like coals. And for what should she be there if not for evil? Tell me that."

"Is it possible?" his wife cried, incredulous, yet willing to believe.

The girl left her ducks, the wineshop-keeper his door, the women their cabins, and came and stood round the bearer of such strange news: very welcome news in a raw frost-bitten dawn; when a day was beginning that would otherwise have had nothing more wonderful in it than tidings of how a litter of black pigs throve, and how a brown horse had fared with the swelling in the throat.

They were very dull there from year's end to year's end; once a month, may be, a letter would come in from some soldier-son or brother, or a pedlar coming to buy eggs would bring likewise some stray rumour from the outer world;—beyond this there was no change, they heard nothing, and saw nothing, seldom moving a league away from that stone crucifix, round which their little homes were clustered.

The man Flandrin had nothing truly to tell; he had fled horrified to be challenged, in the twilight and the snow, by a creature of such evil omen. But when he had got an audience, he was too true an orator and not such a fool as to lose it for such a little beggarly matter as the truth; and his tongue clacked quickly of all which his fears and fancies had conceived, until he had talked himself and his listeners into the full belief that Manon Dax being belated had encountered the evil glance of the daughter of all evil, and had been slain thereby in most cruel sorcery.

Now, in the whole neighbourhood, there was nothing too foul to be credible of the begotten of the fiend—a fiend whom all the grown men and women remembered so well in his earthly form, when he had come to ruin poor Reine Flamma's body and soul, with his eyes like jewels, and his strength passing the strength of all men.

The people listened, gaping, and wonderstruck, and forgetting the bitterness of the cold, being warmed with those unfailing human cordials of foul suspicion and of gratified hatred. Some went off to their daily labour, being unable to spare time for more gossip; but divers women who had nothing to occupy them remained about Flandrin.

A shrivelled dame, who owned the greatest number of brood-hens in the village, and who had only one son, a priest, and who was much respected and deferred to by her neighbours, spoke first when Flandrin had ended his tale for the seventh time, it being a little matter to him that his two hungry cows would be lowing all the while vainly for their morning meal.

"Flandrin, you have said well, beyond a doubt; the good soul has been struck dead by sorcery. But, you have forgot one thing, the children are there, and that devil of Yprès is with them. We—good Christians and true—should not let such things be. Go, and drive her out and bring the young ones hither."

Flandrin stood silent.

It was very well to say that the devil should be driven out, but it was not so well to be the driver.

"That is as it should be," assented the other woman. "Go, Flandrin, and we—we will take the little souls in for this day, and then give them to the public charity, better cannot be done. Go."

"But mind that thou dost strike that beast, Folle-Farine, sharply!" cried his wife.

"If thou showest her the cross, she will have to grovel and flee," said another.

"Not she," grumbled the old dame, whose son was a priest. "One day my blessed son, who is nearly a saint, Heaven knows, menaced her with his cross, and she stood straight, and fearless, and looked at it, and said, 'By that sign you do all manner of vileness in this world, and say you are safe to be blest in another; I know!' and so laughed and went on. What are you to do with a witch like that,—eh?"

"Go, Flandrin," shrieked the women in chorus, "Go! Every minute you waste the little angels are nearer to hell!"

"Come yourselves with me, then," said Flandrin, sullenly. "I will not go after those infants, it is not a man's work."

In his own mind he was musing on a story which his priests had often told him, of swine into which exorcised devils had entered, and despatched swiftly down a slope to a miserable end; and he thought of his own pigs, black, fat, and happy, worth so much to him in the market.

Better, he mused, that Manon Dax's grand-children should be the devil's prey, than those, his choicest, swine.

The women jeered him, menaced him, flouted him, besought him. But vainly—he would not move alone. He had become possessed with the terrors his own fancy had created; and he would not stir a step for all their imprecations.

"Let us go ourselves, then!" screamed his wife at length, flourishing above her head the broom with which she had swept the snow. "Men are ever cowards. It shall never be said of me, that I left those babes to the fiend while I gave my own children their porridge by the fire!"

There was a sentiment in this that stirred all her companions to emulation. They rushed into their homes, snatched a shovel, a staff, a broom, a pig-stick, each whatever came uppermost, and dragging Flandrin in the midst, went down the sloping frozen road between its fringe of poplars.

They were not very sure in their own minds, why they went, nor for what they went; but they had a vague idea of doing what was wise and pious, and they had a great hate in their hearts against the child. They sped as fast as the slippery road would let them, and their tongues flew still faster than their feet; the cold of the daybreak made them sharp and keen on their prey, as the air was on themselves; they screamed fable on fable hoarsely, their voices rising shrilly above the whistling of the winds, and the creaking of the trees, and they inflamed each other with ferocious belief in the sorcery they were to punish.

They were in their way virtuous; they were content on very little; they toiled hard from their birth to their grave; they were most of them chaste wives and devoted mothers, they bore privation steadily, and they slaved in fair weather and foul without a complaint. But they were narrow of soul, greedy of temper, bigoted and uncharitable, and, when they thought themselves or their offspring menaced, implacable.

They were of the stuff that would be burned for a creed, and burn others for another creed.

It is the creed of the vast majority of every nation; the priests and lawgivers of every nation have always told their people that it is a creed holy and honourable—how can the people know that it is at once idiotic and hellish?

Folle-Farine sat within on the damp hay under the broken roof, and watched the open door.

The children were still asleep. The eldest one in his sleep had turned and caught her hand, and held it.

She did not care for them. They had screamed, and run behind the woodstack, or their grandam's skirts, a hundred times when they had seen her on the road or in the orchard.

But she was sorry for them; almost as sorry as she was for the little naked woodpigeons when their nests were scattered on the ground in a tempest, or for the little starveling rabbits when they screamed in their holes for the soft white mother that was lying, tortured and twisted, in the jaws of a steel-trap.

She was sorry for them—half roughly, half tenderly sorry—with some shame at her own weakness, and yet too sincerely sorry to be able to persuade herself to leave them to their fate there, all alone with their dead. For in the savage heart of Taric's daughter there was an innermost corner wherein her mother's nature slept.

She sat there quite still, watching the porch, and listening for footsteps.

The snow was driven in encircling clouds by the winds; the dense fog of the dawn lifted itself off the surrounding fields; the branches of the trees were beautiful with hanging icicles; from the meadow hard-by there wailed unceasingly the mournful moaning of Flandrin's cattle, deserted of their master, and hungry in their wooden sheds.

She heard a distant convent clock strike six: no one came. Yet she had resolved not to leave the children all alone, though Flamma should come and find her there, and thrash her for her absence from his tasks. So she sat still, and waited.

After a little she heard the crisp cracking of many feet on the frozen snow and ice-filled ruts of the narrow road; she heard a confused clatter of angry voices breaking harshly on the stillness of the winter morning.

The light was stronger now, and through the doorway she saw the little passionate crowd of angry faces as the women pressed onward down the hill with Flandrin in their midst.

She rose, and looked out at them, quietly.

For a minute they paused—irresolute, silent, perplexed: at the sight of her they were half daunted; they felt the vagueness of the crime they came to bring against her.

The wife of Flandrin recovered speech first, and dared them to the onslaught.

"What!" she screamed, "nine good Christians fearful of one daughter of hell? Fie! for shame! Look; my leaden Peter is round my neck! Is he not stronger than she any day?"

In a moment more, thus girded at and guarded at the same time, they were through the door and stood on the mud floor of the hearth, close to her, casting hasty glances at the poor dead body on the hearth, whose fires they had left to die out all through that bitter winter.

They came about her in a fierce, gesticulating, breathless troop, flourishing their sticks in her eyes, and casting at her all their various charges in one breath. Flandrin stood a little aloof, sheepishly on the threshold, wishing that he had never said a word of the death of Manon Dax to his good wife and neighbours.

"You met that poor saint and killed her in the snow with your witcheries!" one cried.

"You have stifled that poor babe where it lay!" cried another.

"A good woman like that!" shrieked a third, "who was well and blithe and praising God only a day ago, for I saw her myself come down the hill for our well water!"

"It is as you did with the dear little Rémy, who will be lame all his life, through you," hissed a fourth. "You are not fit to live; you spit venom like a toad."

"Are you alive, my angels?" said a fifth, waking the three children noisily, and rousing their piercing cries. "Are you alive after that witch has gazed on you? It is a miracle! The Saints be praised!"

Folle-Farine stood mute and erect for the moment, not comprehending why they thus with one accord fell upon her. She pointed to the bodies on the hearth, with one of those grave and dignified gestures which were her birthright from the old oriental race.

"She was cold and hungry," she said curtly, her mellow accent softening and enriching the provincial tongue which she had learned from those amidst whom she dwelt. "She had fallen, and was dying. I brought her here. The young child was killed by the snow. I stayed with the rest because they were frightened, and alone. There is no more to tell. What of it?"

"Thou hadst better come away. What canst thou prove?" whispered Flandrin to his wife.

He was afraid of the storm he had invoked, and would fain have stilled it. But that was beyond his power. The women had not come forth half a league in the howling winds of a midwinter daybreak only to go back with a mere charity done, and with no vengeance taken.

They hissed, they screamed, they hurled their rage at her; they accused her of a thousand crimes; they filled the hut with clamour as of a thousand tongues; they foamed, they spat, they struck at her with their sticks; and she stood quiet, looking at them, and the old dead face of Manon Dax which lay upward in the dim light.

The eldest boy struggled in the grasp of the peasant woman who had seized him, and stretched his arms, instead, to the one who had fed him, and whose hand he had held all through his restless slumber in that long and dreary night. The woman covered his eyes with a scream.

"Ah—h!" she moaned, "see how the innocent child is bewitched! It is horrible!"

"Look on that;—oh, infernal thing!" cried Flandrin's wife, lifting up her treasured figure of Peter. "You dare not face that blessed image. See—see all of you—how she winces, and turns white!"

Folle-Farine had shrunk a little as the child had called to her. Its gesture of affection was the first that she had ever seen towards her in any human thing.

She laughed aloud as the image of Peter was thrust in her face. She saw it was some emblem and idol of their faith, devoutly cherished. She stretched her hand out, wrenched it away, trampled on it, and tossed it through the doorway into the snow, where it sank and disappeared. Then she folded her arms, and waited for them.

There was a loud shriek at the blasphemy of the impious act; then they rushed on her.

They came inflamed with all the fury which abject fear and bigoted hatred can beget in minds of the lowest and most brutal type. They were strong, rude, ignorant, fanatical peasants, they abhorred her, they believed no child of theirs safe in its bed while she walked abroad alive. Beside such women, when in wrath and riot, the tiger and the hyæna are as the lamb and the dove.

They set on her with furious force, flung her, trod on her, beat her, kicked her with their woodshod feet, with all the malignant fury of the female animal that fights for its offspring's and its own security.

Strong though she was, and swift, and full of courage, she had no power against the numbers who had thrown themselves on her, and borne her backward by dint of their united effort, and held her down to work their worst on her.

She could not free herself nor return their blows, nor lift herself to wrestle with them; she could only deny them the sweetness of wringing from her a single cry, and that much she did.

She was mute while the rough hands flew at her, the sticks struck at her, the heavy feet were driven against her body, the fingers clutched at her long hair, and twisted and tore at it—she was quite mute throughout.

"Prick her in the breast, and see if the devil be still in her. I have heard say there is no better way to test a witch!" cried Flandrin's wife, writhing in rage for the outrage to the Petrus.

Her foes needed no second bidding; they had her already prostrate in their midst, and a dozen eager hands seized a closer grip upon her, pulled her clothes from her chest, and, holding her down on the mud floor, searched with ravenous eyes for the signet marks of hell.

The smooth skin baffled them; its rich and tender hues were without spot or blemish.

"What matter; what matter?" hissed Rose Flandrin. "When our fathers hunted witches in the old time, did they stop for that? Draw blood, and you will see."

She clutched a jagged rusty nail from out the wall, and leaned over her prey.

"It is the only babe that will ever cling to thee!" she cried, with a laugh, as the nail drew blood above the heart.

Still Folle-Farine made no sound and asked no mercy.

She was powerless, defenceless, flung on her back amidst her tormentors, fastened down by treading feet and clenching hands; she could resist in nothing, she could not stir a limb, still she kept silence, and her proud eyes looked unquailing into the hateful faces bent to hers.

The muscles and nerves of her body quivered with a mighty pang, her chest heaved with the torture of indignity, her heart fluttered like a wounded bird—not at the physical pain, but at the shame of these women's gaze, the loathsome contact of their reckless touch. The iron pierced deeper, but they could not make her speak.

Except for her eyes, that glowed with a dusky fire as they glanced to and fro, seeking escape, she might have been a statue of olive wood, flung down by ruffians to make a bonfire.

"If one were to drive the nail to the head, she would not feel!" cried the women, in furious despair, and were minded, almost, to put her to that uttermost test.

Suddenly from the doorway Flandrin raised an alarm:

"There is our notary close at hand, on the road on his mule! Hist! Come out quickly. You know how strict he is, and how he forbids us ever to try and take the law into our own keeping. Quick—as you love your lives—quick!"

The furies left their prey, and scattered and fled, the notary was a name of awe to them, for he was a severe man, but just.

They seized the children, went out with them into the road, closed the hut door behind them, and moved down the hill; the children wailing sadly, and the eldest trying to get from them and go back.

The women looked mournful and held their heads down, and comforted the little ones; Flandrin himself went to his cattle in the meadow.

"Is anything amiss?" the old white-haired notary asked, stopping his favourite grey mule at sight of the little cavalcade.

The women, weeping, told him that Manon Dax was dead, and the youngest infant likewise—of cold, in the night, as they supposed. They dared to say no other thing, for he had many times rebuked them for their lack of charity and their bigoted cruelties and superstitions, and they were quaking with fear lest he should by any chance enter the cottage and see their work.

"Flandrin, going to his cow, saw her first, and he came to us and told us," they added, crossing themselves fervently, and hushing little Bernardou, who wanted to get from them and return; "and we have taken the poor little things to carry them home; we are going to give them food, and warm them awhile by the stove, and then we shall come back and do all that is needful for the beloved dead who are within."

"That is well. That is good and neighbourly of you," said the notary, who liked them all, having married them all, and registered all their children's births, and who was a good old man though stern; kindly and very honest.

He promised them to see for his part that all needed by the law and by the church should be done for their old lost neighbour, and then urged his fat mule into a trot, for he had been summoned to a rich man's sick bed in that early winter morning, and was in haste lest the priest should be beforehand with him there.

"How tender the poor are to the poor! Those people have not bread enough for themselves, and yet they burden their homes with three strange mouths. Their hearts must be true at the core, if their tongues sometimes be foul," he mused, as he rode the mule down through the fog.

The women went on, carrying and dragging the children with them, in a sullen impatience.

"To think we should have had to leave that fiend of Yprès!" they muttered in their teeth. "Well, there is one thing, she will not get over the hurt for days. Her bones will be stiff for many a week. That will teach her to leave honest folk alone."

And they traversed the road slowly; muttering to one another.

"Hold thy noise, thou little pig!" cried Flandrin's wife, pushing Bernardou on before her. "Hold thy noise, I tell you, or I will put you in the black box in a hole in the ground, along with thy great-grandmother."

But Bernardou wept aloud, refusing to be comforted or terrified into silence. He was old enough to know that never more would the old kindly withered brown face bend over him as he woke in the morning, nor the old kindly quavering voice croone him country ballads and cradle songs at twilight by the bright wood fire.

Little by little the women carrying the children crept down the slippery slope, half ice and half mud in the thaw, and entered their own village, and therein were much praised for their charity and courage.

For when they praise, as when they abuse, villages are loud of voice and blind of eye, much as are the cities.

Their tongues, and those of their neighbours, clacked all day long, noisily and bravely, of their good and their great deeds; they had all the sanctity of martyrdom, and all the glory of victory, in one.

True, they had left all their house and field work half done;—"but the Holy Peter will finish it in his own good time, and avenge himself for his outrage," mused the wife of Flandrin, sorrowing over her lost Petrus in the snowdrift, and boxing the ears of little Bernardou, as he huddled in her chimney corner, to make him cease from his weeping.

When they went back with their priest at noon to the

hut of old Manon Dax to make her ready for her burial, they trembled inwardly lest they should find their victim there, and lest she should lift up her voice in accusation against them. Their hearts misgave them sorely. Their priest, a cobbler's son, and almost as ignorant as themselves, save that he could gabble a few morsels of bad Latin, would be, they knew, on their own side; but they were sensible that they had let their fury hurry them into acts which could easily be applauded by their neighbours, but not so easily justified to the law.

"For the law is over good," said Rose Flandrin, "and takes the part of all sorts of vile creatures. It will protect a rogue, a brigand, a bullock, a dog, a witch, a devil—anything,—except now and then an honest woman."

But their fears were groundless; she was gone; the hut when they entered it had no tenants except the lifeless famished bodies of the old grandam and the year-old infant.

When Folle-Farine had heard the hut door close, and the steps of her tormentors die away down the hill, she had tried vainly several times to raise herself from the floor, and had failed.

She had been so suddenly attacked and flung down and trampled on, that her brain had been deadened, and her senses had gone for the first sharp moment of the persecution.

As she lifted herself slowly, and staggered to her feet, and saw the blood trickle where the nail had pierced her breast, she understood what had happened to her; and her face grew savage and dark, and her eyes fierce and lustful, like the eyes of some wild beast rising wounded in his lair.

It was not for the hurt she cared; it was the shame of defeat and outrage that stung her like a whip of asps.

She stood awhile looking at the dead face of the woman she had aided.

"I tried to help you," she thought. "I was a fool. I might have known how they pay any good done to them."

She was not surprised; her mind had been too deadened by a long course of ill usage to feel any wonder at the treatment with which she had been repaid.

She hated them with the mute unyielding hatred of her race, but she hated herself more because she had yielded to the softness of sorrow and pity for any human thing; and more still because she had not been armed and on her guard, and had suffered them to prevail and to escape without her vengeance.

"I will never come abroad without a knife in my girdle again," she thought—this was the lesson that her charity had brought her as its teaching.

She went out hardening her heart, as she crept through the doorway into the snow and the wind, so that she should not leave one farewell word or token of gentleness with the dead, that lay there so tranquil on the ashes of the hearth.

"She lied, even in her last breath," thought Folle-Farine. "She said that her God was good!"

She could hardly keep on her own homeward way. All her limbs were stiff and full of pain. The wound in her chest was scarcely more than skin deep, yet it smarted sorely and bled still. Her brain was dull, and her ears were filled with strange noises from the force with which she had been flung backward on her head.

She had given her sheepskin to the children, as before her Phratos had done; and one of the peasants had carried the youngest away in it. The sharpness of the intense cold froze the blood in her as she crawled through a gap in the poplar hedge, and under the whitened brambles and grasses, beyond, to get backward to the mill by the path that ran through the woods and pastures.

The sun had risen, but was obscured by fog, through which it shed a dull red ray here and there above the woods in the east.

It was a bitter morning, and the wind, though it had abated, was still rough, and drove the snow in clouds of powder hither and thither over the fields. She could only move very slowly, very stiffly; the thorns tearing her, the snow blinding her, the icicles lacerating her bare feet as she moved.

She wondered, dimly, why she lived. It seemed to her that the devil, when he had made her, must have made her out of sport and cruelty, and then tossed her into the world to be a scapegoat and a football for any creature that might need one.

That she might end her own life never occurred to her; her intelligence was not awake enough to see that she need not have borne its burden one hour more, so long as there had been one pool in the woods deep enough to drown her under its green weeds and lily leaves any cool summer night. Nay,—that she had but to lie down, then and there, where she was, beneath the ice-dropping trees, and let the sleep that weighed so heavily on her eyelids come, dreamless and painless, and there would be an end of all for her, as for the frozen rabbits and the birds that strewed the upland meadows, starved and stiff.

She did not know;—and had she known, wretched though existence was to her, death would not have allured her. She saw that the dead might be slapped on their cheek, and could not lift their arm to strike again—

a change that would not give her vengeance could have had no sweetness and no succour for her. The change she wanted was to live, and not to die.

By tedious and painful efforts, she dragged herself home by the way of the lanes and pastures; hungry, lame, bleeding, cold and miserable, with her eyes burning, and her hands and her head hot with fever.

She made her way into the mill-yard and tried to commence her first morning's work; the drawing of water from the well for the beasts and for the house, and the sweeping down of the old wide court round which the sheds and storehouses ran.

She never dreamed of asking either for food or pity, either for sympathy or remission of her labours. She set to work at once, but for the only time since Phratos had brought her thither, the strength and vigour of her frame had been beaten.

She was sick and weak; her hand sank off the handle of the windlass; and she dropped stupidly on the stone edge of the well, and sat there leaning her head on her hands.

The mastiff came and licked her face tenderly. The pigeons left the meal flung to them on the snow, and flew merrily about her head in pretty fluttering caresses. The lean cat came and rubbed its cheek softly against her, purring all the while. The woman Pitchou saw her, and she called out of the window to her master.

"Flamma! there is thy gad-about, who has not been a' bed all night."

The old man heard, and came out of his mill to the well in the courtyard.

"Where hast been?" he asked sharply of her. "Pitchou says thou hast not lain in thy bed all night long. Is it so?"

Folle-Farine lifted her head slowly, with a dazed stupid pain in the look of her eyes.

"Yes, it is true," she answered, doggedly.

"And where hast been then?" he asked, through his clenched teeth; enraged that his servant had been quicker of eye and of ear than himself.

A little of her old dauntless defiance gleamed in her face through its stupor and languor, as she replied to him with effort in brief phrases.

"I went after old Manon Dax, to give her my supper. She died in the road, and I carried her home. And the youngest child was dead too. I stayed there because the children were alone; I called to Flandrin and told him; he came with his wife and other women, and they said I had killed old Dax; they set on me, and beat me, and pricked me for a witch. It is no matter. But it made me late."

In her glance upward, even in the curtness of her words, there was an unconscious glimmer of appeal, a vague fancy that for once she might, perhaps, meet with approval and sympathy, instead of punishment and contempt. She had never heard a kind word from him, nor one of any compassion, and yet a dim unuttered hope was in her heart, that for once he might condemn her persecutors and pardon her.

But the hope was a vain one, like all which she had cherished since first the door of the mill-house had opened to admit her.

Flamma only set his teeth tighter. In his own soul he had been almost ashamed of his denial to his old neighbour, and had almost feared, that it would lose him the good will of that good heaven which had sent him so mercifully such a sharp year of famine to enrich him. Therefore, it infuriated him, to think that this offspring of a foul sin should have had pity and charity, where he had lacked them.

He looked at her and saw with grim glee, that she was black and blue with bruises, and that the linen which she held together across her bosom had been stained with blood.

"Flandrin and his wife are honest people, and pious," he said, in answer to her. "When they find a wench out of her bed at night, they deal rightly with her, and do not hearken to any lies that she may tell them of feigned alms-giving to cover her vices from their sight. I thank them that they did so much of my work for me. They might well prick thee for a witch; but they will never cut so deep into thy breast, as to be able to dig the mark of the devil out of it. Now, up and work, or it will be the worse for thee."

She obeyed him.

There during the dark winter's day, the pain which she endured, with her hunger and the cold of the weather, made her fall thrice, like a dead thing, on the snow of the court, and the floors of the sheds. But she lay insensible till the youth in her brought back consciousness, without aid; in those moments of faintness, no one noticed her save the dog, who came and crept to her to give her warmth, and strove to wake her with the kisses of his rough tongue.

She did her work as best she might; neither Flamma nor his servant once spoke to her.

"My women dealt somewhat roughly with thy wench at break of day, good Flamma," said the man Flandrin, meeting him in the lane that afternoon, and fearful of offending the shrewd old man who had so many of his neighbours in his grip. "I hope thou wilt not take it amiss? The girl maddened my dame—spitting on her Peter, and throwing the blessed image away in a ditch."

"The woman did well," said Flamma, coldly, driving his grey mare onward through the fog.

Flandrin could not tell whether he were content, or were displeased.

Claudis Flamma himself, hardly knew which he was, himself; he held her as the very spawn of hell itself, and yet it was loathsome to him, that his neighbours should also know, and say, that a devil had been the only fruit of that fair offspring of his own, whom he and they had so long held as a saint.

The next day and the next, and the next again after that, she was too ill to stir; they beat her and called her names, but it was of no use; they could not get work out of her; she was past it, and beyond all rousing of their sticks, or of their words.

They were obliged to let her be. She stayed for nearly four days in the hay in her loft; devoured with fever, and with every bone and muscle in pain. She had a pitcher of water by her and drank continually, thirstily, like a sick dog. With rest and no medicine but the cold spring water, she recovered; she had been delirious in a few of the hours, and had dreamed of nothing but of the old life in the Liébana, and of the old sweet music of Phratos. She remained there untended, shivering and fever-stricken, until the strength of her youth returned to her. She rose on the fifth day weaker, but otherwise little the worse; with the soft sad songs of her old friend the viol ringing always through her brain.

The fifth day from the death of Manon Dax, was the day of the new year.

There was no work being done at the mill; the wheel stood still, locked fast, for the deep stream was close bound in ice; frost had returned, and the country was white with snow two feet deep, and bleak and bare, and rioted over by furious cross winds.

Flamma and Pitchou were in the kitchen when she entered it; they looked up, but neither spoke to her. In being ill—for the first time since they had had to do with her,—she had committed, for the millionth time, a crime.

There was no welcome for her in that cheerless place, where scarcely a spark of fire was allowed to brighten the hearth, and where the hens, straying in from without, sat with ruffled feathers, chilled and moping, and where, the old Black Forest clock in the corner, had stopped from the intense cold.

There was no welcome for her—she went out into the air, thinking the woods, even at midwinter, could not be so lonesome as was that cheerless house.

The sun was shining through a rift in the stormy clouds, and the white roofs, and the ice-crusted waters, and the frosted trees, were glittering in its light.

There were many dead birds about the paths. Claudis Flamma had thought their famine-time a good one, in which to tempt them with poisoned grain.

She wondered where the dog was who never had failed to greet her,—a yard farther on she saw him.

He was stretched stiff and lifeless beside the old barrel that had served him as a kennel; his master had begrudged him the little straw needful to keep him from the hurricanes of those bitter nights; and he had perished quietly, without a moan, like a sentinel slain at his post —frozen to death in his old age after a life of faithfulness repaid with blows.

She stood by him a while with dry eyes, but with an aching heart. He had loved her, and she had loved him; and many a time she had risked a stroke of the lash to save it from his body; and many a time she had sobbed herself to sleep in her earlier years, with her arms curled round him, as round her only friend and only comrade in bondage and in misery. . . .

She stooped down; kissed him softly on his broad grizzled forehead, and lifted his corpse into a place of shelter, and covered it tenderly, so that he should not be left to the crows and the kites, until she should be able to make his grave in those orchards in which he had loved so well to wander, and in which he and she had spent all their brief hours of summer liberty and leisure.

She shuddered as she looked her last on him; and filled in the snow above his tomb, under the old twisted pear tree, beneath which, he and she had so often sat together in the long grasses, consoling one another for scant fare and cruel blows by the exquisite mute sympathy which can exist betwixt the canine and the human animal when the two are alone, and love and trust each other, only, out of all the world.

Whilst the dog had lived, she had had two friends; now that he slept for ever in the old grey orchard, she had but one left.

She went to seek this one.

Her heart ached for a kind glance—for a word that should be neither of hatred nor of scorn. It was seldom that she allowed herself to know such a weakness. She had dauntless blood in her; she came of a people that despised pity, and who knew how to live hard and to die hard, without murmur or appeal. Yet she had clung to the old mastiff, who was savage to all save herself; so she still clung to the old man Marcellin, who to all save herself was a terror and a name of foul omen.

He was good to her in his own fierce and rugged way; and they had the kinship of the proscribed; and they loved one another in a strange, silent, savage manner, as a yearling wolf cub and an aged grizzled bear might love each other in the depths of a forest, where the foot of the hunter and the fangs of the hound were alike against the young and the old.

She had not seen him for six days. She felt ill, and weak, and cold, and alone. She thought she would go to him in his hut, and sit a little by his lonely hearth, and hear him tell strange stories of the marvellous time when he was young, and the world was drunk with a mad sweet dream which was never to come true upon earth.

Her heart was in wild revolt, and a fierce futile hate gnawed ever in it. She had become used to the indignities of the populace, and the insults of all the people who went to and fro her grandsire's place; but each one pierced deeper and deeper than the last, and left a longer scar, and killed more and more of the gentler and better instincts which had survived in her through all the brutalising debasement of her life.

She could not avenge the outrage of Rose Flandrin and her sisterhood, and being unable to avenge it, she shut her mouth and said nothing of it, as her habit was. Nevertheless it festered and rankled in her; and now and then the thought crossed her—why not take a flint and a bit of tow, and burn them all in their beds as they slept in that little hollow at the foot of the hill?

She thought of it often—would she ever do it? She did not know.

It had a taint of cowardice in it; yet a man that very winter had fired a farmstead for far less an injury, and had burned to death all who had lain therein that night. Why should she not kill and burn these also? They had never essayed to teach her to do better, and when she had tried to do good to one of them, the others had set on her as a witch.

In the afternoon of this first day of the year she had to pass through their hamlet to seek Marcellin.

The sun was low and red; the dusky light glowered over the white meadows and through the leafless twilight of the woods; here and there a solitary tree of holly reared itself, scarlet and tall, from the snowdrifts; here and there a sheaf of arrowy reeds pierced the sheets of ice that covered all the streams and pools.

The little village lay with its dark round roofs, cosy and warm, with all the winter round. She strode through it erect, and flashing her scornful eyes right and left; but her right hand was inside her skirt, and it gripped fast the handle of a knife. For such was the lesson which the reward for her charity had taught her — a lesson not lightly to be forgotten, nor swiftly to be unlearned again.

In its simple mode, the little place, like its greater neighbours, kept high festival for a fresh year begun.

Its crucifix rose, bare and white, out of a crown of fir boughs and many wreaths of ruddy berries. On its cabin windows the light of wood cracking and blazing within glowed brightly. Through them she saw many of their interiors as she went by in the shadow without.

In one the children knelt in a circle round the fire, roasting chestnuts in the embers with gay shouts of laughter. In another, they romped with their big sheep-dog, decking him with garlands of ivy and laurel.

In one little brown room a betrothal party made merry; in another, that was bright with Dutch tiles, and hung round with dried herbs and fruits, an old matron had her arm round the curly head of a sailor lad, home for a short glad hour.

In the house of Flandrin a huge soup-pot smoked with savoury odour, and the eyes of his wife were soft with a tender mirth as she watched her youngest-born playing with a Punch, all bells and bright colours, and saw the elder ones cluster round a gilded Jesus of sugar.

In the wine-shop, the keeper of it, having taken to himself a wife that day, kept open house to his friends, and he and they were dancing to the music of a horn and a fiddle, under rafters bedecked with branches of fir, with many-hued ribands, and with little oil lamps that blew to and fro in the noise of the romp. And all round were the dark still woods, and in the midst rose the crucifix; and above, on the height of the hill, the little old hut of Manon Dax stood dark and empty.

She looked at it all, going through it, with her hand on her knife.

"One spark," she thought, playing with the grim temptation that possessed her—"one spark on the dry thatch, and what a bonfire they would have for their feasting!"

The thought was sweet to her.

Injustice had made her ravenous and savage. When she had tried to do well, and to save life, these people had accused her of taking it by evil sorcery.

She felt a longing to show them what evil indeed she could do, and to see them burn, and to hear them scream vainly, and then to say to them with a laugh, as the flames licked up their homes and their lives, "Another time, take care how you awake a witch!"

Why did she not do it? She did not know; she had brought out a flint and tinder in the pouch that hung at her side. It would be as easy as to pluck a sere leaf; she knew that.

She stood still and played with her fancy, and it was horrible and sweet to her — so sweet because so horrible.

How soon their mirth would be stilled!

As she stood thinking, there, and in her fancy seeing the red glare that would light up that peaceful place, and hearing the roar of the lurid flames that would drown the music, and the laughter, and the children's shouts, out of the twilight there rose to her a small dark thing, with a halo round its head: the thing was little Bernardou, and the halo was the shine of his curling hair in the lingering light.

He caught her skirts in his hands, and clung to her and sobbed.

"I know you — you were good that night. The people all say you are wicked, but you gave us your food, and held my hand. Take me back to gran'mère — oh, take me back!"

She was startled and bewildered.

This child had never mocked her, but he had screamed and run from her in terror, and had been told a score of stories that she was a devil, who could kill his body and soul.

"She is dead, Bernardou," she answered him; and her voice was troubled, and sounded strangely to her as she spoke for the first time to a child without being derided or screamed at in fear.

"Dead! What is that?" sobbed the boy. "She was stiff and cold, I know, and they put her in a hole; but she would waken, I know she would, if she only heard *us*. We never cried in the night but she heard in her sleep, and got up and came to us. Oh, do tell her — do, do tell her!"

She was silent; she did not know how to answer

him, and the strangeness of any human appeal made to her bewildered her and held her mute.

"Why are you out in the cold, Bernardou?" she asked him suddenly, glancing backward through the lattice of the Flandrins' house, through which she could see the infants laughing and shaking the puppet with the gilded bells.

"They beat me; they say I am naughty, because I want gran'mère," he said, with a sob. "They beat me often, and oh! if she knew, she would wake and come. Do tell her—do! Bernardou will be so good, and never vex her, if only she will come back!"

His piteous voice was drowned in tears.

His little life had been hard; scant fare, cold winds, and naked limbs had been his portion; yet the life had been bright and gleeful to him, clinging to his grandam's skirts as she washed at the tub or hoed in the cabbage-ground, catching her smile when he brought her the first daisy of the year, running always to her open arms in any hurt, sinking to sleep always with the singing of her old ballads on his ear.

It had been a little life, dear, glad, kindly, precious to him, and he wept for it; refusing to be comforted by sight of a gilded puppet in another's hand, or a sugared Jesus in another's mouth, as they expected him to be.

It is the sort of comfort that is always offered to the homeless, and they are always thought ungrateful if they will not be consoled by it.

"I wish I could take you, Bernardou!" Folle-Farine murmured, with a momentary softness that was exquisitely tender in its contrast to her haughty and fierce temper. "I wish I could."

For one wild instant the thought came to her to break from her bonds, and take this creature who was as lonely as herself, and to wander away and away into that unknown land which stretched around her, and of which she knew no more than one of the dark leaves knew that grew in the snow-filled ditch.

But the thought passed unuttered; she knew neither where to go nor what to do.

Her few early years in the Liébana were too dream-like and too vaguely remembered to be any guide to her; and the world seemed only to her in her fancies as a vast plain, dreary and dismal, in which every hand would be against her, and every living thing be hostile to her. Beside, the long habitude of slavery was on her, and it is a yoke that eats into the flesh too deeply to be wrenched off without many an effort.

As she stood thinking, with the child's eager hands clasping her skirts, a shrill voice called from the wood-stack and dung-heap outside Flandrin's house:

"Bernardou! Bernardou! thou little plague. Come within. What dost do out there in the dark? Mischief, I will warrant."

The speaker strode out, and snatched and bore and clutched him away; she was the sister of Rose Flandrin, who lived with them, and kept the place and the children in order.

"Thou little beast!" she muttered, in fury. "Dost dare talk to the witch that killed thy grandmother? Thou shalt hie to bed, and sup on a fine whipping. Thank God, thou goest to the hospital to-morrow! Thou wouldst bring a dire curse on the house in reward for our alms to thee."

She dragged him in and slammed-to the door, and his cries echoed above the busy shouts and laughter of the Flandrin family, gathered about the tinselled Punch and the sugared Jesus, and the soup-pot, that stewed them a fat farm-yard goose for their supper.

Folle-Farine listened awhile, with her hand clenched on her knife; then she toiled onward through the village, and left it and its carols and carousings behind her in the red glow of the sinking sun.

She thought no more of setting their huts in a blaze; the child's words had touched and softened her; she remembered the long patient bitter life of the woman who had died of cold and hunger in her eighty-second year, and yet who had thus died saying to the last, "God is good."

"What is their God?" she mused. "They care for him, and he seems to care nothing for them whether they be old or young."

Yet her heart was softened, and she would not fire the house in which little Bernardou was sheltered.

His was the first gratitude that she had ever met with, and it was sweet to her as the rare blossom of the edelweiss to the traveller upon the highest Alpine summits—a flower full of promise, born amidst a waste.

The way was long to where Marcellin dwelt, but she walked on through the fields that were in summer all one scarlet glow of poppies, and were now a white sheet of frozen water.

The day was over, the evening drew nigh, the sound of innumerable bells in the town echoed faintly from the distance, over the snow: all was still.

On the night of the new year the people had a care that the cattle in the byres, the sheep in the folds, the dogs in the kennels, the swine in the styes, the old carthorses in the sheds, should have a full meal and a clean bed, and be able to rejoice.

In all the country round there were only two that were forgotten—the dead in their graves, and the daughter of Taric.

Folle-Farine was cold, hungry, and exhausted, for the fever had left her enfeebled; and from the coarse food of the mill-house her weakness had turned.

But she walked on steadily.

At the hut where Marcellin dwelt she knew that she would be sure of one welcome, one smile; one voice that would greet her kindly; one face that would look on her without a frown.

It would not matter, she thought, how the winds should howl and the hail drive, or how the people should be merry in their homes and forgetful of her and of him. He and she would sit together over the little fire, and give back hate for hate and scorn for scorn, and commune with each other, and want no other cheer or comrade.

It had been always so since he had first met her at sunset amongst the poppies, then a little child of eight years old. Every new-year's night she had spent with him in his hovel; and in their own mute way they had loved one another, and drawn closer together, and been almost glad, though often pitcher and platter had been empty, and sometimes even the hearth had been cold.

She stepped bravely against the wind, and over the crisp firm snow, her spirits rising as she drew near the only place that had ever opened its door gladly to her coming; her heart growing lighter as she approached the only creature to whom she had ever spoken her thoughts without derision or told her woes without condemnation.

His hut stood by itself in the midst of the wide pastures, and by the side of a stream.

A little light was wont to twinkle at that hour through the crevices of its wooden shutter; this evening all was dark, the outline of the hovel rose like a rugged mound against the white wastes round it. The only sound was the far-off chiming of the bells that vibrated strangely on the rarefied sharp air.

She crossed the last meadow where the sheep were folded for the night, and went to the door and pushed against it to open it—it was locked.

She struck it with her hand.

"Open, Marcellin—open quickly. It is only I."

There was no answer.

She smote the wood more loudly, and called to him again.

A heavy step echoed on the mud floor within; a match was struck, a dull light glimmered; a voice she did not know muttered drowsily, "Who is there?"

"It is I, Marcellin," she answered. "It is not night. I am come to be an hour with you. Is anything amiss?"

The door opened slowly, an old woman, whose face was strange to her, peered out into the dusk. She had been asleep on the settle by the fire, and stared stupidly at the flame of her own lamp.

"Is it the old man, Marcellin, you want?" she asked.

"Marcellin, yes—where is he?"

"He died four days ago. Get you gone; I will have no tramps about my place."

"Died!"

Folle-Farine stood erect, without a quiver in her face or in her limbs; but her teeth shut together like a steel clasp, and all the rich and golden hues of her skin changed to a sickly ashen pallor.

"Yes, why not?" grumbled the old woman. "To be sure men said that God would never let him die, because he killed St. Louis; but myself I never thought that. I knew the devil would not wait more than a hundred years for him—you can never cheat the devil, and he always seems stronger than the saints—somehow. You are that thing of Yprès, are you not? Get you gone!"

"Who are you? Why are you here?" she gasped.

Her right hand was clenched on the door-post, and her right foot was set on the threshold, so that the door could not be closed.

"I am an honest woman and a pious; and it befouls me to dwell where he dwelt," the old peasant hissed in loud indignation. "I stood out a whole day, but when one is poor, and the place is offered quit of rent, what can one do?—and it is roomy and airy for the fowls, and the priest has flung holy water about it and purified it, and I have a Horse-shoe nailed up, and a St. John in the corner. But be off with you, and take your foot from my door."

Folle-Farine stood motionless.

"When did he die; and how?" she asked in her teeth.

"He was found dead on the road, on his heap of stones, the fourth night from this," answered the old woman, loving to hear her own tongue, yet dreading the one to whom she spoke. "Perhaps he had been hungered, I do not know; or more likely the devil would not wait any longer; anyways, he was dead—the hammer in his hand. Max Liében, the man that travels with the wooden clocks, found him. He lay there all night. Nobody would touch him. They say they saw the mark of the devil's claws on him. At last they got a dungcart, and that took him away before the sun rose. He died just under the great Calvary—it was like his blasphemy. They have put him in the common ditch. I think it shame to let the man that slew a saint be in the same grave with all the poor honest folk who feared God, and were Christians though they might be beggars and outcasts. Get you gone, you be as vile as he. If you want him go ask your father the foul fiend for him—they are surely together now."

And she drove the door to, and closed it, and barred it firmly within.

"Not but what the devil can get through the chinks," she muttered, as she turned the wick of her lamp up higher.

Folle-Farine went back over the snow; blind, sick, feeling her way through the twilight as though it were the darkness of night.

"He died alone—he died alone," she muttered, a thousand times, as she crept shivering through the gloom; and, she knew, that now her own fate was yet more desolate. She knew that now she lived alone without one friend on earth.

The death on the open highway; the numbness, and stillness, and deafness to all the maledictions of men; the shameful bier made at night on the dung-cart, amidst loathing glances and muttered curses; the nameless grave in the common ditch with the beggar, the thief, the harlot, and the murderer;—these, which were so awful to all others, seemed to her as sweet as to sink to sleep on soft unshorn grass, whilst rose leaves are shaken in the wind, and fall as gently as kisses upon the slumberer.

For she in her youth and in the splendour of her strength, and in the blossom of her beauty, gorgeous as a passion-flower in the sun, envied bitterly the old man who had died at his work on the public road, hated by his kind, and weighted with the burden of nigh a hundred years.

Since his death was not more utterly lonely and desolate than was her life; and to all taunts and to all curses the ears of the dead are deaf.

BOOK III.

"L'Artiste est un dieu tombé, qui se souvient du temps quand il créa un monde."

CHAPTER I.

NIGHT had come; a dark night of earliest spring. The wild day had sobbed itself to sleep after a restless life with fitful breath of storm and many sighs of shuddering breezes.

The sun had sunk, leaving long tracks of blood-red light across one-half the heavens.

There was a sharp crisp coldness as of lingering frost in the gloom and the dulness. Heavy clouds, as yet unbroken, hung over the cathedral and the clustering roofs around it in dark and starless splendour.

Over the great still plains which stretched eastward and southward, black with the furrows of the scarce-budded corn, the wind blew hard; blowing the river and the many streamlets spreading from it into foam; driving the wintry leaves, which still strewed the earth thickly, hither and thither in legions; breaking boughs that had weathered the winter hurricanes, and scattering the tender blossoms of the snowdrops and the earliest crocuses in all the little moss-grown garden ways.

The smell of wet grass, of the wood-born violets, of trees whose new life was waking in their veins, of damp earths turned freshly upwards by the plough, were all blown together by the riotous breezes.

Now and then a light gleamed through the gloom where a little peasant boy lighted home with a torch some old priest on his mule, or a boat went down the waters with a lamp hung at its prow. For it grew dark early, and people used to the river read a threat of a flood on its face.

A dim glow from the west, which was still tinged with the fire of the sunset, fell through a great square window set in a stone building, and striking across the sicklier rays of an oil lamp reached the opposing wall within.

It was a wall of grey stone, dead and lustreless like the wall of a prison-house, over whose surface a spider as colourless as itself dragged slowly its crooked hairy limbs loaded with the moisture of the place, which was an old tower, of which the country folk told strange tales, where it stood among the rushes on the left bank of the stream.

A man watched the spider as it went.

It crept on its heavy way across the faint crimson reflection from the glow of the sunken sun.

It was fat, well-nourished, lazy, content; its home of dusky silver hung on high, where its pleasure lay in weaving, clinging, hoarding, breeding. It lived in the dark; it had neither pity nor regret; it troubled itself neither for the death it dealt to nourish itself, nor for the light without, into which it never wandered; it spun and throve and multiplied.

It was an emblem of the man who is wise in his generation; of the man whom Cato the elder deemed divine; of the Majority and the Mediocrity who rule over the earth and enjoy its fruits.

This man knew that it was wise; that those who were

like to it were wise also: wise with the only wisdom which is honoured of other men.

He had been unwise—always; and therefore he stood watching the sun die, with hunger in his soul, with famine in his body.

For many months he had been half famished, as were the wolves in his own northern mountains in the winter solstice. For seven days he had only been able to crush a crust of hard black bread between his teeth. For twenty hours he had not done even so much as this. The trencher on his tressel was empty; and he had not wherewithal to re-fill it.

He might have found some to fill it for him no doubt. He lived amidst the poor, and the poor to the poor are good, though they are bad and bitter to the rich. But he did not open either his lips or his hand. He consumed his heart in silence; and his vitals preyed in anguish on themselves without his yielding to their torments.

He was a madman; and Cato, who measured the godliness of man by what they gained, would have held him accursed;—the madness that starves and is silent for an idea is an insanity, scouted by the world and the gods. For it is an insanity unfruitful; except to the future. And for the future who cares,—save these madmen themselves?

He watched the spider as it went.

It could not speak to him as its fellow once spoke in the old Scottish story. To hear as that captive heard, the hearer must have hope, and a kingdom,—if only in dreams.

This man had no hope; he had a kingdom indeed, but it was not of earth; and, in an hour of sheer cruel bodily pain, earth alone has dominion and power and worth.

The spider crawled across the grey wall; across the glow from the vanished sun; across a coil of a dead passion-vine, that strayed loose through the floor; across the classic shapes of a great cartoon drawn in chalks upon the dull rugged surface of stone.

Nothing arrested it; nothing retarded it, as nothing hastened it. It moved slowly on; fat, lustreless, indolent, hueless; reached at length its den, and there squatted aloft, loving the darkness; its young swarming around, its prey held in its forceps, its nets cast about.

Through the open casement there came on the rising wind of the storm, in the light of the last lingering sunbeam, a beautiful night-moth, begotten by some cruel hot-house heat in the bosom of some frail exiled tropical flower.

It swam in on trembling pinions, and alighted on the golden head of a gathered crocus that lay dying on the stones—a moth that should have been born to no world save that of the summer world of a Midsummer Night's Dream.

A shape of Ariel and Oberon; slender, silver, purple, roseate, lustrous-eyed, and gossamer-winged.

A creature of woodland waters, and blossoming forests; of the yellow chalices of kingcups and the white breasts of river lilies, of moonbeams that strayed through a summer world of shadows, and dew-drops that glistened in the deep folded hearts of roses. A creature to brush the dreaming eyes of a poet, to nestle on the bosom of a young girl sleeping: to float earthwards on a falling star, to slumber on a lotus leaf.

A creature that amidst the still soft hush of woods and waters still tells, to those who listen, of the world when the world was young.

The moth flew on, and poised on the fading crocus

leaves which spread out their pale gold on the level of the grey floor.

It was weary, and its delicate wings drooped; it was storm-tossed, wind-beaten, drenched with mist and frozen with the cold; it belonged to the moon, to the dew, to the lilies, to the forget-me-nots, and to the night; and it found that the hard grip of winter had seized it whilst yet it had thought that the stars and the summer were with it. It lived before its time,—and it was like the human soul, which being born in the darkness of the world dares to dream of light, and, wandering in vain search of a sun that will never rise, falls and perishes in wretchedness.

It was beautiful exceedingly; with the brilliant tropical beauty of a life that is short-lived. It rested a moment on the stem of the pale flower, then with its radiant eyes fastened on the point of light which the lamp thrust upward, it flew on high; and, spreading out its transparent wings and floating to the flame, kissed it, quivered once, and died.

There fell among the dust and cinder of the lamp a little heap of shrunken fire-scorched blackened ashes.

The wind whirled them upward from their rest, and drove them forth into the night to mingle with the storm-scourged grasses, the pale dead violets, the withered snow-flowers, with all things frost-touched and forgotten.

The spider sat aloft, sucking the juices from the fettered flies, teaching its spawn to prey and feed; content in squalor and in plenitude; in sensual sloth, and in the increase of its body and its hoard.

He watched them both: the success of the spider, the death of the moth; trite as a fable; ever repeated as the tides of the sea; the two symbols of humanity; of the life which fattens on greed and gain, and the life which perishes of divine desire.

Then he turned and looked at the cartoons upon the wall; shapes grand and dim, the children of his genius, a genius denied by men.

His head sank on his chest, his hand tore the shirt away from his breast, which the pangs of a bodily hunger that he scorned devoured, indeed, but which throbbed with a pain more bitter than that of even this lingering and ignoble death. He had genius in him, and he had to die like a wolf on the Armorican wolds, yonder westward, when the snows of winter hid all offal from its fangs.

It was horrible.

He had to die for want of the crust that beggars gnawed in the kennels of the city; he had to die of the lowest and commonest need of all—the sheer animal need of food.

"*J'avais quelque chose là!*" was, perhaps, the most terrible of all those death-cries of despair which the guillotine of Thermidor wrung from the lips of the condemned. For it was the despair of the bodily life for the life of the mind which died with it.

When a man clings to life for life's sake, because it is fair and sweet, and good to the sight and the senses, there may be weakness in his shudder at its threatening loss. But when a man is loth to lose life, although it be hard and joyless and barren of all delights, because this life gives him power to accomplish things greater than he, which yet without him must perish, there is the strength in him, as there is the agony, of Prometheus.

With him it must die also: that deep dim greatness within him which moves him, despite himself; that nameless unspeakable force, which compels him to create and to achieve; that vision by which he beholds worlds beyond him not seen by his fellows.

Weary of life indeed he may be; of life material, and full of subtlety; of passion, of pleasure, of pain; of the kisses that burn, of the laughs that ring hollow, of the honey that so soon turns to gall, of the sickly fatigues and the tired cloyed hunger that are the portion of men upon earth. Weary of these he may be; but still if the gods have breathed on him and made him mad, with the madness that men have called genius, there will be that in him greater than himself, which he knows,—and cannot know without some fierce wrench and pang,—will be numbed and made impotent, and drift away, lost for evermore, into that eternal Night which is all that men behold of death.

It was so with this man now.

Life was barren of all delight for him, full of privation, of famine, of obscurity, of fruitless travail and of vain desire; yet because he believed that he had it in him to be great, or rather because, with a purer and more impersonal knowledge, he believed that it was within his power to do that which, when done, the world would not willingly let die, it was loathsome to him to perish thus of the sheer lack of food, as any toothless snake would perish in its swamp.

He stood opposite to the great white cartoons on which his soul had spent itself; creations which seemed but vague and ghostly in the shadows of the chamber, but in which he saw, or at the least believed he saw, the title-deeds of his own heirship to the world's kingdom of fame.

For himself he cared nothing; but for them—he smiled bitterly as he looked: "They will light some bakehouse fire to pay those that may throw my body in a ditch," he thought.

And yet the old passion had so much dominion still that he instinctively went nearer to his latest and best-loved creations, and took the white chalks up and worked once more by the dull sullen rays of the lamp behind him.

They would be torn down on the morrow and thrust for fuel into some housewife's kitchen-stove. What matter?

He loved them; they were his sole garniture and treasure; in them his soul had gathered all its dreams and all its pure delights: so long as his sight lasted he sought to feed it on them; so long as his hand had power he strove to touch, to caress, to enrich them.

Even in such an hour as this, the old sweet trance of Art was upon him.

He was devoured by the deadly fangs of long fast; streaks of living fire seemed to scorch his entrails; his throat and lungs were parched and choked; and ever and again his left hand clenched on the bones of his naked chest as though he could wrench away the throes that gnawed it. He knew that worse than this would follow; he knew that tenfold more torment would await him; that limbs as strong, and muscles as hard, and manhood as vigorous as his, would only yield to such death as this slowly, doggedly, inch by inch, day by day. He knew; and he knew that he could not trust himself to go through that uttermost torture without once lifting his voice to summon the shame of release from it. Shame—since release would needs be charity.

He knew full well; he had seen all forms of death; he had studied its throes, and portrayed its horrors. He knew that before dawn—it might be before midnight—

this agony would grow so great that it would conquer him; and that to save himself from the cowardice of appeal, the shame of besought alms, he would have to use his last powers to drive home a knife hard and sure through his breast-bone. Yet he stood there, almost forgetting this, scarcely conscious of any other thing than of the passion that ruled him.

Some soft curve in a girl's bare bosom, some round smooth arm of a sleeping woman, some fringe of leaves against a moonlit sky, some broad-winged bird sailing through shadows of the air, some full-orbed lion rising to leap on the nude soft indolently-folded limbs of a dreaming virgin, palm-shadowed in the East;—all these he gazed on and touched, and looked again, and changed by some more inward curve or deepened line of his chalk stylus.

All these usurped him; appealed to him; were well beloved and infinitely sad; seemed ever in their whiteness and their loneliness to cry to him,—"Whither dost thou go? Wilt thou leave *us* alone?"

And as he stood, and thus caressed them with his eyes and touch, and wrestled with the inward torment which grew greater and greater as the night approached, the sudden sickly feebleness of long hunger came upon him; the grave-like coldness of his fireless chamber slackened and numbed the flowing of his veins; his brain grew dull and all its memory ceased, confused and blotted. He staggered once, wondering dimly and idly as men wonder in delirium, if this indeed were death: then he fell backwards senseless on his hearth.

The last glow of day died off the wall. The wind rose louder, driving in through the open casement a herd of withered leaves. An owl flew by, uttering weary cries against the storm.

On high the spider sat, sucking the vitals of its prey, safe in its filth and darkness; looking down ever on the lifeless body on the hearth, and saying in its heart,—"Thou Fool!"

CHAPTER II.

As the night fell, Folle-Farine, alone, steered herself down the water through the heart of the town, where the buildings were oldest, and where on either side there loomed through the dusk, carved on the black timbers, strange masks of satyr and of faun, of dragon and of griffin, of fiend and of martyr.

She sat in the clumsy empty market-boat, guiding the tiller rope with her foot.

The sea flowing in stormily upon the coast sent the tide of the river inland with a swift impetuous current, to which its sluggish depths were seldom stirred. The oars rested unused in the bottom of the boat; she glided down the stream without exertion of her own, quietly, easily, dreamily.

She had come from a long day's work, lading and unlading timber and grain for her taskmaster and his fellow farmers, at the river wharf at the back of the town, where the little sea-trawlers and traders, with their fresh salt smell and their brown sails crisp from fierce sea winds, gathered for traffic with the corn barges and the egg-boats of the land.

Her day's labour was done, and she was repaid for it by the free effortless backward passage home through the shadows of the water-streets; where in the overhanging buildings, ever and anon, some lantern swinging on a cord from side to side, or some open casement arched above a gallery, showed the dark sad wistful face of some old creature kneeling in prayer before a crucifix, or the gold ear-rings of some laughing girl leaning down with the first frail violets of the year fragrant in her bodice.

The cold night had brought the glow of wood-fires in many of the dwellings of that poor and picturesque quarter; and showed many a homely interior through the panes of the oriel and lancet windows, over which brooded sculptured figures seraph-winged, or carven forms helmeted and leaning on their swords.

In one of them there was a group of young men and maidens gathered round the wood nut-burning, the lovers seeking each other's kiss as the kernels broke the shells; in another, some rosy curly children played at soldiers with the cuirass and sabre which their grandsire had worn in the army of the empire; in another, before a quaint oval old-fashioned glass, a young girl all alone made trial of her wedding wreath upon her fair forehead, and smiled back on her own image with a little joyous laugh that ended in a sob; in another, a young bearded workman carved ivory beside his hearth, whilst his old mother sat knitting in a high oak chair; in another, a sister of charity, with a fair Madonna's face, bent above a little pot of home-bred snowdrops, with her tears dropping on the white heads of the flowers, whilst the sick man of whom she had charge, slept and left her a brief space for her own memories, her own pangs, her own sickness, which was only of the heart—only—and therefore hopeless.

All these Folle-Farine saw, going onward in the boat on the gloom of the water below.

She did not envy them; she rather, with her hatred of them, scorned them. She had been freeborn, though now she was a slave; the pleasures of the home and hearth she envied no more than she envied the imprisoned bird its seed and water, its mate and song, within the close cage bars.

Yet they had a sort of fascination for her. She wondered how they felt, these people who smiled and span, and ate and drank, and sorrowed and enjoyed, and were in health and disease, at feast and at funeral, always together, always bound in one bond of a common humanity; these people, whose God on the cross never answered them; who were poor, she knew; who toiled early and late; who were heavily taxed; who fared hardly and scantily; yet who for the main part contrived to be mirthful and content, and to find some sunshine in their darkened hours, and to cling to one another, and in a way be glad.

Just above her was the corner window of a very ancient house, encrusted with blazonries and carvings. It had been a prince bishop's palace; it was now the shared shelter of half a score of lace weavers and of ivory workers, each family in their chamber, like a bee in its cell.

As the boat floated under one of the casements, she saw that it stood open; there was a china cup filled with house-born primroses on the broad sill; there was an antique illuminated Book of Hours lying open beside the flowers; there was a strong fire-light shining from within; there was an old woman asleep and smiling in her dreams beside the hearth; by the open book was a girl, leaning out into the chill damp night, and looking down the street as though in search for some expected and thrice-welcome guest.

She was fair to look at, with dark hair twisted under her towering white cap, and a peach-like cheek and throat, and her arms folded against her blue 'kerchief crossed upon her chest.

Into the chamber, unseen by her, a young man stole across the shadows, and came unheard behind her and bent his head to hers, and kissed ere she knew that he was there. She started with a little happy cry and pushed him away with pretty provocation; he drew her into his arms and into the chamber; he shut-to the lattice, and left only a dusky reflection from within shining through the panes made dark by age and dust.

Folle-Farine had watched them; as the window closed her head dropped, she was stirred with a mournful, passionate, contemptuous wonder: what was this love that was about her everywhere, and yet with which she had no share? She only thought of it with haughtiest scorn; and yet—

There had come a great darkness on the river, a surly roughness in the wind; the shutters were now closed in many of the houses of the water-street, and their long black shadows fell across the depth that severed them, and met and blended in the twilight.

The close of this day was stormy; the wind blew the river swiftly; the heavy raw mists were setting in from the sea as the night descended. She did not heed these; she liked the wild weather best; she loved the rush of a chill wind amongst her hair, and the moisture of blown spray upon her face; she loved the manifold phantasies of the clouds, and the melodies of the blast coming over the sands and the rushes. She loved the swirl and rage of the angry water, and the solitude that closed in round her with the darkness.

The boat passed onward through the now silent town; only in one other place a light glowed through the unshuttered lattices that were ruddy and emblematic with the paintings of the Renaissance. It was the window of the gardener's wife.

At that season there could bloom neither saxifrage nor carnation; but some green-leaved winter shrub with rosy laden berries had replaced them, and made a shining frame all round the painted panes.

The fair woman was within; her delicate head rose out of the brown shadows round, with a lamp burning above it and a little oval mirror before. Into the mirror she was gazing with a smile, whilst with both hands about her throat she clasped some strings of polished shells brought to her from the sea.

"How white and how warm and how glad she is!" thought Folle-Farine, looking upward; and she rowed in the gloom through the sluggish water with envy at her heart.

She was growing harder, wilder, worse, with every day; more and more like some dumb fierce forest beast, that flees from every step and hates the sound of every voice.

Since the night that they had pricked her for a witch, the people had been more cruel to her than ever; they cast bitter names at her as she went by; they hissed and hooted her as she took her mule through their villages, or passed them on the road with her back bent under some load of faggots, or of winter food; once or twice they stoned her, and chance alone had saved her from injury.

For it was an article of faith in all the hamlets round that she had killed old Manon Dax. The Flandrins said so, and they were good pious people who would not lie. Every dusky evening when the peasantry, through the doors of their cabins, saw the gleam of her red girdle and the flash of her hawk's eyes, where she plodded on through the mist on her tyrant's errands, they crossed themselves and told each other for the hundredth time the tale of her iniquities over their pan of smoking chestnuts,

It had hardened her tenfold; it had made her brood on sullen dreams of a desperate vengeance.

Marcellin, too, was gone; his body had been eaten by the quicklime in the common ditch, and there was not even a voice so stern as his to bid her a good morrow. He had been a harsh man, of dark repute and bitter tongue; but in his way he had loved her; in his way, with the eloquence that had remained to him, and by the strange stories that he had told her of that wondrous time wherein his youth had passed, when men had been as gods and giants, and women either horrible as the Medusa, or sublime as the Iphigenia, he had done something to awaken her mind; to arouse her hopes; to lift her up from the torpor of toil, the lusts of hatred, the ruinous apathy of despair. But he was dead; and she was alone; and was abandoned utterly to herself.

She mourned for him with a passionate pain that was all the more despairing, because no sound of it could ever pass her lips to any creature.

To and fro continually she went by the road on which he had died alone; by the heap of broken stones, by the wooden crucifix, by the high hedge and the cornlands beyond. Every time she went the blood beat in her brain, the tears swelled in her throat; she hated with a hatred that consumed her and was ready to ripen into any deadly deed, the people who had shunned him in his life, and in his death derided and insulted him, and given him such burial as they gave the rotten carcase of some noxious beast.

Her heart was ripe for any evil that should have given her vengeance; a dull cold sense of utter desolation and isolation was always on her; the injustice of the people began to turn her blood to gall, her courage into cruelty;

there began to come upon her the look of those who brood upon a crime.

It was, in truth, but the despairing desire to live that stirred within her; to know, to feel, to roam, to enjoy, to suffer still, if need be; but to suffer something else than the endless toil of the field-ox and tow-horse, something else than the unavenged blow that pays the ass and the dog for their services.

The desire to be free grew upon her with all the force and fury inherited from her father's tameless and ever wandering race; if a crime could have made her free she would have seized it.

She was in the prison of a narrow and hated fate; and from it she looked out on the desert of an endless hate, which stretched around her without one blossom of love, one well spring of charity, rising in its deathlike waste.

The dreamy imaginations, the fantastic pictures, that had been so strong in her in her early years, were still there, though distorted by ignorance and inflamed by despair. Though, in her first poignant grief for him, she had envied Marcellin his hard-won rest, his grave in the public ditch of the town, it was not in her to desire to die. She was too young, too strong, too restless, too impatient, and her blood of the desert and the forest was too hot.

What she wanted was to live. Live as the great moor bird did that she had seen float one day over these pale, pure, blue skies, with its mighty wings outstretched in the calm grey weather; which came none knew whence, and which went none knew whither; which poised silent and stirless against the clouds; then called with a sweet wild love-note to its mate, and waited for him as he sailed in from the misty shadows where the sea lay; and with him rose yet higher and higher in the air; and passed westward, cleaving the fields of light, and so vanished;—a queen of the wind, a daughter of the sun; a creature of freedom, of victory, of tireless movement, and of boundless space, a thing of heaven and of liberty.

* * * * *

The evening became night; a night rough and cold almost as winter.

There was no boat but hers upon the river, which ran high and strong. She left the lights of the town behind her, and came into the darkness of the country. Now and then the moon shone a moment through the storm wrack, here and there a torch glimmered, borne by some wayfarer over a bridge.

There was no other light.

The bells of the cathedral chiming a miserere, sounded full of woe behind her in the still sad air.

There stood but one building between her and her home, a square strong tower built upon the edge of the stream, of which the peasants told many tales of horror. It was of ancient date, spacious, and very strong. Its upper chambers were used as a granary by the farm-people who owned it; the vaulted hall was left unused by them, partly because the river had been known to rise high enough to flood the floor; partly because legend had bequeathed to it a ghastly repute of spirits of murdered men who haunted it.

No man or woman in all the country round dared venture to it after nightfall; it was all that the stoutest would do to fetch and carry grain there at broad day; and the peasant who, being belated, rowed his market-boat past it when the moon was high, moved his oar with one trembling hand, and with the other crossed himself unceasingly.

To Folle-Farine it bore no such terror.

The unconscious pantheism breathed into her earliest thoughts, with the teachings of Phratos, made her see a nameless mystical and always wondrous beauty in every blade of grass that fed on the dew, and with the light, rejoiced; in every bare brown stone that flashed to gold in bright brook waters, under a tuft of weed; in every hill-side stream that leaping and laughing sparkled in the sun; in every wind that wailing went over the sickness of the weary world.

For such a temper, no shape of the day or the night, no mystery of life or of death can have terror; it can dread nothing, because every created thing has in it a divine life and an eternal mystery.

As she and the boat passed out into the loneliness of the country, with fitful moon gleams to light its passage, the weather and the stream grew wilder yet.

There were on both sides strips of the silvery inland sands, beds of tall reeds, and the straight stems of poplars, ghostlike in the gloom. The tide rushed faster; the winds blew more strongly from the north; the boat rocked, and now and then was washed with water, till its edges were submerged.

She stood up in it, and gave her strength to its guidance; it was all that she could do to keep its course straight, and steer it so that it should not grate upon the sand, nor be blown into the tangles of the river reeds. For herself she had no care, she could swim like any cygnet; and, for her own sport, had spent hours in water at all seasons. But she knew that to Claudis Flamma the boat was an honoured treasure, since to replace it would have cost him many a hard-earned and well loved piece of money.

As she stood thus upright in the little tossing vessel, against the darkness and the winds, she passed the solitary building; it had been placed so low down against the shore that its front walls, strong of hewn stone, and deep bedded in the soil, were half submerged in the dense growth of the reeds and of the willowy osiers which grew up and brushed the great arched windows of its haunted hall. The lower half of one of the seven latticed windows had been blown wide open; a broad square casement, braced with iron bars, looking out upon the river, and lighted by a sickly glimmer of the moon.

Her boat was swayed close against the wall, in a sudden lurch, caused by a fiercer gust of wind and higher wave of the strong tide; the rushes entangled it; it grounded on the sand; there was no chance, she knew, of setting it afloat again without her leaving it to gain a footing on the sand, and use her force to push it off into the current.

She leaped out without a moment's thought amongst the rushes, with her kirtle girt up close above her knees. She sank to her ankles in the sand, and stood to her waist in the water.

But she was almost as light and sure of foot as a moor-gull, when it lights upon the treacherous mosses of a bog; and standing on the soaked and shelving bank, she thrust herself with all her might against her boat, dislodged it, and pushed it out once more afloat.

She was about to wade to it and spring into it, before the stream had time to move it farther out, when an owl flew from the open window behind her. Unconsciously she turned her head to look whence the bird had come.

She saw the wide dark square of the opened casement; the gleam of a lamp within the cavern-like vastness of the vaulted hall. Instinctively she paused, drew closer, and forgot the boat.

The stone sills of the seven windows were level with the topmost sprays of the tall reeds and the willowy underwood; they were, therefore, level with herself. She saw straight in; saw, so far as the pale uncertain fusion of moon and lamp rays showed them, the height and width of this legend-haunted place; vaulted and pillared with timber and with stone; dim and lonely as a cathedral crypt, and with the night-birds flying to and fro in it, as in a ruin, seeking their nests in its rafters and in the capitals of its columns.

No fear, but a great awe fell upon her. She let the boat drift on its way unheeded; and stood there at gaze like a forest doe.

She had passed this grain tower with every day or night that she had gone down the river upon the errands of her taskmaster; but she had never looked within it once, holding the peasants' stories and terrors in the cold scorn of an intrepid courage.

Now, when she looked, she, for the first time believed—believed that the dead lived and gathered there.

White, shadowy, countless shapes loomed through the gloom, all motionless, all noiseless, all beautiful, with the serene yet terrible loveliness of death.

In their midst burned a lamp; as the light burns night and day in the tombs of the kings of the east.

Her colour paled, her breath came and went, her body trembled like a leaf; yet she was not afraid. An ecstasy of surprise and faith smote the dull misery of her life. She saw at last another world than the world of toil in which she had laboured without sigh and with-

sigh, to gaze on her; to her, they seemed to live with that life of the air, of the winds, of the stars, of silence and solitude, and all the nameless liberties of death, of which she dreamed when, shunned, and cursed, and hungered, she looked up to the skies at night from a sleepless bed.

They were indeed the dead: the dead of that fair time when all the earth was young, and men communed with their deities, and loved them, and were not afraid. When their gods were with them in their daily lives; and when in every breeze that curled the sea, in every cloud that darkened in the west, in every water-course that leaped and sparkled in the sacred cedar groves, in every bee-sucked blossom of wild thyme that grew purple by the marble temple steps, the breath and the glance of the gods were felt, the footfall and the voice of the gods were heard.

They were indeed the dead: the dead who—dying earliest, whilst yet the earth was young enough to sorrow for its heroic lives, to embalm them, to remember them, and, to count them worthy of lament—perished in their bodies, but lived for ever immortal in the traditions of the world.

From every space of the sombre chamber some one of these gazed on her through the mist.

Here the silver dove of Argos winged her way through the iron jaws of the dark sea-gates; here the white Io wandered, in exile and unresting, for ever scourged on by the sting in her flesh, as a man by the genius in him.

Here the glad god whom all the woodlands loved, played in the moonlight, on his reeds, to the young stags that couched at his feet in golden beds of daffodils and asphodel. Here over a darkened land the great Demeter moved, bereaved and childless, bidding the vine be barren, and the fig trees stay fruitless, and the seed of the sown furrows lie strengthless to multiply and fill the sickles with the ripe increase.

Here the women of Thebes danced upon Cithæron in the mad moonless nights, under the cedars, with loose hair on the wind, and bosoms that heaved and brake through their girdles of fawnskin. Here at his labour, in Pheræ, the sungod toiled as a slave; the highest wrought as the lowest; while wise Hermes stood by and made mirth of the kingship that had bartered the rod of dominion for the mere music which empty air could make in a hollow reed.

Here, too, the brother gods stood, Hypnos and Oneiros, and Thanatos; their bowed heads crowned with the poppy and moonwort, the flowering fern, and the amaranth, and, pressed to their lips, a white rose, in the old sweet symbol of silence; fashioned in the same likeness, with the same winged feet which yet fall so softly, that no human ears hear their coming; the gods that most of all have pity on men, the gods of the Night and of the Grave.

These she saw; not plainly, but through the wavering shadows, and the halo of the vapours which floated, dense and silvery as smoke, in from the misty river.

Their lips were dumb, and for her they had no name nor story, and yet they spoke to her with familiar voices. She knew them, she knew that they were gods, and yet were dead; and in the eyes of the forest-god, who piped upon his reeds, she saw the eyes of Phratos look on her with their tender laughter, and their unforgotten love.

Just so had he looked so long ago—so long!—in the deep woods at moonrise, when he had played to the bounding fawns, to the leaping waters, to the listening trees, to the sleeping flowers.

They had called him an outcast—and lo!—she found him a god.

She sank on her knees, and buried her face in her hands, and wept—wept with grief for the living lost for ever, wept with joy that the dead for ever lived.

Tears had rarely sprung to her proud rebellious eyes; she deemed them human things, things of weakness and of shame; she had thrust them back and bitten her lips till the blood came, in a thousand hours of pain, rather than that men should be able to see them and exult. The passion had its way for once, and spent itself, and passed; she rose trembling and pale; with her eyes wet and dimmed in lustre, like stars that shine through rain. She looked around her fearfully.

She thought that the gods might rise in wrath against her, even as mortals did, for daring to be weary of her life.

As she rose, she saw for the first time before the cold hearth the body of a man.

It was stretched straightly out on the stone floor; the chest was bare; upon the breast the right hand was clenched close and hard; the limbs were in profound repose; the head was lit by the white glimmer from the moon; the face was calm and colourless, and full of sadness.

In the dim strange light it looked white as marble, colossal as a statue, in that passionless rest, that dread repose.

Instinctively she drew nearer to him; breathless and allured she bent forward and looked closer on his face.

He was a god, like all the rest, she thought; but dead—not as they were dead, with eyes that still rejoiced in the light of cloudless suns, and with lips that still smiled with a serene benignity and an eternal love,

—but dead, as mortals die, without hope, without release, with their breath frozen on their tired lips, and bound on their hearts eternally the burden of their sin and woe.

She leaned down close by his side, and looked on him—sorrowful, because, he alone of all the gods was stricken there, and he alone had the shadow of mortality upon him.

Looking thus she saw that his hands were clenched upon his chest, as though their latest effort had been to tear the bones asunder, and wrench out a heart that ached beneath them; she saw that this was not a divine, but a human form,—dead indeed as the rest were, but dead by a man's death of assassination, or disease, or suicide, or what men love to call the "act of heaven," whereby they mean the self-sown fruit of their own faults and follies.

Had the gods slain him—being a mortal—for his entrance there?

Marcellin in legends had told her of such things.

He was human; with a human beauty; which yet white and cold and golden, full of serenity and sadness, was like the sun-god's yonder, and very strange to her whose eyes had only rested on the sunburnt, pinched, and rugged faces of the populace around her.

That beauty allured her; she forgot that he had against her the crime of that humanity which she hated. He was to her like some noble forest beast, some splendid bird of prey, struck down by a bolt from some murderous bow, strengthless and senseless, yet majestic even in its fall.

"The gods slew him because he dared to be too like to themselves," she thought, "else he could not be so beautiful,—he,—only a man, and dead?"

The dreamy intoxication of fancy had deadened her

to all sense of time or fact. The exaltation of nerve and brain made all fantastic phantasies seem possible to her as truth.

Herself, she was strong; and desolate no more, since the eyes of the immortals had smiled on her, and bade her welcome there; and she felt an infinite pity on him, inasmuch as with all his likeness to them he yet, having incurred their wrath, lay helpless there as any broken reed.

She bent above him her dark rich face, with a soft compassion on it; she stroked the pale heavy gold of his hair, with fingers brown and lithe, but infinitely gentle; she fanned the cold pain of his forehead, with the breath of her rose-like mouth; she touched him, stroked him, gazed on him, as she would have caressed and looked on the velvet hide of the stag, the dappled plumage of the hawk, the white leaf of the lily.

A subtle, vague pleasure stole on her, a sharp sweet sorrow moved her,—for he was beautiful, and he was dead.

"If they would give him back his life?" she thought; and she looked for the glad forest god playing on his reed amidst the amber asphodels, he who had the smile and the glance of Phratos. But she could see his face no more.

The wind rose, the moon was hidden, all was dark save the flicker of the flame of the lamp; the storm had broken, and the rain fell: she saw nothing now but the bowed head of Thanatos, holding the rose of silence to his lips.

On her ear there seemed to steal a voice from the darkness, saying:

"One life alone can ransom another. Live immortal with us; or for that dead man—perish."

She bowed her head where she knelt in the darkness; the force of an irresistible fate seemed upon her; that sacrifice which is at once the delirium and divinity of her sex, had entered into her.

She was so lowly a thing; a creature so loveless and cursed; the gods, if they took her in pity, would soon scorn her as men had scorned; whilst he whom they had slain there—though so still, so white and mute, so powerless,—he looked a king amongst men, though the gods for his daring had killed him.

"Let him live!" she murmured. "As for me,—I am nothing—nothing. Let me die as the Dust dies—what matter?"

The wind blew the flame of the lamp into darkness; the moon still shone through the storm on to the face of Thanatos.

He alone heard. He—the only friend who, come he early or late, fails no living thing at the last.

He alone remained, and waited for her: he, whom alone of all the gods—for this man's sake—she chose.

CHAPTER III.

When the trance of her delirious imagination passed, they left her tranquil, but with the cold of death seeming to pass already from the form she looked on into hers. She was still crouching by his body on the hearth; and knew what she had chosen, and did not repent.

He was dead still;—or so she thought;—she watched him with dim dreaming eyes, watched him as women do who love.

She drew the fair glistening hair through her hands; she touched the closed and blue-veined eyelids tenderly;

she laid her ear against his heart to hearken for the first returning pulses of the life she had bought back to him.

It was no more to her the dead body of a man, unknown, unheeded, a stranger, and because a mortal, of necessity to her a foe. It was a nameless wondrous mystic force and splendour to which she had given back the pulse of existence, the light of day; which was no more the gods', nor any man's, no more the prey of death, nor the delight of love; but hers—hers—shared only with the greatness she had bought for him.

Even as she looked on him she felt the first faint flutter in his heart; she heard the first faint breath upon his lips.

His eyes unclosed and looked straight at hers, without reason or lustre in them, clouded with a heavy and delirious pain.

"To die—of hunger—like a rat in a trap!" he muttered in his throat, and strove to rise; he fell back, senseless, striking his head upon the stones.

She started; her hands ceased to wander through his hair, and touch his cold lips as she would have touched the cup of a flower; she rose slowly to her feet. She had heard; and the words, so homely and so familiar in the lives of all the poor, pierced the wild faiths and visions of her heated brain, as a ray of the clear daybreak pierces through the purple smoke from altar fires of sacrifice.

The words were so terrible, and yet so trite; they cleft the mists of her dreams as tempered steel cleaves folds of gossamer.

"To die—of hunger!"

She muttered the phrase after him—shaken from her stupor by its gaunt and common truth.

It roused her to the consciousness of all his actual needs.

Her heart rebelled even against her newly found immortal masters, since, being in wrath, they could not strike him swiftly with their vengeance, but had killed him thus with these lingering and most bitter pangs, and had gathered there as to a festival to see him die.

As she stooped above him, she could discern the faint earthy cavernous odour, which comes from the languid lungs and empty chest of one who has long fasted, almost unto death.

She had known that famine odour many a time ere then; in the hut of Manon Dax, and by the hedge rows, and in the ditches, that made the sick beds of many another, as old, as wretched, and as nobly stubborn against alms; in times of drought or in inclement winters, the people in all that country side suffered continually from the hunger torment; she had often passed by men and women, and children, crouching in black and wretched cabins, or lying fever stricken on the cold stony fields, glad to gnaw a shred of sheepskin, or suck a thorny bramble of the fields to quiet the gnawing of their entrails.

She stood still beside him, and thought.

All light had died; the night was black with storm; the shadowy shapes were gone; there were the roar of the rushing river, and the tumult of the winds and rains upon the silence; all she saw was this golden head; this colourless face; this lean and nerveless hand that rested on the feebly beating heart;—these she saw still as she would have seen the white outlines of a statue in the dark.

He moved a little, with a hollow sigh.

"Bread,—bread,—bread!" he muttered. "To die for bread!—"

At the words, all the quick resource and self-reliance,

which the hard life she led had sharpened and strengthened in her, awoke amidst the dreams and passions, and meditations of her mystical faiths, and her poetic ignorance.

The boldness and the independence of her nature roused themselves; she had prayed for him to the gods, and to the gods given herself for him; that was well—if they kept their faith. But if they forsook it? The blood rushed back to her heart with its old proud current; alone, she swore to herself to save him. To save him in the gods' despite.

In the street that day, she had found the half of a roll of black bread. It had lain in the mud, none claiming it: a sulky lad passed it in scorn, a beggar with gold in his wallet kicked it aside with his crutch; she took it and put it by for her supper; so often some stripe or some jibe replaced a begrudged meal for her at Flamma's board.

That was all she had. A crust dry as a bone, which could do nothing towards saving him, could be of no more use to pass those clenched teeth, and warm those frozen veins, than so much of the wet sand gathered up from the river shore. Neither could there be any wood, which, if brought in and lit, would burn. All the timber was green and full of sap, and all, for a score square leagues around, was at that hour drenched with water.

She knew that the warmth of fire to dry the deadly dampness in the air, the warmth of wine to quicken the chillness and the torpor of the reviving life, were what were wanted beyond all other things. She had seen famine in all its stages, and she knew the needs and dangers of that fell disease.

There was not a creature in all the world, who would have given her so much as a loaf or a faggot; even if the thought of seeking human aid had ever dawned on her.

As it was, she never even dreamed of it; every human hand,—to the rosy fist of the smallest and fairest child, —was always clenched against her; she would have sooner asked for honey from a knot of snakes, or sought a bed of roses in a swarm of wasps, as have begged mercy or aid at any human hearth.

She knew nothing, either, of any social laws that might have made such need as this, a public care on public alms. She was used to see men, women, and children perishing of want; she had heard people curse the land that bore, and would not nourish them. She was habituated to work hard for every bit or drop that passed her lips; she lived amidst multitudes who did the same; she knew nothing of any public succour to which appeal could in such straits be made.

If bread were not forthcoming, a man or a woman had to die for lack of it, as Manon Dax and Marcellin had done; that seemed to her a rule of fate, against which there was no good in either resistance or appeal.

What could she do? she pondered. Whatever she would do, she knew that she had to do quickly. Yet she stood irresolute.

To do anything, she had to stoop herself down to that sin to which no suffering or privation of her own had even tempted her.

In a vague fierce fashion, unholpen and untaught, she hated all sin.

All quoted it as her only birthright; all told her that she was embued with it body and soul; all saw it in her slightest acts, in her most harmless words; and she abhorred this, the one gift which men cast to her as her only heirloom, with a strong scornful loathing which stood her in the stead of virtue.

With an instinctive cynicism which moved her continually, yet to which she could have given no name, she had loved to see the children and the maidens,—those who held her accursed, and were themselves held so innocent and just,—steal the ripe cherries from the stalk, pluck the forbidden flowers that nodded over the convent walls, pierce through the boundary fence to reach another's pear, speak a lie softly to the old greyheaded priest, and lend their ripe lips to a soldier's rough salute, whilst she, the daughter of hell, pointed at, despised, shunned as a leper, hunted as a witch,—kept her hands soilless and her lips untouched.

It was a pride to her, to say in her teeth, "I am stronger than they," when she saw the stolen peach in their hand, and heard the lying word on their tongue. It had a savage sweetness for her, the will with which she denied herself the luxurious fruit that, unseen, she could have reached a thousand times from the walls when her throat was parched and her body empty; with which she uttered the truth, and the truth alone, though it brought the blows of the cudgel down on her shoulders; with which she struck aside in disdain, the insolent eyes, and mocking mouths of the youths, who would fain have taught her, that if beggared of all other things, she was at least rich in form and hue.

She hated sin, for sin seemed to her only a human word for utter feebleness; she had never sinned for herself, as far as she knew; yet to serve this man, on whose face she had never looked before that night, she was ready to stoop to the thing which she abhorred.

She had been so proud of her freedom from all those frailties of passion, and greed, and self pity, with which the souls of the maidens around her were haunted;—so proud, with the chaste, tameless arrogance of the women of her race, that was bred in their blood, and taught them as their first duty, by the oriental and jealous laws of their vengeful and indolent masters.

She had been so proud!—yet this cleanliness of hand and heart, this immunity from her enemies' weakness, this independence which she had worn as a buckler of proof against all blows, which she had girded about her as a zone of purity more precious than gold—this, the sole treasure she had, she was about to surrender for the sake of a stranger.

It was a greater gift, and one harder to give, than the mortal life she had offered for his to the gods.

As she kneeled on the stone floor beside him, her heart was torn with a mute and violent struggle; her bent face grew dark and rigid, her haughty brows knit together in sadness and conflict.

In the darkness he moved a little; he was unconscious, yet ever, in that burning stupor, one remembrance, one regret, remained with him.

"That the mind of a man can be killed for the want of the food thrown to swine!" he muttered drearily, in the one gleam of reason that shone through the delirium of his brain.

The words were broken, disjointed, almost inarticulate; but they stung her to action as the spur stings a horse.

She started erect, and crossed the chamber, leapt through the open portion of the casement, and lighted again without, knee deep in water. She lost her footing and fell, entangled in the rushes; but she rose and climbed in the darkness to where the roots of an oak stump stretched into the stream, and, gaining the shore, ran as well as the storm and the obscurity allowed her, along the bank, straight towards Yprès.

It was a wild and bitter night; the rushing of the foaming river went by her all the way; the path was flooded; she was up to her ankles in water at every step, and was often forced to wade through channels a foot deep.

She went on straight towards her home, unconscious of cold, of fatigue, of her wet clinging clothes, of the water that splashed unseen in the black night up against her face as her steps sank into some shaking strip of marsh, some brook that, in the rising of the river, ran hissing and swelling to twice its common height.

All she was sensible of was of one inspiration, one purpose, one memory that seemed to give her the wings of the wind, and yet to clog her feet with the weight of lead,—the memory of that white sad senseless face, lying beneath the watch of the cruel gods.

She reached Yprès, feeling and scenting her way by instinct, as a dog does, all through the tumult of the air and against the force of the driving rains. She met no living creature; the weather was too bad for even a beggar to be afoot in it, and even the stray and homeless beasts had sought some shelter from a ruined shed or crumbling wall.

As softly as a leaf may fall she unloosed the latch of the orchard, stole through the trees, and took her way in an impenetrable gloom, with the swift sure flight of one to whom the place had long been as familiar by night as day.

The uproar of wind and rain would have muffled the loudest tread. The shutters of the mill-house were all closed; it was quite still. Flamma and his serving people were all gone to their beds, that they might save by sleep the cost of wood and candle.

She passed round to the side of the house, climbed up the tough network of a tree of ivy, and without much labour loosed the fastenings of her own loft window, and entering there passed through the loft into the body of the house.

Opening the door of the landing-place noiselessly, she stole down the staircase, making no more sound than a hare makes stealing over mosses to its form. The ever-wakeful lightly-sleeping ears of a miser were near at hand; but even they were not aroused; and she passed down unheard.

She went hardily, fearlessly, her mind once set upon the errand. She did not reason with herself, as more timorous creatures might have done, that being half starved, and paid not at all, as recompense for strong and continual labour, she was but about to take a just due withheld, a fair wage long overdue. She only resolved to take what another needed by a violence which she had never employed to serve her own needs, and having resolved went to execute her resolution with the unhesitating dauntlessness that was bred in her, flesh and bone.

Knowing all the turns and steps of the obscure passages, she quickly found her way to the store chambers where such food and fuel as were wanted in the house were stored.

The latter was burnt and the former eaten sparingly and grudgingly, but the store of both was at this season of the year fairly abundant.

It had more than once happened that the mill had been cut off from all communication with the outer world by floods that had reached its upper casements, and

Claudis Flamma was provided against any such accidents; the more abundantly as he had more than once found it a lucrative matter in such seasons of inundation to lower provisions from his roof to boats floating below when the cotters around were in dire need and ready to sell their very souls for a bag of rice or string of onions.

Folle-Farine opened the shutter of the store room and let in the faint grey glimmer from the clearing skies.

A bat which had been resting from the storm among the rafters fluttered violently against the lattice; a sparrow driven down the chimney in the hurricane flew up from one of the shelves with a twittering outcry.

She paused to open the lattice for them both, and set them free to fly forth into the still sleeping world; then she took an old rush basket that hung upon a nail, and filled it with the best of such homely food as was to be found there—loaves, and meats, and rice, and oil, and a flask of the richest wine—wine of the south, of the hue of the violet, sold under secrecy at a high charge and profit.

That done, she tied together as large a bundle of brushwood and of faggots as she could push through the window, which was broad and square, and thrust it out by slow degrees; put her basket through likewise, and lowered it carefully to the ground; she followed them herself with the agility born of long practice, and dropped on the grass beneath.

She waited but to close and refasten the shutter from without, then threw the mass of faggots on her shoulders, and carrying in her arms the osier basket, took her backward way through the orchards to the river.

She had not taken either bit or drop for her own use.

She was well used to carry burdens as heavy as the mules bore, and to walk under them unassisted for many leagues to the hamlets and markets round about. But even her strength of bronze had become fatigued; she felt frozen to the bone; her clothes were saturated with water, and her limbs were chill and stiff. Yet she, trudged on, unblenching and unpausing, over the soaked earth, and through the swollen water and the reeds, keeping always by the side of the stream, that was so angry in the darkness; by the side of the grey flooded sands, and the rushes that were blowing with a sound like the sea.

She met no living creature except a fox, who rushed between her feet, holding in its mouth a screaming chicken.

Once she stumbled and struck her head and breast with a dull blow against a pile of wood which, in the furious weather, was unseen by her. It stunned her for the instant, but she rallied and looked up with eyes as used to pierce the deepest gloom as any goshawk's; she discerned the outline of the Calvary, towering high and weird-like above the edge of the river, where the priests and people had placed it, so that the boatmen could abase themselves and do it honour as they passed the banks.

The lantern on the cross shone far across the stream, but shed no light upon the path she followed.

At its foot she had stumbled and been bruised upon her errand of mercy; the reflection of its rays streamed across to the opposing shore, and gave help to a boat load of smugglers landing stolen tobacco in a little creek.

She recovered herself and trudged on once more along the lonely road.

"How like their god is to them!" she thought; the wooden crucifix was the type of her persecutors; of those who flouted and mocked her, who flung and pierced her as a witch; who cursed her because she was not of their people.

The cross was the hatred of the world incarnated to her; it was in Christ's name that Marcellin's corpse had been cast on the dung and in the ditch; it was in Christ's name that the women had avenged on her the pity which she had shown to Manon Dax; it was in Christ's name that Flamma had scourged her because she would not pass rotten figs for sweet. For the name of Christ is used to cover every crime, by the peasant who cheats his neighbour of a copper coin, as by the sovereign who massacres a nation for a throne.

She left the black cross reared there against the rushes, and plodded on through sand and rain and flood, bearing her load:—in Christ's name they would have seized her as a thief.

The storm abated a little, and every now and then a gleam of moonlight was shed upon the flooded meadows. She gained the base of the tower, and by means of the length of rope let, by degrees, the firewood and the basket through the open portion of the window on to the floor below, then again followed them herself.

Her heart thrilled as she entered.

Her first glance to the desolate hearth showed her that the hours of her absence had brought no change there.

The gods had not kept faith with her, they had not raised him from the dead.

"They have left it all to me," she thought, with the old strange sweet yearning in her heart over this life that she had bought with her own.

She first flung the faggots and brushwood on the hearth, and set them on fire to burn, fanned by the breath of the wind. Then she poured out a little of the wine, and kneeled down by him, and forced it drop by drop through his colourless lips, raising his head upon her as she kneeled.

The wine was pure and old; it suffused his attenuated frame as with a rush of new blood; under her hand his heart moved with firmer and quicker movement.

She broke bread in the wine and put the soaked morsels to his mouth as softly as she would have fed some little shivering bird made nestless by the hurricane.

He was unconscious still, but he swallowed what she held to him, without knowing what he did; a slight warmth gradually spread over his limbs; a strong shudder shook him. His eyes looked dully at her through a film of exhaustion and of sleep.

"J'avais quelque chose là!" he muttered, incoherently, his voice rattling in his hollow chest, as he raised himself a little on one arm. "J'avais quelque chose là!" and with a sigh he fell back once more—his head tossing in uneasiness from side to side.

Amidst the heat and mists of his aching brain, one thought remained with him—that he had created things greater than himself, and that he died like a dog, powerless to save them. The saddest dying words that the air ever bare on its breath—the one bitter vain regret of every genius that the common herds of men stamp out under leaden hoofs, as they slay their mad cattle or their drunken mobs—stayed on the blurred confusion of his mind, which, in its stupor and its helplessness, still knew that once it had been strong to create—that once it had been clear to record—that once it had dreamed the dreams that save men from the life of the swine—that once it had told to the world the truth divested of lies,—and that none had seen, none had listened to, none had believed.

There is no more terrible woe upon earth than the woe of the stricken brain, which remembers the days of its strength, the living light of its reason, the sunrise of its proud intelligence, and knows that these have passed away like a tale that is told; like a year that is spent; like an arrow that is shot to the stars, and flies aloft, and falls in a swamp; like a fruit that is too well loved of the sun, and so, over-soon ripe, is dropped from the tree and forgot on the grasses, dead to all joys of the dawn and the noon and the summer, but still alive to the sting of the wasp, to the fret of the aphis, to the burn of the drought, to the theft of the parasite.

She only dimly understood, and yet she was smitten with awe and reverence at that endless grief which had no taint of cowardice upon it, but was pure as the patriot's despair, impersonal as the prophet's agony.

For the first time the intellect in her consciously awoke. For the first time she heard a human mind find voice even in its stupor and its wretchedness to cry aloud, in reproach to its unknown Creator:

"I am *yours!* Shall I perish with the body? Why have ever bade me desire the light and seek it, if for ever you must thrust me into the darkness of negation? Shall I be Nothing?—like the muscle that rots, like the bones that crumble, like the flesh that turns to ashes, and blows in a film on the winds? Shall I die so? I?—the mind of a man, the breath of a god?"

Time went by; the chimes from the cathedral tolled dully through the darkness, over the expanse of the flood.

The light from the burning wood shone redly and fitfully. The sigh and moan of the tossed rushes, and of the water birds, awakened and afraid, came from the outer world on the winds that blew through the desolation of the haunted chamber. Grey owls flew in the high roof, taking refuge from the night. Rats hurried noiseless and eager over the stones of the floor, seeking stray grains that fell through the rafters from the granaries above.

She noticed none of these things; she never looked up nor around; all she heard was the throb of the delirious words on the silence, all she saw was the human face in the clouded light through the smoke from the flame.

The glow of the fire shone on the bowed head of Thanatos, the laughing eyes of Pan, Hermes' fair cold derisive face, and the majesty of the Lykegênês toiling in the ropes that bound him to the mill-stones to grind bread, for the mortal appetites and the ineloquent lips of men.

But at the gods she barely looked; her eyes were bent upon the human form before her.

She crouched beside him, half kneeling and half sitting: her clothes were drenched, the fire scorched, the draughts of the air-froze her; she had neither eaten nor drunk since the noon of the day; but she had no other remembrance than of this life which had the beauty of the sun-king and the misery of the beggar.

He lay long, restless, unconscious, muttering strange sad words, at times of sense, at times of folly, but always, whether lucid or delirious, words of rebellion against his fate, of a despairing lament for the soul in him that would be with the body quenched.

After awhile the feverish mutterings of his voice grew lower and less frequent; his eyes seemed to become sensible of the glare of the fire, and to contract and close in a more conscious pain; after a yet longer time he ceased to stir so restlessly, ceased to sigh and shudder; he grew quite still, his breath came tranquilly, his head fell back, and he sank to a deep sleep.

The personal fears, the womanly terrors, which would have assailed creatures at once less savage and less innocent never moved her for an instant. That there was any strangeness in her action, any peril in this solitude, she never dreamed. Her heart, bold with the blood of Taric, could know no physical fear; and her mind at once ignorant and visionary, her temper at once fierce and unselfish, kept from her all thought of those suspicions, which would fall on and chastise an act like hers; suspicions such as would have made women less pure and less dauntless tremble at that lonely house, that night of storm, that unknown fate which she had taken into her own hands, unwitting and unheeding whether good or evil might be the issue thereof.

To her he was beautiful, he suffered, she had saved him from death, and he was hers: and this was all that she remembered. She dealt with him as she would have done with some forest beast or bird that she should have found frozen in the woods of winter.

His head had fallen on her, and she crouched unwearied in the posture that gave him easiest rest. With a touch so light that it could not awaken him, she stroked the lustreless gold of his hair, and from time to time felt for the inaudible beating of his heart.

Innumerable dreams, shapeless, delicious, swept through her brain, as the echoes of some music, faint yet unutterably sweet, that half arouses and half soothes some sleeper in a grey drowsy summer dawn.

For the first time since the melodies of Phratos had died for ever from off her ear she was happy.

She did not ask wherefore,—neither of herself nor of the gods did she question whence came this wonder-flower of her nameless joy. She only sat quiet, and let the hours drift by, and watched this stranger as he slept, and was content.

So the night passed.

Whilst yet it seemed night still, the silence trembled with the pipe of waking birds, the darkness quivered with the pale first rays of dawn.

Over the flood and the fields the first light broke. From the unseen world behind the mist, faint bells rang in the coming day.

He moved in his sleep, and his eyes unclosed, and looked at her face as it hung above him, like some drooped rose heavy with the too great sweetness of a summer shower.

It was but the gaze of a moment, and his lids dropped again, weighted with the intense weariness of a slumber that held all his senses close in its leaden chains. But the glance, brief though it was, had been conscious; —under it a sudden flush passed over her, a sudden thrill stirred in her, as the life stirs in the young woodlands at the near coming of the spring. For the first time since her birth she became wholly human.

A sharp terror made her tremble like a leaf; she put his head softly from her on the ground, and rose, quivering, to her feet.

It was not the gods whom she feared, it was herself. She had never once known that she had beauty, any more than the flower knows it blowing on the wind. She had passed through the crowds of fair and market, not knowing why the youths looked after her with cruel eyes all aglow. She had walked through them, indifferent and unconscious, only thinking that they wanted to hunt her down as an unclean beast, and dared not, because her teeth were strong.

She had taken a vague pleasure in the supple grace of her own form, as she saw it mirrored in some woodland pool where she had bathed amidst the water-lilies; but it had been only such an instinctive and unstudied pleasure as the swan takes in seeing her silver breast shine back to her, on the glassy current adown which she sails.

Now,—as she rose and stood, as the dawn broke, beside him, on the hearth, and heard the birds' first waking notes, that told her the sun was even then touching the edge of the veiled world to light, a hot shame smote her, and the womanhood in her woke.

She looked down on herself and saw that her soaked skirts were knotted above her knees, as she had bound them when she had leaped from the boat's side; that her limbs were wet and glistening with river water, and the moisture from the grasses, and the sand and shingle of the shore; and that the linen of her vest, threadbare with age, left her arms bare to the shoulders, and showed, through its rents, the gleam of her warm brown skin and the curves of her shining shoulders.

A sudden horror came upon her, lest he should awake again and see her as she was;—wet, miserable, half clothed, wind-tossed like the rushes, outcast and ashamed.

She did not know that she had beauty in her; she did not know that even as she was, she had an exquisite grace in her savage loveliness, as storm-birds have in theirs against the thunder-cloud and the lightning blaze of their water-world in tempest.

She felt a sudden shrinking from all chance of his clearer and more conscious gaze; a sudden agony of shy dread, and longing to hide herself under the earth, or take refuge in the depths of the waters, rather than meet the eyes to which she had given back the light of life cast on her in abhorrence and in scorn. That he could have any other look for her, she had no thought.

She had been an outcast amongst an alien people too long to dream that any human love or gratitude or praise could ever fall on her. She had been too long cursed by every tongue, to dream that any human voice could ever arise in honour or in welcome to a thing so despised and criminal as she. For the gift which she had given this man too would only live to curse her;—that she had known when she had offered it.

She drew her rude garments closer, and stole away with velvet footfall, through the twilight of the dawn; her head hung down, and her face was flushed as with some great guilt.

With the rising of the day all her new joy was dead. With the waking of the world, all her dreams shrank back into secrecy and shame. The mere timid song of the linnet in the leafless bushes seemed sharp on her ear, calling on her to rise and go and toil with the beasts of the share and the shaft, as the creature of labour, of exile, of namelessness, and of despair, that men had made her.

At the casement, she turned and cast one lingering glance upon him where he slept; then once more she launched herself into the dusky and watery mists of the cold dawn.

She had made no more sound in her passing than a bird makes in its flight.

The sleeper never stirred, but dreamed on motionless, in the darkness and the silence, and the drowsy warmth.

He dreamed indeed, of a woman's form half-bare, golden of hue like a fruit of the south, blue veined, and flushed to changing rose heats, like an opal's fire; with limbs strong and yet slender, gleaming wet with water, and brown arched feet shining with silvery sands; with mystical eyes, black as night and amorous-lidded; and a mouth like the half-closed bud of a flower, which sighing seemed to breathe upon him the fragrance of dim cedar-woods shrouded in summer rains, of honey-weighted heather blown by moorland winds, of almond-blossoms shed like snow against a purple sea; of all things air-born, sun-fed, fair and free.

But he saw these only as in a dream; and, as a dream, when he awakened they had passed.

Though still dark from mists and heavy clouds, the dawn grew on to morning as she went noiselessly away over the grey sands, the wet shore paths, the sighing rushes.

The river-meadows were all flooded, and on the opposite banks the road was impassable; but on her side she could still find footing, for the ground there had a steeper rise, and the swollen tide had not reached in any public roadway too high for her to wade, or draw herself by the half merged bushes through it on the homeward tracks to Yprès.

The low sun was hidden in a veil of water. The old convent-bells of all the country-side rang through the mists. The day was very young as yet; but the life of the soil and the stream was waking as the birds were. Boats went by on the current, bearing a sad freightage of sheep drowned in the night, and ruined peasants, whose little wealth of stack and henhouse had been swept down by the unlooked-for tide.

From the distant banks, the voices of women came muffled through the fog, weeping and wailing for some lost lamb, choked by the water in its fold, or some pretty breadth of garden, just welcome to their sight with snowdrops and with violets, that had been laid desolate and washed away.

Through the clouds of vapour that curled in a dense opaque smoke from the wet earth, there loomed the dusky shapes of oxen; their belled horns sending forth a pleasant music from the gloom. On the air, there was an odour from soaked grasses and upturned sods, from the breath of the herds lowing hock deep in water, from the green knots of broken primrose roots sailing by on the brown rough river.

A dying bush of grey lavender swept by on the stream; it had the fresh earth of its lost garden home still about it; and in its stems a robin had built her little nest. The nest streamed in tatters and ruin on the wind, the robin flew above the wreck fluttering and uttering shrill notes of woe.

Folle-Farine saw nothing.

She held on her way blindly, mutely, mechanically, by sheer force of long habit. Her mind was in a trance; she was insensible of pain or cold, of hunger or fever, of time or place.

Yet she went straight home, as the horse being blinded will do, to the place where its patience and fealty have never been recompensed with any other thing than blows.

As she had groped her way through the gloom of the night, and found it, though the light of the roadside Christ had been turned from her, so in the same blind manner she had groped her way to her own conceptions of honesty and duty. She hated the bitter and cruel old man, with a slave's hatred, mute and enduring, that nothing could have changed; but all the same she served him faithfully. She was an untamed animal indeed, that he had yoked to his ploughshare; but she did her work loyally and doggedly; and whenever she had shaken her neck free of the yoke, she returned and thrust her head through it again, whether he scourged her back to it or not.

It was partially from the force of habit which is strong upon all creatures; it was partially from a vague instinct in her to work out her right to the begrudged shelter which she received, and not to be beholden for it for one single hour to any charity.

The mill was at work in the twilight when she reached it.

Claudis Flamma screamed at her from the open door of the loft, where he was weighing corn for the grinding.

"You have been away all night long!"

She was silent; standing below in the wet garden.

He cast a foul word at her, new upon his lips. She was silent all the same; her arms crossed on her breast, her head bent.

"Where is the boat?—that is worth more than your body. And soul you have none."

She raised her head and looked upward.

"I have lost the boat."

She thought that, very likely, he would kill her for it. Once when she had lost an osier basket, not a hundredth part the cost of this vessel, he had beaten her till every bone in her frame had seemed broken for many a week. But she looked up quietly, standing there amongst the dripping bushes and the cheerless grassy ways.

That she never told a lie, he above in the loft knew by long proof; but this was in his sight only of a piece with the strength born in her from the devil; the devil had in all ages told so many truths to the confusion of the saints of God.

"Drifted where?"

"I do not know—on the face of the flood,—with the tide."

"You had left it loose?"

"I got out to push it off the sand. It had grounded. I forgot it. It went adrift."

"What foul thing were you at meanwhile?"

She was silent.

"If you do not say, I will cut your heart out with a hundred stripes!"

"You can."

"I can! you shall know truly that I can! Go, get the boat—find it above or below water—or to the town prison you go as a thief."

The word smote her with a sudden pang. For the first time her courage failed her. She turned and went in silence at his bidding.

In the wet daybreak, through the swollen pools and the soaked thickets, she searched for the missing vessel; knowing well that it would be scarcely less than a miracle which could restore it to her; and that the god upon the cross worked no miracles for her;—a child of sin.

For several hours she searched; hungry, drenched, ready to drop with exhaustion, as she was used to see the over-driven cattle sink upon the road.

She passed many peasants; women on their mules, men in their barges, children searching for such flotsam and jetsam as the water might have flung upon the land from the little flooded gardens, and the few riverside cabins, which it had invaded in the night. She asked tidings of the boat from none of these. What she could not do for herself, it never occurred to her that others could do for her. It was an ignorance that was strength.

At length, to her amaze, she found it; saved for her

by the branches of a young tree, which, being blown down, had fallen into the stream, and had caught the boat hard and fast as in a net.

At sore peril to herself, she dislodged it with infinite labour from the entanglement of the boughs, and at scarce less peril, rowed on her homeward way upon the swollen force of the turbid river; full against the tide which again was flowing inland, from the sea that beat the bar, away to the northward, in the full sunrise.

It was far on in the forenoon, as she drew near the orchards of Yprès, brown in their leaflessness, and with grey lichens blowing from their boughs, like hoary beards of trembling paupers shaking in the icy breaths of charity.

She saw that Claudis Flamma was at work amidst his trees, pruning and delving in the red and chilly day.

She went up the winding stairs, planks green and slippery with wet river weeds, which led straight through the apple orchards to the mill.

"I have found the boat," she said, standing before him; her voice was faint and very tired, her whole body drooped with fatigue, her head for once was bowed.

He turned with his billhook in his hand. There was a leap of gladness at his heart; the miser's gladness over recovered treasure; but he showed such welcome neither in his eye nor words.

"It is well for you that you have," he said with bitter meaning. "I will spare you half the stripes:—strip."

Without a word of remonstrance, standing before him in the grey shadow of the lichens, and the red mists of the morning, she pushed the rough garments from her breast and shoulders, and vanquishing her weakness, drew herself erect to receive the familiar chastisement.

"I am guilty—this time," she said to herself as the lash fell:—she was thinking of her theft.

CHAPTER IV.

A SCORE of years before, in a valley of the far north, a group of eager and silent listeners stood gathered about one man, who spoke aloud with fervent and rapturous oratory.

It was in the green Norwegian spring, when the silence of the winter world had given way to a million sounds of waking life from budding leaves and nesting birds, and melting torrents and warm winds, fanning the tender primrose into being, and wooing the red Alpine rose to blossom.

The little valley was peopled by a hardy race of herdsmen and of fishers; men who kept their goat flocks on the steep sides of the mountains, or went down to the deep waters in search of a scanty subsistence. But they were a people simple, noble, grave, even in a manner heroic and poetic, a people nurtured on the old grand songs of a mighty past, and holding a pure faith in the traditions of a great sea-sovereignty. They listened, breathless, to the man who addressed them, raised on a tribune of rough rock, and facing the ocean, where it stretched at the northward end of the vale; a man peasant-born himself, but gifted with a native eloquence; half-poet, half-preacher; fanatic and enthusiast; one who held it as his errand to go to and fro the land, raising his voice against the powers of the world, and of wealth, and who spoke against these with a fervour and force which, to the unlearned and impressionable multitudes that heard him, seemed the voice of a genius heaven-sent.

When a boy he had been a shepherd, and dreaming in the loneliness of the mountains, and by the side of the deep hill-lakes far away from any sound or steps of human life, a madness, innocent, and in its way beautiful, had come upon him.

He believed himself born to carry the message of grace to the nations; and to raise up his voice against those passions whose fury had never assailed him, and against those riches whose sweetness he had never tasted. So he had wandered from city to city, from village to village; mocked in some places, revered in others; protesting always against the dominion of wealth, and speaking with a strange pathos and poetry which thrilled the hearts of his listeners, and had in it, at times, almost the menace and the mystery of a prophet's upbraiding.

He lived very poorly; he was gentle as a child; he was a cripple and very feeble; he drank at the wayside rills with the dogs; he lay down on the open fields with the cattle; yet he had a power in him that had its sway over the people, and held the scoffers and the jesters quiet under the spell of his tender and flute-like voice.

Raised above the little throng upon the bare red rock, with the green fiords and the dim pine-woods stretching round him as far as his eye could reach, he preached, now, to the groups of fishers and herdsmen, and foresters and hunters; protesting to this simple people against the force of wealth, and the lust of possession, as though he preached to princes and to conquerors.

He told them of what he had seen in the great cities through which he had wandered; of the corruption and the vileness, and the wantonness; of the greed in which the days and the years of men's lives were spent; of the amassing of riches for which alone the nations cared, so that all loveliness, all simplicity, all high endeavour, all innocent pastime, were abjured and derided amongst them. His voice was sweet and full as the swell of music as he spoke to them, telling them one of the many fables and legends, of which he had gathered a full harvest, in the many lands that had felt his footsteps.

This was the parable he set before them that day, whilst the rude toilers of the forests and the ocean stood quiet as little children, hearkening with upturned faces and bated breath, as the sun went down behind the purple pines.

"There lived once in the east, a great king; he dwelt far away, amongst the fragrant fields of roses, and in the light of suns that never set.

"He was young, he was beloved, he was fair of face and form; and the people as they hewed stone, or brought water, said amongst themselves, 'Verily, this man is as a god; he goes where he lists, and he lies still or rises up as he pleases; and all fruits of all lands are culled for him; and his nights are nights of gladness, and his days, when they dawn, are all his to sleep through or spend as he wills.' But the people were wrong. For this king was weary of his life.

"His buckler was sown with gems, but his heart beneath it was sore. For he had been long bitterly harassed by foes who descended on him as wolves from the hills in their hunger, and he had been long plagued with heavy wars and with bad rice harvests, and with many troubles to his nation that kept it very poor, and forbade him to finish the building of new marble palaces, and the making of fresh gardens of delight, on which his heart was set. So he, being weary of a barren land and of an empty treasury, with all his might prayed to the gods that all he touched might turn to gold, even as he had heard had happened to some magician long before in other ages. And the gods gave him the thing he craved; and his treasury overflowed. No king had ever been so rich, as this king now became in the short space of a single summer-day.

"But it was bought with a price.

"When he stretched out his hand to gather the rose that blossomed in his path, a golden flower scentless and stiff was all he grasped. When he called to him the carrier-dove that sped with a scroll of love words across the mountains, the bird sank on his breast a carven piece of metal. When he was athirst and shouted to his cup-bearer for drink, the red wine ran a stream of molten gold. When he would fain have eaten, the pulse and the pomegranate grew alike to gold between his teeth. And lo! at eventide, when he sought the silent chambers of his harem, saying, 'here at least shall I find rest,' and bent his steps to the couch whereon his best beloved slave was sleeping, a statue of gold was all he drew into his eager arms, and cold shut lips of sculptured gold were all that met his own.

"That night the great king slew himself, unable any more to bear this agony; since all around him was desolation, even though all around him was wealth.

"Now the world is too like that king, and in its greed of gold it will barter its life away.

"Look you,—this thing is certain—I say that the world will perish, even as that king perished, slain as he was slain, by the curse of its own fulfilled desire.

"The future of the world is written. For God has

granted their prayer to men. He has made them rich and their riches shall kill them.

"When all green places have been destroyed in the builder's lust of gain:—when all the lands are but mountains of brick, and piles of wood and iron:—when there is no moisture anywhere; and no rain ever falls:—when the sky is a vault of smoke; and all the rivers reek with poison:—when forest and stream, and moor and meadow, and all the old green wayside beauty are things vanished and forgotten:—when every gentle timid thing of brake and bush, of air and water, has been killed, because it robbed them of a berry or a fruit:—when the earth is one vast city, whose young children behold neither the green of the field nor the blue of the sky, and hear no song but the hiss of the steam, and know no music but the roar of the furnace:—when the old sweet silence of the country-side, and the old sweet sounds of waking birds, and the old sweet fall of summer showers, and the grace of a hedgerow bough, and the glow of the purple heather, and the note of the cuckoo and cushat, and the freedom of waste and of woodland, are all things dead, and remembered of no man:—then the world, like the Eastern king, will perish miserably of famine and of drought, with gold in its stiffened hands, and gold in its withered lips, and gold everywhere:—gold that the people can neither eat nor drink, gold that cares nothing for them, but mocks them horribly:—gold for which their fathers sold peace and health, and holiness and liberty:—gold that is one vast grave."

His voice sank, and the silence that followed was only filled with the sound of the winds in the pinewoods, and the sound of the sea on the shore.

The people were very still and afraid; for it seemed to them that he had spoken as prophets speak, and that his words were the words of truth.

Suddenly on the awe-stricken silence an answering voice rang, clear, scornful, bold, and with the eager and fearless defiance of youth.

"If I had been that king, I would not have cared for woman, or bird, or rose. I would have lived long enough to enrich my nation and mass my armies, and die a conqueror. What would the rest have mattered? You are mad, O Preacher! to rail against gold. You flout a god that you know not, and that never has smiled upon you."

The speaker stood outside the crowd with a dead sea-bird in his hand; he was in his early boyhood, he had long locks of bright hair that curled loosely on his shoulders, and eyes of northern blue, that flashed like steel in their scorn.

The people, indignant and terrified at the cold rough words which blasphemed their prophet, turned with one accord to draw off the rash doubter from that sacred audience place, but the Preacher stayed their hands with a gesture, and looked sadly at the boy.

"Is it thee, Arslàn—dost thou praise gold?—I thought thou hadst greater gods."

The boy hung his head and his face flushed.

"Gold must be power always," he muttered. "And without power what is life?"

And he went on his way out from the people, with the dead bird, which he had slain with a stone that he might study the exquisite mysteries of its silvery hues.

The Preacher followed him dreamily with his glance.

"Yet he will not give his life for gold," he murmured. "For there is that in him greater than gold, which will not let him sell it, if he would."

CHAPTER V.

And the words of the Preacher had come true; so true that the boy Arslàn, grown to manhood, had dreamed of fame, and followed the genius in him, and having failed to force the world to show faith in him, had dropped down dying on a cold hearth, for sheer lack of bread, under the eyes of the gods.

It had long been day when he awoke.

The wood smouldered, still warming the stone chamber. The owls that nested in the ceiling of the hall were beating their wings impatiently against the closed casements, blind with the light and unable to return to their haunts and homes. The food and the wine stood beside him on the floor; the fire had scared the rats from theft.

He raised himself slowly, and by sheer instinct ate and drank with the avidity of long fast. Then he stared around him blankly, blinded like the owls.

It seemed to him that he had been dead; and had risen from the grave.

"It will be to suffer it all over again in a little space," he muttered dully.

His first sensation was disappointment, anger, weariness. He did not reason. He only felt.

His mind was a blank.

Little by little a disjointed remembrance came to him. He remembered that he had been famished in the coldness of the night, had endured much torment of the body, had fallen headlong and lost his consciousness. This was all he could recall.

He looked stupidly for awhile at the burning logs; at the pile of brambles; at the flask of wine, and the simple stores of food. He looked at the grey closed window, through which a silvery daylight came. There was not a

So the shame of this ransom from death far outweighed with him the benefit.

"Why could they not let me be?" he cried in his soul against those unknown lives which had weighed his own with the fetters of obligation. "Rather death than a debt! I was content to die; the bitterness was passed. I should have known no more. Why could they not let me be!"

And his heart was hard against them. They had stolen his only birthright—freedom.

Had he craved life so much as to desire to live by shame he would sooner have gone out into the dusky night and have snatched food enough for his wants from some rich husbandman's granaries, or have stabbed some miser at prayers, for a bag of gold:—rather crime than the debt of a beggar.

So he reasoned; stung and made savage by the scourge of enforced humiliation. Hating himself because, in obedience to mere animal craving, he had taken and eaten, not asking whether what he took was his own.

He had closed his mouth, living, and had been ready to die mute, glad only that none had pitied him; his heart hardened itself utterly against this unknown hand which had snatched him from death's dreamless ease and ungrudged rest, to awaken him to a humiliation that would be as ashes in his teeth so long as his life should last.

He arose slowly, and staggered to the casement.

He fancied he was delirious, and had distempered visions of the food so long desired. He knew that he had been starving long—how long? Long enough for his brain to be weak and visited with phantoms. Instinctively he touched the long round rolls of bread, the shape of the wine flask, the wicker of the basket: they were the palpable things of common life; they seemed to tell him that he had not dreamed.

Then it was charity? His lips moved with a curse. That was his only thanksgiving.

The windows were unshuttered; through them he looked straight out upon the rising day—a day rainless and pale, and full of cool softness, after the deluge of the rains.

The faint sunlight of a spring that was still chilled by winter was shed over the flooded fields and swollen streams; snow-white mists floated before the languid passage of the wind; and the moist land gave back, as in a mirror, the leafless trees, the wooden bridges, the belfries and the steeples, and the strange sad bleeding Christs.

On all sides near, the meadows were sheets of water, the woods seemed to drift upon a lake; a swan's nest was washed past on broken rushes, the great silvery birds beating their heavy wings upon the air, and pursuing their ruined home with cries. Beyond, everything was veiled in the twilight of the damp grey vapour; a world half seen, half shrouded, lovely exceedingly, filled with all divine possibilities and all hidden powers: a world such as Youth beholds with longing eyes in its visions of the future.

"A beautiful world!" he said to himself; and he smiled wearily as he said it.

Beautiful, certainly; in that delicious shadow; in that vague light: in that cloud-like mist, wherein the earth met heaven.

Beautiful, certainly; all those mystical shapes rising from the sea of moisture which hid the earth and all the things that toiled on it. It was beautiful, this calm, dim, morning world, in which there was no sound except the distant ringing of unseen bells; this veil of vapour, whence sprang these fairy and fantastic shapes that cleft the watery air; this colourless transparent exhalation, breathing up from the land to the sky, in which all homely things took grace and mystery, and every common and familiar form became transfigured.

It was beautiful; but this landscape had been seen too long and closely by him for it to have power left to cheat his senses.

Under that pure and mystical veil of the refracted rain things vile, and things full of anguish, had their being:—the cattle in the slaughter-houses; the drunkards in the hovels; disease and debauch and famine; the ditch, that was the common grave of all the poor; the hospital, where pincers and knives tore the living nerves in the inquisition of science; the fields, where the women toiled bent, cramped, and hideous; the dumb driven beasts, patient and tortured, for ever blameless, yet for ever accursed;—all these were there beneath that lovely veil, through which there came so dreamily the slender shafts of spires and the chimes of half heard bells.

He stood and watched it long, so long that the clouds descended and the vapours shifted away, and the pale sunrays shone clearly over a disenchanted world, where roof joined roof and casement answered casement, and the figures on the crosses became but rude and ill-carved daubs; and the cocks crew to one another, and the herdsmen swore at their flocks, and the oxen flinched at the goad, and the women went forth to their field work; and all the charm was gone.

Then he turned away.

The cold fresh breath of the morning had breathed upon him, and driven out the dull, delicious fancies that had possessed his brain. The simple truth was plain before him: that he had been seen by some stranger in his necessity and succoured.

He was thankless; like the suicide, to whom unwelcome aid denies the refuge of the grave, calling him back to suffer, and binding on his shoulders the discarded burden of life's infinite weariness and woes.

He was thankless; for he had grown tired of this fruitless labour, this abortive combat; he had grown tired of seeking credence and being derided for his pains, while other men prostituted their powers to base use and public gain, receiving as their wages honour and applause; he had grown tired of toiling to give beauty and divinity to a world which knew them not when it beheld them.

He had grown tired, though he was yet young, and had strength, and had passion, and had manhood. Tired —utterly, because he was destitute of all things save his genius, and in that none were found to believe.

"I have tried all things, and there is nothing of any worth." It does not need to have worn the imperial purples and to be lying dying in old age to know thus much in all truth and all bitterness.

"Why did they give me back my life?" he said in his heart, as he turned aside from the risen sun.

He had striven to do justly with this strange, fleeting, unasked gift of existence, which comes, already warped, into our hands, and is broken by death ere we can set it straight.

He had not spent it in riot or madness, in lewd love or in gambling greed; he had been governed by great desires, though these had been fruitless, and had spent his strength to a great end, though this had been never reached.

As he turned from looking out upon the swollen stream that rushed beneath his windows, his eyes fell upon the opposite wall, where the white shapes of his cartoons were caught by the awakening sun.

The spider had drawn his dusty trail across them; the rat had squatted at their feet; the darkness of night had enshrouded and defaced them; yet with the morning they arose, stainless, noble, undefiled.

Amongst them there was one colossal form, on which the sun poured with its full radiance.

This was the form of a captive grinding at a millstone; the majestic symmetrical supple form of a man who was also a god.

In his naked limbs there was a supreme power; in his glance there was a divine command; his head was lifted as though no yoke could ever lie on that proud neck; his foot seemed to spurn the earth as though no mortal tie had ever bound him to the sod that human steps bestrode: yet at the corn-mill he laboured, grinding wheat like the patient blinded oxen that toiled beside him.

For it was the great Apollo in Pheræ.

The hand which awoke the music of the spheres had been blood-stained with murder; the beauty which had the light and lustre of the sun had been darkened with passion and with crime; the will which no other on earth or in heaven could withstand had been bent under the chastisement of Zeus.

He whose glance had made the black and barren slopes of Delos to laugh with fruitfulness and gladness, —he whose prophetic sight beheld all things past, present, and to come, the fate of all unborn races, the doom of all unspent ages,—he, the Far-Striking King, laboured here beneath the curse of crime, greatest of all the gods, and yet a slave.

In all the hills and vales of Greece his Io pæan sounded still.

Upon his holy mountains there still arose the smoke of fires of sacrifice.

With dance and song the Delian maidens still hailed the divinity of Lêtô's son.

The waves of the pure Ionian air still rang for ever with the name of Delphinios.

At Pytho and at Clarus, in Lycia and in Phokis, his oracles still breathed forth upon their fiat terror or hope into the lives of men; and still in all the virgin forests of the world the wild beasts honoured him wheresoever they wandered, and the lion and the boar came at his bidding from the deserts to bend their free necks and their wills of fire meekly to bear his yoke in Thessaly.

Yet he laboured here at the corn-mill of Admetus; and watching him at his bondage there stood the slender, slight, wing-footed Hermes, with a slow, mocking smile upon his knavish lips, and a jeering scorn in his keen eyes, even as though he cried:

"O, brother, who would be greater than I! For what hast thou bartered to me the golden rod of thy wealth and thy dominion over the flocks and the herds? For seven chords strung on a shell—for a melody not even thine own! For a lyre out-shone by my syrinx hast thou sold all thine empire to me. Will human ears give heed to thy song now thy sceptre has passed to my hands? Immortal music only is left thee, and the vision foreseeing the future. O god! O hero! O fool! what shall these profit thee now?"

Thus to the artist by whom they had been begotten the dim white shapes of the deities spoke. Thus he saw them, thus he heard, whilst the pale and watery sunlight lit up the form of the toiler in Pheræ.

For even as it was with the divinity of Delos, so is it likewise with the genius of a man, which, being born of a god, yet is bound as a slave to the grind-stone. Since even as Hermes mocked the Lord of the Unerring Bow, so is genius mocked of the world, when it has bartered the herds, and the grain, and the rod that metes wealth, for the seven chords that no ear, dully mortal, can hear.

And as he looked upon this symbol of his life, the captivity and the calamity, the strength and the slavery of his existence overcame him; and for the first hour since he had been born of a woman Arslàn buried his face in his hands and wept.

He could bend great thoughts to take the shapes that he chose, as the chained god in Pheræ bound the strong kings of the desert and forest to carry his yoke; yet, like the god, he likewise stood fettered to the mill to grind for bread.

CHAPTER VI.

A VALLEY long and narrow, shut out from the rest of the living world by the ramparts of stone that rose on either side to touch the clouds; dense forests of pines, purple as night, where the erl-king rode and the bear-king reigned; at one end mountains, mist, and gloom, at the other end the ocean; brief days with the sun shed on a world of snow, in which the sounds of the winds and the moans of the wolves alone were heard in the solitude; long nights of marvellous magnificence with the stars of the arctic zone glowing with an unbearable lustre above a sea of phosphorescent fire; those were Arslàn's earliest memories—those had made him what he was.

In that pine-clothed Norwegian valley, opening to the sea, there were a few homesteads gathered together round a little wooden church, with great torrents falling above them, and a profound loneliness around; severed by more than a day's journey from any other of the habitations of men.

There a simple idyllic life rolled slowly on through the late and lovely spring times, when the waters loosened and the seed sprouted, and the white blossoms broke above the black ground: through the short and glorious summers, when the children's eyes saw the elves kiss the roses, and the fairies float on the sunbeam, and the maidens braided their fair hair with blue cornflowers to dance on the eve of St. John: through the long and silent winters, when an almost continual night brooded over all things, and the thunder of the ocean alone answered the war of the wind-torn forests, and the blood-red blaze of the northern light gleamed over a white still mountain world, and within doors, by the warm wood fire, the youths sang Scandinavian ballads, and the old people told strange Sagas, and the mothers, rocking their new-born sons to sleep, prayed God for mercy to have on all human lives drowning at sea and frozen in the snow.

In this Alpine valley, hidden amidst stupendous walls of stone, bottomless precipices, and summits that touched the clouds, there was a cottage even smaller and humbler than most, and closest of all to the church. It was the house of the pastor. The old man had been born there, and had lived there all the years of his life save a few that he had passed in a town as a student; and he had wedded a neighbour who, like himself, had known no other home than this one village. He was gentle, patient, simple, and full of tenderness; he worked like his people all the week through, in the open weather, amongst his fruit-trees, his little breadth of pasturage, his herb-garden, and his few sheep. On the seventh day he preached to the people the creed that he himself believed in with all the fond, unquestioning, implicit faith of the young children who lifted to him their round wondering eyes.

He was good; he was old: in his simple needs and his undoubting hopes he was happy; all the living things of his little world loved him, and he loved them. And fate lit on him to torture him, as it is its pleasure to torture the innocent.

It sent him a daughter who was fair to sight, and had a voice like music; a form lithe and white, with hair of gold, and eyes like her own planets. She had never seen any other spot save her own valley; but she had the old Bersercker blood in her veins, and she was restless; the sea tempted her with an intense power; she desired passionately, without knowing what she desired.

The simple pastoral work, the peaceful household labours, the girls' garland of alpine flowers, the youths' singing in the brief rose twilight, the saga told the thousandth time around the lamp in the deep mid-winter silence; these things would not suffice for her. The old Scandinavian madness was in her veins. And one day the sea tempted her too utterly; beyond her strength,—as a lover, after a thousand vain entreaties, one day tempts a woman, and one day finds her weak.

The sea vanquished her, and she went—whither?

They hardly knew: to these old people the world that lay behind their mountain fortress was a blank. It might be a paradise; it might be a prison. They could not tell. They suffered their sorrow meekly; they never cursed her; they did not even curse their fate because they had given life to a woman child.

After awhile they heard of her.

She wrote them tender and glowing words; she was well, she was proud, she was glad, she had found those who told her that she had a voice which was as a gift of gold, and that she might sing in triumph to the nations. Such tidings came from time to time; brief welcome words, first teeming with hope, then delirious with triumph, yet ever ending with a short sad sigh of conscience, a prayer for pardon—pardon for what? The letters never said: perhaps only for the sin of desertion.

The slow salt tears of age fell on these glowing pages in which the heart of a young, vain-glorious, tender creature stamped itself; but the old people never spoke of them to others. "She is happy, it does not matter for us." This was all they said, yet this gentle patience was a martyrdom too sharp to last; when that year closed the mother was in her grave, and the old man left alone.

The long silent winter came, locking the valley within its fortress of ice, severing it from all the rest of the breathing human world; and the letters ceased. He would not let them say that she had forgotten; he chose to think that the severance was due to the wall of snow which was built up between them rather than to any division of her ingratitude and oblivion.

The sweet sudden Norwegian spring came, all the white and golden flowers breaking up from the hard crust of the soil, and all the loosened waters rushing with a shout of liberty to join the sea.

The summer followed with the red mountain roses blossoming by the brooks, and the green mountain grasses blowing in the wind, with the music of the herd-bells ringing down the passes, and the sound of the fife and of the reed-pipe calling the maidens to the dance.

In the midst of the summer, one night, when all the stars were shining above the valley, and all the children slept under the roofs with the swallows, and not a soul was stirring, save where here and there a lover watched a light glow in some lattice underneath the eaves, a half-dead woman dragged herself feebly under the lime-tree shadows of the pastor's house, and struck with a faint cry upon the door and fell at her father's feet, broken and senseless. Before the full day had dawned she had given birth to a male child; and died as her son's eyes opened to the morning light.

He inherited no name, and they called him after his grandsire, Arslàn.

When his dead daughter lay stretched before him in the sunlight, with her white large limbs folded to rest, and her noble fair face calm as a mask of marble, the old pastor knew little—nothing—of what her life through these two brief years had been. Her lips had scarcely breathed a word since she had fallen senseless on his threshold. That she had had triumph he knew; that she had fallen into dire necessities he saw.

Whether she had surrendered art for the sake of love, or whether she had lost the public favour by some caprice of the public, whether she had been eminent or obscure in her career, whether it had abandoned her or she had abandoned it, he could not tell, and he knew too little of the world to be able to learn.

That she had travelled her weary way homeward to her native mountains that her son might not perish amidst strangers, he knew; but no more. Nor was more ever known by any living soul. In life there are so many histories which are like broken boughs that strew the ground after a storm, snapped short at either end, so that none know the crown of them nor the root.

The child whom she had left grew in goodliness and strength and stature, until the people said that he was like that child-king, whom their hero Frithiof raised upon his buckler above the multitude: and who was not afraid, but boldly gripped the brazen shield, and smiled fearlessly at the noonday sun.

He had his mother's golden Scandinavian beauty; the beauty of sculpture, white as the snow, of unusual height, and largely moulded; and his free life amidst the ice fields and the pinewoods, and on the wild northern seas, developed both health and strength to their uttermost perfection.

The people admired and wondered at him; they did not love him. The lad was cold, dauntless, silent; he repelled their sympathies and disdained their pastimes. He chose rather to be by himself than with them. He was never cruel; but he was never tender; and when he did speak he spoke with a sort of eloquent scorn and caustic imagery that seemed to them extraordinary in one so young. But his grandfather loved him greatly; and reared him tenderly and wisely; and braced him with a scholar's lore and with a mountaineer's exposure, so that both brain and body had their due.

He was a simple childlike broken old man; but in this vigorous youth that unfolded itself beside him his age seemed to strike fresh root, and he had wisdom and skill enough to guide its development justly. The desire of his soul was that his grandson should succeed him in the spiritual charge of that tranquil valley, and thus escape the dire perils of the cities in which the mother's life had been caught and consumed like a moth's in flame. But Arslàn's eyes looked ever across the ocean with that look in them which had been in his mother's, and when the old man spoke of this holy and peaceful future, he was silent.

Moreover, he—who had never beheld but the rude paintings on panels of pine that decorated the little red church under the firs and lindens,—he had the gift of art in him.

He had few and rough means only with which to make his crude and unguided essays; but the delirium of it was on him, and the peasants of his village gazed awe-stricken and adoring before the things which he drew on every piece of pine-wood, on every smooth breadth of sea-worn granite, on every bare surface of lime-washed wall that he could find at liberty for his usage.

When they asked him what, in his manhood, he would do, he said little. "I will never leave the old man," he made answer; and he kept his word. Up to his twentieth year he never quitted the valley. He studied deeply, after his own manner, but nearly all his days were passed in the open air alone; in the pure cold air of the highest mountain summits, amidst the thunder of the furious torrents; in the black recesses of lonely forests, where none, save the wolf and the bear, wandered with him; or away on the vast expanse of the sea, where the storm drove the great arctic waves like scourged sheep, and the huge breakers seized the shore as a panther its prey.

On such a world as this, and in the marvellous nights of the north, his mind fed itself and gained its full powers. The feeble life of the old man held him to this lonely valley that seemed filled with the coldness, the mystery, the unutterable terror and majesty of the arctic pole, to which it looked; but, unknown to him, it thus fettered him likewise where alone the genius in him could take its full shape and full stature.

Unknown to him, in these years it took the depth, the strength, the patience, the melancholy, the virility of the North; took these never to be lost again.

In the twentieth winter of his life an avalanche engulfed the pastor's house, and the little church by which it stood; covering both beneath a mountain of earth and snow and rock and riven trees. Some of the timbers withstood the shock, and the roof remained standing uncrushed above their heads. The avalanche fell some little time after midnight: there were only present in the dwelling himself, the old man, and a serving woman.

The woman was killed on her bed by the fall of a beam upon her; he and the pastor still lived: lived in perpetual darkness without food or fuel, or any ray of light.

The wooden clock stood erect, uninjured; they could hear the hours go by in slow succession. The old man was peaceful and even cheerful; praising God often; and praying that help might come to his beloved one. But his strength could not hold out against the icy cold, the long hunger, the dreadful blank around. He died ere the first day had wholly gone by, at even-song; saying still that he was content, and still praising God who had rewarded his innocence with shame, and recompensed his service with agony. For two more days and nights, Arslàn remained in his living tomb, enshrouded in eternal gloom, alone with the body of his grandfather, stretching out his hands ever and again to meet that icy touch rather than be without companionship.

On the morning of the third day the people of the village, who had laboured ceaselessly, reached him; and he was saved.

As soon as the spring broke, he left the valley and passed over the mountains, seeking a new world. His old familiar home had become hateful to him; he had no tie to it save two low graves, still snow-covered underneath a knot of tall stone-pines; the Norsc passion of wandering was in his veins as it had been in his mother's before him; he mutely desired freedom, colour, knowledge, art, fame, as she had desired them, and he went: turning his face from that lowly green nest lying like a lark's between the hills.

He did not go as youth mostly goes, blind with a divine dream of triumph: he went, consciously, to a bitter combat as the sea kings of old, whose blood ran in his veins, and whose strength was in his limbs, had gone to war, setting their prow hard against the sharp salt waves and in the teeth of an adverse wind.

He was not without money. The pastor, indeed, had died almost penniless; he had been always poor, and had given the little he possessed to those still poorer. But the richest landowner in the village, the largest possessor of flocks and herds, dying childless, had bequeathed his farm and cattle to Arslàn; having loved the lad's dead mother silently and vainly. The value of these realised by sale gave to Arslàn, when he became his own master, what, in that valley at least, was wealth; and he went without care for the future on this score into the world of men; his mind full of dreams and the beautiful myths of dead ages; his temper compounded of poetry and of coldness, of enthusiasm and of scepticism; his one passion a supreme ambition, pure as snow in its instinct, but half savage in its intensity.

From that spring, when he had passed away from his birthplace as the winter snows were melting on the mountain sides, and the mountain flowers were putting forth their earliest buds under the pine boughs, until the time that he now stood solitary, starving, and hopeless before the mocking eyes of his Hermes, twelve years had run their course, and all through them he had never once again beheld his native land.

Like the Scandinavian Regner, he chose rather to perish in the folds, and by the fangs, of the snakes that devoured him than return to his country with the confession of defeat. And despite the powers that were in him, his life had been a failure, an utter failure—as yet.

In his early youth he had voyaged often, with men who went to the extreme north in search of skins and such poor trade as they could drive with Esquimaux or Koraks; he had borne their dangers and their poverty, their miseries and their famine, for sake of seeing what they saw;—the pathless oceans of the ice realm, the trailing pines alone in a white snow world, the red moon fantastic and horrible in a sky of steel, the horned clouds of reindeer rushing through the endless night, the arch of the aurora spanning the heavens with their fire. He had passed many seasons of his boyhood in the silence, the solitude, the eternal desolation, and the mute mystery of that Arctic world, which for no man has either sympathy or story; and in a way he had loved it, and was often weary for it; in a way its spirit remained with him always; and its inexorable coldness, its pitiless indifference to men's wants and weakness, its loneliness and its purity, and its scorn, were in all the works of his hand; blended in a strange union with the cruelty, and the voluptuousness, and the gorgeousness of colour, which gave to everything he touched the glow and the temper of the east.

Thus, what he did pleased none; being for one half the world too chill, and being for the other half too sensual.

The world had never believed in him; and he found

himself in the height and the maturity of his powers condemned to an absolute obscurity. Not one man in a million knew his name.

During these years he had devoted himself to the study of art with an undeviating subservience to all its tyrannies.

He had studied humanity in all its phases; he had studied form with all the rigid care that it requires; he had studied colour in almost every land that lies beneath the sun; he had studied the passions in all their deformities, as well as in all their beauties; he had spared neither himself nor others in pursuit of knowledge. He had tried most vices, he had seen all miseries, he had spared himself no spectacle, however loathsome; he had turned back from no license, however undesired, that could give him insight into or empire over human raptures and affliction. Neither did he spare himself any labour however costly, however exhausting, to enrich his brain with that varied learning, that multifarious science which he held needful to every artist who dared to desire greatness.

The hireling beauty of the wanton, the splendour of the sun and sea, the charnel lore of anatomy, the secrets of dead tongues and buried nations, the horrors of the lazar wards and pest-houses, the glories of golden deserts and purple vineyards, the flush of love on a young girl's cheek, the rottenness of corruption on a dead man's limbs, the hellish riot of a brothel, the divine calm of an eastern night; all things alike he studied, without abhorrence as without delight, indifferent to all save for one end,—knowledge and art.

So entirely and undividedly did this possess him that it seemed to have left him without other passions; even as the surgeon dissects the fair lifeless body of some beautiful dead woman, regardless of loveliness or sex, only intent on the secret of disease, the mystery of formation, which he seeks therein, so did he study the physical beauty of women and their mortal corruption, without other memories than those of art. He would see the veil fall from off the limbs of a creature lovely as a goddess, and would think only to himself—"How shall I render this so that on my canvas it shall live once more?"

One night, in the hot, close streets of Damascus, a man was stabbed,—a young Maronite—who lay dying in the roadway, without sign or sound, whilst his assassins fled; the silver Syrian moon shining full on his white and scarlet robe, his calm, up-turned face, his lean hand knotted on the dagger he had been spared no time to use; a famished street dog smelling at his blood.

Arslàn, passing through the city, saw and paused beside him; stood still and motionless, looking down on the outstretched figure; then drew his tablets out and sketched the serene, rigid face, the flowing, blood-soaked robes, the hungry animal mouthing at the wound. Another painter, his familiar friend, following on his steps, joined him a little later, and started from his side in horror—

"My God! what do you do there?" he cried. "Do you not see?—the man is dying."

Arslàn looked up—"I had not thought of that," he answered.

It was thus always with him.

He was not cruel. To animals he was humane, to women gentle, to men serene; but his art was before all things with him, and with humanity he had little sympathy: and if he had passions, they had wakened no more than as the drowsy tigress wakes in the hot hush of noon, half indifferent, half lustful, to strike fiercely what comes before her, and then, having slain, couches herself and sleeps again.

But for this absolute surrender of his life, his art had as yet recompensed him nothing.

Men did not believe in him; what he wrought saddened and terrified them; they turned aside to those who fed them on simpler and on sweeter food.

His works were great, but they were such as the public mind deems impious. They unveiled human corruption too nakedly, and they shadowed forth visions too exalted, and satires too unsparing, for them to be acceptable to the multitude. They were compounded of an idealism clear and cold as crystal, and of a reality cruel and voluptuous as love. They were penetrated with an acrid satire and an intense despair: the world caring only for a honied falsehood and a gilded gloss in every art, would have none of them.

So for these twelve long years his labour had been waste, his efforts fruitless. Those years had been costly to him in purse;—travel, study, gold flung to fallen women, sums spent on faithless friends, utter indifference to whosoever robbed him so long as he was left in peace to pursue lofty aims and high endeavours—all these did their common work on wealth which was scanty in the press of the world, though it had appeared inexhaustible on the shores of the north sea.

His labours also were costly, and they brought him no return.

The indifference to fortune in a man of genius looks, to a man of the world, the stupor of idiotcy: from such a stupor he was shaken one day to find himself face to face with beggary.

His works were seen by few, and these few were antagonistic to them.

All ways to fame were closed to him, either by the envy of other painters, or by the apathies and the antipathies of the nations themselves. In all lands he was repulsed; he roused the jealousy of his compeers and the terror of the multitudes. They hurled against him the old worn-out cry that the office of art was to give pleasure, not pain; and when his money was gone, so that he could no longer, at his own cost, expose his works to the public gaze, they and he were alike obliterated from the public marts; they had always denied him fame, and they at last thrust him quickly into oblivion, and abandoned him to it without remorse, and even with contentment.

He could, indeed, with the facile power of eye and touch that he possessed, have easily purchased a temporary ease and evanescent repute, if he had given the world from his pencil those themes for which it cared, and descended to the common spheres of common art. But he refused utterly to do this. The best and greatest thing in him was his honesty to the genius wherewith he was gifted; he refused to prostitute it; he refused to do other than to tell the truth as he saw it.

"This man blasphemes; this man is immoral," his enemies had always hooted against him. It is what the world always says of those who utter unwelcome truths in its unwilling ears.

So the words of the old Skald by his own northern sea shores came to pass; and at length, for the sake of art, it came to this, that he perished for want of bread.

For seven days he had been without food, except the winter berries which he broke off the trees without, and such handfuls of wheat as fell through the disjointed timbers of the ceiling, for whose possession he disputed with the rats.

The sheer absolute poverty, which leaves the man whom it has seized without so much as even a crust wherewith to break his fast, is commoner than the world in general ever dreams. For he was now so poor that for many months he had been unable to buy fresh canvas on which to work, and had been driven to chalk the outlines of the innumerable fancies that pursued him upon the bare smooth grey stone walls of the old granary in which he dwelt.

He let his life go silently away without complaint, and without effort, because effort had been so long unavailing, that he had discarded it in a contemptuous despair.

He accepted his fate, seeing nothing strange in it, and nothing pitiable; since many better men than he had borne the like. He could not have altered it without beggary or theft, and he thought either of these worse than itself.

There were hecatombs of grain, bursting their sacks, in the lofts above; but when, once on each eighth day, the maltster owning them sent his men to fetch some from the store, Arslàn let the boat be moored against the wall, be filled with barley, and be pushed away again down the current, without saying once to the rowers, "Wait; I starve!"

And yet, though like a miser amidst his gold, his body starved amidst the noble shapes and the great thoughts that his brain conceived and his hand called into substance, he never once dreamed of abandoning for any other the career to which he had dedicated himself from the earliest days that his boyish eyes had watched the fires of the Arctic lights glow above the winter seas.

Art was to him as mother, brethren, mistress, offspring, religion—all that other men hold dear. He had none of these, he desired none of them; and his genius sufficed to him in their stead.

It was an intense and reckless egotism, made alike cruel and sublime by its intensity and purity, like the egotism of a mother in her child. To it, as the mother to her child, he would have sacrificed every living creature; but to it also, like her, he would have sacrificed his very existence as unhesitatingly. But it was an egotism which, though merciless in its tyranny, was as pure as snow in its impersonality; it was untainted by any grain of avarice, of vanity, of selfish desire; it was independent of all sympathy; it was simply and intensely the passion for immortality:—that sublime selfishness, that superb madness, of all great minds.

Art had taken him for its own, as Demeter, in the days of her desolation, took the child Demophoon to nurture him as her own on the food of gods, and to plunge him through the flames of a fire that would give him immortal life. As the pusillanimous and sordid fears of the mortal mother lost to the child for evermore the possession of Olympian joys and of perpetual youth, so did the craven and earthly cares of bodily needs hold the artist back from the radiance of the life of the soul, and drag him from the purifying fires. Yet he had not been utterly discouraged; he strove against the Metanira of circumstance; he did his best to struggle free from the mortal bonds that bound him; and, as the child Demophoon mourned for the great goddess that had nurtured him, refusing to be comforted, so did he turn from the base consolations of the senses and the appetites, and beheld ever before his sight the ineffable majesty of that Mater Dolorosa who once and for ever had anointed him as her own.

Even now as the strength returned to his limbs and the warmth to his veins, the old passion, the old worship, returned to him.

The momentary weakness which had assailed him passed away. He shook himself with a bitter impatient scorn for the feebleness into which he had been betrayed; and glanced around him still with a dull wonder as to the strange chances which the past night had brought. He was incredulous still; he thought that his fancy, heated by long fasting, might have cheated him; that he must have dreamed; and that the food and fuel which he saw must surely have been his own.

Yet reflection told him that this could not be; he remembered that for several weeks his last coin had been spent; that he had been glad to gather the birds' winter berries to crush beneath his teeth, and gather the dropped corn from the floor to quiet the calm of hunger; that for many a day there had been no fire on the hearth, and that only a frame which long sunless northern winters had braced to such hardihood in early youth, had enabled him to resist and endure the cold. Therefore, it must be charity. Charity!—as the hateful truth came home to him, he met the eyes of the white, slender, winged Hermes: eyes that from out that colourless and smiling face seemed to mock him with a cruel contempt.

His was the old, old story—the rod of wealth bartered for the empty shell that gave forth music.

Hermes seemed to know it and to jeer him.

Hermes, the mischief-monger, and the trickster of men; the inventive god who spent his days in cajoling his brethren, and his nights in the mockery of mortals; the messenger of heaven who gave Pandora to mankind; Hermes, the eternal type of unscrupulous Success, seemed to have voice and cry to him:—"Oh fool, fool, fool!

who listens for the music of the spheres and disdains the only melody that men have ears to hear—the melody of gold!"

Arslân turned from the great cartoon of the gods in Pheræ, and went out into the daylight, and stripped and plunged into the cold and turbulent stream. Its chillness and the combat of its current braced his nerves and cleared his brain.

When he was clad, he left the grain-tower with the white forms of its gods upon its walls, and walked slowly down the bank of the river. Since life had been forced back upon him he knew that it was incumbent upon his manhood to support it by the toil of his hands if men would not accept the labour of his brain.

Before, he had been too absorbed in his pursuit, too devoted to it, body and soul, to seek to sustain existence by the sheer manual exertion which was the only thing that he had left untried for self-maintenance. In a manner too he was too proud; not too proud to labour, but too proud to easily endure to lay bare his needs to the knowledge of others. But now, human charity must have saved him; a charity which he hated as the foulest insult of his life; and he had no chance save to accept it like a beggar bereft of all shame, or to seek such work as would give him his daily bread.

So he went; feebly, for he was still weak from the length of his famine.

The country was well known to him, but the people not at all. He had come by hazard on the old ruin where he dwelt, and had stayed there full a year.

These serene blue skies, these pale mists, these corn-clad slopes, these fields of plenteous abundance, these quiet homesteads, these fruit-harvests of this Norman plain were in a contrast intense, yet soothing, to all that his life had known. These old quaint cities, these little villages that seemed always hushed with the sound of bells, these quiet streams on which the calm sunlight slept so peacefully, these green and golden lands of plenty that stretched away to the dim grey distant sea,—all these had had a certain charm for him.

He had abided with them, partly because amidst them it seemed possible to live on a handful of wheat and a draught of water, unnoticed and unpitied, partly because, having come thither on foot through many lands and by long hardship, he had paused there weary and incapable of farther effort.

Whilst the little gold he had had on him had lasted he had painted innumerable transcripts of its ancient buildings, and of its summer and autumnal landscapes. And of late—through the bitter winter—of late it had seemed to him that it was as well to die here as elsewhere.

When a man knows that his dead limbs will be huddled into the common ditch of the poor, the nameless, and the unclaimed, and that his dead brain will only serve for soil to feed some little rank wayside poisonous weed, it will seldom seem of much moment in what earth the ditch be dug, by what feet the sward be trod.

He went now on his way seeking work; he did not care what, he asked for any that might serve to use such strength as hunger had left in him, and to give him his daily bread. But this is a great thing to demand in this world, and so he found it.

They repulsed him everywhere.

They had their own people in plenty, they had their sturdy, tough, weather-beaten women, who laboured all day in rain, or snow, or storm, for a pittance, and they had these in larger numbers than their field-work needed. They looked at him askance; this man with the eyes of arctic blue and the grave gestures of a king, who only asked to labour as the lowest amongst them. He was a stranger to them; he did not speak their tongue with their accent; he looked, with that white beauty and that lofty stature, as though he could crush them in the hollow of his hand.

They would have none of him.

"He brings misfortune!" they said amongst themselves; and they would have none of him.

He had an evil name with them. They said at eventide by their wood-fires that strange things had been seen since he had come to the granary by the river.

Once he had painted, from the pretty face of a stonecutter's little fair son, a study of the wondrous child Zagreus gazing in the fatal mirror; the child was laughing, and happy, and healthful at noon, crowned with carnations and river lilies, and by sunset he was dead—dead like the flowers that were still amongst his curls.

Once a girl had hired herself as model to him for an Egyptian wanton, half a singer and half a gipsy—handsome, lithe, fantastic, voluptuous: the very night she left the granary she was drowned in crossing a wooden bridge of the river, which gave way under the heavy tramp of a fantoccini player who accompanied her.

Once he had sketched, for the corner of an oriental study, a rare-plumaged bird of the south, which was the idol of a water-carrier of the district, and the wonder of all the children round: and from that date the bird had sickened, and drooped, and lost its colours, and pined until it died.

The boy's death had been from a sudden seizure of one of the many ills of infancy; the dancing-girl's had come from a common accident due to the rottenness of old worn water-soaked timber; the mocking-bird's had arisen from the cruelty of captivity and the chills of northern winds; all had been the result of simple accident and of natural circumstance. But they had sufficed to fill with horror the minds of a peasantry always bigoted and strongly prejudiced against every stranger; and it became to them a matter of implicit credence that whatsoever living thing should be painted by the artist Arslàn would assuredly never survive to see the rising of the morrow's sun.

In consequence, for leagues around they shunned him; not man, nor woman, nor child would sit to him as models; and now, when he sought the wage of a daily labour amongst them, he was everywhere repulsed. He had long repulsed human sympathy, and in its turn it repulsed him.

At last he turned and retraced his steps, baffled and wearied; his early habits had made him familiar with all manner of agricultural toil; he would have done the task of the sower, the herdsman, the hewer of wood, or the charcoal-burner; but they would none of them believe this of one with his glance and his aspect: and solicitation was new to his lips and bitter there as gall.

He took his way back along the line of the river; the beauty of the dawn had gone, the day was only now chilly, heavy with a rank moisture from the steaming soil. Broken boughs and uprooted bushes were floating on the turgid water, and over all the land there hung a sullen fog.

The pressure of the air, the humidity, the colourless stillness that reigned throughout, weighed on lungs which for a score of years had only breathed the pure strong rarified air of the north; he longed with a sudden passion to be once more amidst his native mountains under the clear steel-like skies, and beside the rush of the vast wild seas. Were it only to die as he looked on them, it were better to die there than here.

He longed, as men in deserts thirst for drink, for one breath of the strong salt air of the north, one sight of the bright keen sea-born sun as it leapt at dawn from the waters.

The crisp cold nights, the heavens which shone as steel, the forests filled with the cry of the wolves, the mountains which the ocean ceaselessly assailed, the mighty waves which marched erect like armies, the bitter Arctic wind which like a sabre cleft the darkness; all these came back to him beloved and beautiful in all their cruelty, desired by him, with a sick longing for their freshness, for their fierceness, for their freedom.

As he dragged his tired limbs through the grasses and looked out upon the sullen stream that flowed beside him, an oar struck the water, a flat black boat drifted beneath the bank, a wild swan disturbed rose with a hiss from the sedges.

The boat was laden with grain; there was only one rower in it, who steered by a string wound round her foot.

She did not lift her face as she went by him; but her bent brow and her bosom grew red, and she cut the water with a swifter, sharper stroke; her features were turned from him by that movement of her head, but he saw the eastern outline of the cheek and chin, the embrowned velvet of the skin, the half-bare beauty of the heaving chest and supple spine bent back in the action of the oars, the long slender arched shape of the naked foot, round which the cord was twined;—their contour and their colour struck him with a sudden surprise.

He had seen such oftentimes, eastwards, on the banks of golden rivers, treading, with such feet as these, the sands that were the dust of countless nations; bearing, on such shoulders as these, earthen water-vases that might have served the feasts of Pharaohs; showing such limbs as these against the curled palm branches and the deep blue sky upon the desert's edge.

But here!—a face of Asia amongst the corn-lands of Northern France? It seemed to him strange; he looked after her with wonder.

The boat went on down the stream without any pause; the sculls cleaving the heavy tide with regular and resolute monotony; the golden piles of the grain and the brown form of the bending figure soon hidden in the clouds of river-mist.

He watched her, only seeing a beggar-girl rowing a skiff full of corn down a sluggish stream. There was nothing to tell him that he was looking upon the saviour of his body from the thralls of death; if there had been, in his mood, then, he would have cursed her.

The boat glided into the fog which closed behind it: a flock of water-birds swam out from the rushes and darted at some floating kernels of wheat that had fallen over the vessel's side; they fought and hissed, and flapped and pecked amongst themselves over the chance plunder; a large rat stole amidst them unnoticed by them in their exultation, and seized their leader and bore him struggling and beating the air with blood-stained wings away to a hole in the bank; a mongrel dog, prowling on the shore, hearing the wild duck's cries, splashed into the sedges, and swam out and gripped the rat by the neck in bold sharp fangs, and bore both rat and bird, bleeding and dying, to the land; the owner of the mongrel, a peasant, making ready the ground for colza in the low-lying fields, snatched the duck from the dog to bear it home for his own eating, and kicked his poor beast in the ribs for having ventured to stray without leave and to do him service without permission.

"The dulcet harmony of the world's benignant law!" thought Arslàn, as he turned aside to enter the stone archway of his own desolate dwelling, "To live one must slaughter—what life can I take?"

At that moment the setting sun pierced the heavy veil of the vapour, and glowed through the fog.

The boat, now distant, glided for a moment into the ruddy haze, and was visible; the water around it, like a lake of flame, the white steam above it, like the smoke of a sacrifice fire.

Then the sun sank, the mists gathered closely once more, all light faded, and the day was dead.

He felt stifled and sick at heart as he returned along the reedy shore towards his dreary home. He wondered dully why his life would not end: since the world would have none of him, neither the work of his brain nor the work of his hands, it seemed that he had no place in it.

He was half resolved to lie down in the water there, amongst the reeds, and let it flow over his face and breast, and kiss him softly and coldly into the sleep of death. He had desired this many times; what held him back from its indulgence was not "the child within us that fears death," of which Plato speaks; he had no such misgiving in him, and he believed death to be a simple rupture and end of all things, such as any man had right to seek and summon for himself; it was rather that the passion of his art was too strong in him, that the power to create was too intense in him, so that he could not willingly consign the forces and the fantasies of his brain to that annihilation to which he would, without thought or pause, have flung his body.

As he entered the haunted hall which served him as his painting-room, he saw a fresh fire of logs upon the hearth, whose leaping flames lighted the place with cheerful colour, and he saw on the stone bench fresh food, sufficient to last several days, and a brass flagon filled with wine.

A curious emotion took possession of him as he looked. It was less surprise at the fact, for his senses told him that it was the work of some charity which chose to hide itself, than it was wonder as to who, in this strange land, where none would even let him earn his daily bread, knew enough or cared enough to supply his necessities thus. And with this there arose the same intolerant bitterness of the degradation of alms, the same ungrateful hatred of the succour that seemed to class him amongst beggars, which had moved him when he had awakened with the dawn.

He felt neither tenderness nor gratitude, he was only conscious of humiliation.

There were in him a certain coldness, strength, and indifference to sympathy, which, whilst they made his greatness as an artist, made his callousness as a man. It might have been sweet to others to find themselves thus remembered and pitied by another at an hour when their forces were spent, their fate friendless, and their hopes all dead. But it was not so to him, he only felt like the desert animal which, wounded, repulses every healing hand, and only seeks to die alone.

There was only one vulnerable, one tender nerve in him, and this was the instinct of his genius. He had been nurtured in hardihood, and had drawn in endurance with every breath of his native air; he would have borne physical ills without one visible pang, and would have been indifferent to all mortal suffering; but for the powers in him, for the art he adored, he had a child's weakness, a woman's softness.

He could not bear to die without leaving behind his life some work the world would cherish.

Call it folly, call it madness, it is both: the ivory Zeus that was to give its sculptor immortality, lives but in tradition; the bronze Athene, that was to guard the Piræus in eternal liberty, has long been levelled with the dust; yet with every age the artist still gives life for fame, still cries "Let my body perish, but make my work immortal!"

It was this in him now which stirred his heart with a new and gentler emotion; emotion which, while half disgust, was also half gladness. This food was alms-given, since he had not earned it, and yet—by means of this sheer bodily subsistence—it would be possible for him to keep alive those dreams, that strength, by which he still believed it in him to compel his fame from men.

He stood before the Phœbus in Pheræ, thinking; it stung him with a bitter torment; it humiliated him with a hateful burden—this debt which came he knew not whence, and which he never might be able to repay. And yet his heart was strangely moved; it seemed to him that the fate which thus wantonly, and with such curious persistence, placed life back into his hands, must needs be one that would bear no common fruit.

He opposed himself no more to it.

He bent his head and broke bread, and ate and drank of the red wine:—he did not thank God or man as he broke his fast; he only looked in the mocking eyes of Hermes, and said in his heart:—

"Since I must live, I will triumph."

And Hermes smiled: Hermes the wise, who had bought and sold the generations of men so long ago, in the golden age, and who knew so well how they would barter away their greatness and their gladness, and their bodies and their souls, for one sweet strain of his hollow reed-pipe, for one sweet glance of his soulless Pandora's eyes.

Hermes—Hermes the liar, Hermes the wise,—knew how men's oaths were kept.

BOOK IV.

"The desire of the moth for the star."

CHAPTER I.

At the close of that day Claudis Flamma discovered that he had been robbed—robbed more than once: he swore and raved and tore his hair for loss of a little bread and meat and oil and a flagon of red wine.

He did not suspect his grand-daughter; accusing her perpetually of sins of which she was innocent, he did not once associate her in thought with the one offence which she had committed. He thought that the window of his storehouse had been forced from the exterior; he made no doubt that his spoiler was some vagabond from one of the river barges. By such tramps his hen-house and his apple-lofts had often previously been invaded.

She heard his lamentations and imprecations in unbroken silence; he did not question her; and without a lie she was able to keep her secret. In her own sight she had done a foul thing—a thing that her own hunger had never induced her to do. She did not seek to reconcile herself to her action by any reflection that she had only taken what she had really earned a thousand times over by her service; her mind was not sufficiently instructed, and was of too truthful a mould to be capable of the deft plea of a sophistry.

She could dare the thing; and do it, and hold her

peace about it, though she should be scourged to speak; but she could not tamper with it to excuse it to herself; for this she had neither the cunning nor the cowardice.

Why had she done it?—done for a stranger what no pressure of need had made her do for her own wants? She did not ask herself; she followed her instinct. He allured her with his calm and kingly beauty, which was like nothing else her eyes had ever seen; and she was drawn by an irresistible attraction to this life which she had bought at the price of her own from the gods. Yet stronger even than this sudden human passion which had entered into her was her dread lest he whom she had ransomed from death should know of his debt to her.

Under such a dread, she never opened her lips to anyone on this thing which she had done. Silence was natural to her; she spoke so rarely, that many in the province believed her to be dumb; no sympathy had ever been shown to her to woo her to disclose either the passions that burned latent in her veins, or the tenderness that trembled stifled in her heart.

Thrice again did she take food and fuel to the water-tower undetected, both by the man whom she robbed, and the man whom she succoured. Thrice again did she find her way to the desolate chamber in its owner's absence and refill the empty platters and warm afresh the cold blank hearth. Thrice again did Claudis Flamma note the diminution of his stores, and burnish afresh his old rusty fowling-piece, and watch half the night on his dark staircase, and prepare with his own hands a jar of poisoned honey and a bag of poisoned wheat, which he placed, with a cruel chuckle of grim glee, to tempt the eyes of his spoilers.

But the spoiler, being of his own household, saw this trap set, and was aware of it.

In a week or two the need for these acts which she hated ceased. She learned that the stranger for whom she thus risked her body and soul, had found a boatman's work upon the water which, although a toil rough and rude, and but poorly paid, still sufficed to give him bread. Though she was herself so pressed with hunger, many a time, that as she went through the meadows and hedgerows she was glad to crush in her teeth the tender shoots of the briars, and the acrid berry of the brambles, she never again, unbidden, touched so much as a mouldy crust thrown out to be eaten by the poultry.

Flamma, counting his possessions greedily night and morning, blessed the saints for the renewed safety of his dwelling, and cast forth the poisoned wheat as a thank-offering to the male birds who were for ever flying to and fro their nested mates in the leafless boughs above the earliest violets, and whose little throats were strangled even in their glad flood of nuptial song, and whose soft bright eyes grew dull in death ere even they had looked upon the springtide sun.

For it was ever thus that Folle-Farine saw men praise God.

She took their death to her own door, sorrowing and full of remorse.

"Had I never stolen the food, these birds might never have perished," she thought, as she saw the rosy throats of the robins and bullfinches turned upward in death on the turf. She blamed herself bitterly with an aching heart.

The fatality which makes human crime recoil on the innocent creatures of the animal world oppressed her with its heavy and hideous injustice. Their God was good, they said: yet for her sin and her grandsire's greed the harmless song-birds died by the score in torment.

"How shall a God be good who is not just?" she thought.

In this mute young lonely soul of hers Nature had sown a strong passion for justice, a strong instinct towards what was righteous. As the germ of a plant born in darkness underground will, by sheer instinct, uncurl its colourless tendrils, and thrust them through crevices and dust, and the close structure of mortared stones, until they reach the light and grow green and strong in it, so did her nature strive, of its own accord, through the gloom enveloping it, towards those moral laws which in all ages and all lands remain the same, no matter what deity be worshipped, or what creed be called the truth.

Her nascent mind was darkened, oppressed, bewildered, perplexed, even like the plant which forcing itself upward from its cellar opens its leaves not in pure air and under a blue sky, but in the reek and smoke and fœtid odours of a city. Yet, like the plant, she vaguely felt that light was somewhere; and as vaguely sought it.

With most days she took her grandsire's boat to and fro the town, fetching or carrying; there was no mode of transit so cheap to him as this, whose only cost was her fatigue. With each passage up and down the river, she passed by the dwelling of Arslàn.

Sometimes she saw him; once or twice, in the twilight, he spoke to her; she only bent her head to hide her face from him, and rowed more quickly on her homeward way in silence. At other times, in his absence, and when she was safe from any detection, she entered the dismal solitudes wherein he laboured, and gazed in rapt and awed amazement at the shapes that were shadowed forth upon the walls.

The service by which he gained his daily bread was on the waters, and took him often leagues away—simple hardy toil, amongst fishers and canal-carriers and bargemen. But it left him some few days, and all his nights, free for art; and never in all the years of his leisure had his fancy conceived and his hand created more exquisite dreams and more splendid phantasies than now in this bitter and cheerless time, when he laboured amidst the poorest for the bare bread of life.

"De belles choses peuvent se faire dans une cave;" and in truth the gloom of the cellar gives birth to an art more sublime than the light of the palace can ever beget.

Suffering shortens the years of the artist, and kills him oftentimes ere his prime be reached; but in suffering alone are all great works conceived. The senses, the passions, the luxuries, the lusts of the flesh, the delirium of the desires, the colours, the melodies, the fragrance, the indolences,—all that make the mere "living of life" delightful, all go to enrich and to deepen the human genius which steeps itself in them; but it is in exile from these that alone it can rise to its greatest.

The grass of the Holy River gathers perfume from the marvellous suns, and the moonless nights, and the gorgeous bloom of the east, from the aromatic breath of the leopard and the perfume of the fallen pomegranate, and the sacred oil that floats in the lamps, and the caress of the girl-bathers' feet, and the myrrh-dropping unguents that glide from the maidens' bare limbs in the moonlight,—the grass holds and feeds on them all. But not till the grass has been torn from the roots, and been crushed, and been bruised and destroyed, can the full odours exhale of all it has tasted and treasured.

Even thus the imagination of man may be great, but it can never be at its greatest until one serpent, with merciless fangs, has bitten it through and through, and impregnated it with passion and with poison,—that one deathless serpent which is Memory.

Arslàn had never been more ceaselessly pursued by innumerable phantasies, and never had given to these a more terrible force, a more perfect utterance, than now, when the despair which possessed him was absolute,— when it seemed to him that he had striven in his last strife with fate, and been thrown never to rise again,— when he kept his body alive by such soulless ceaseless labour as that of the oxen in the fields,—when he saw every hour drift by, barren, sullen, painful,—when only some dull yet staunch instinct of virility held him back from taking his own life in the bleak horror of these fruitless days,—when it seemed to him that his oath before Hermes to make men call him famous was idle as the sigh of a desert wind through the hollow ears of a skull bleaching white on the sand.

Yet he had never done greater things,—never in the long years through which he had pursued and studied art.

With the poor wage that he earned by labour he bought by degrees the tools and pigments lacking to him, and lived on the scantiest and simplest food, that he might have wherewith to render into shape and colour the imaginations of his brain.

And it was on these that the passionate, wondering, half-blinded eyes of Folle-Farine looked with awe and adoration in those lonely hours when, in his absence, she stole into his chamber, and touching nothing, scarcely daring to breathe aloud, crouched on the bare pavement mute and motionless, and afraid with a fear that was the sweetest happiness her brief youth had ever known.

Though her own kind had neglected and proscribed her, with one accord, there had been enough in the little world surrounding her to feed the imaginative senses latent in her,—enough of the old mediæval fancy, of the old ecclesiastical beauty, of the old monastic spirit, to give her a consciousness, though a dumb one, of the existence of art.

Untaught though she was, and harnessed to the dreary mill-wheel round of a hard physical toil, she yet had felt dimly the charm of the place in which she dwelt.

Where the fretted pinnacles rose in hundreds against the sky,—where the common dwellings of the poor were panelled and parquetted and carved in a thousand fashions,—where the graceful and the grotesque and the terrible were mingled in an inextricable, and yet exquisite, confusion,—where the grey squat jug that went to the well, and the jolting beam to which the clothes' line was fastened, and the creaking sign that swung above the smallest wine-shop, and the wooden gallery on which the poorest troll hung out her many-coloured rags, had all some trace of a dead art, some fashioning by a dead hand,—where all these were, it was not possible for any creature dowered by nature with any poetic instinct to remain utterly unmoved and unawakened in their midst.

Of the science and the execution of art she was still absolutely ignorant; the powers by which it was created still seemed a magic incomprehensible, and not human; but its meaning she felt with that intensity which is the truest homage of all homage to its influence.

Day after day, therefore, she returned and gazed on the three gods of forgetfulness, and on all the innumerable forms and fables which bore them company; the virgin field of her unfilled mind receiving the seeds of thought and of fancy that were scattered so largely in this solitude, lying waste, bearing no harvest.

Of these visits Arslàn himself knew nothing; towards him her bold wild temper was softened to the shyness of a doe.

She dreaded lest he should ever learn what she had done; and she stole in and out of the old granary, unseen by all, with the swiftness and the stealthiness which she shared in common with other untamed animals which, like her, shunned all man and woman kind.

And this secret—in itself so innocent, yet for which she would at times blush in her loneliness, with a cruel heat that burnt over all her face and frame—changed her life, transfigured it from its objectless, passionless, brutish dulness and monotony, into dreams and into desires.

For the first time she had in her joy and fear; for the first time she became human.

All the week through he wrought perforce by night; the great windows stood wide open to the bright cold moons of early spring; he worked only with black and white, using colour only at sunrise, or on the rare days of his leisure.

Often at nightfall she left her loft, as secretly as a fox its lair, and stole down the river, and screened herself amongst the grasses, and watched him where he laboured in the mingling light of the moon and of the oil-lamp burning behind him.

She saw these things grow from beneath his hand, these mighty shapes created by him; and he seemed to her like a god, with the power to beget worlds at his will, and all human life in its full stature out from a little dust.

The contrast of this strength, of this power which he wielded, with the helpless exhaustion of the body in which she had found him dying, smote her with a sorrow and a sweetness that were like nothing she had ever known. That a man could summon hosts at his command like this, yet perish for a crust!—that fusion of omnipotence and powerlessness, which is the saddest and the strangest of all the sad strange things of genius, awoke an absorbing emotion in her dormant heart!

She watched him thus for hours in the long nights of a slow-footed spring, in whose mists and chills and heavy dews her inured frame took no more harm than did the green corn shooting through the furrows.

She was a witness to his solitude. She saw the fancies of his brain take form. She saw the sweep of his arm call up on the blank of the wall, or on the pale spaces of the canvas, these images which for her had alike such majesty and such mystery. She saw the faces beam, the eyes smile, the dancing-women rise, the foliage uncurl, the gods come forth from the temples, the nereids glide through the moonlit waters, at his command, and beneath his touch.

She saw him also in those moments when, conceiving no eyes to be upon him, this man, whom mankind denied, loosened rein to the bitterness in him; and, standing weary and heartsick before these creations for which his generation had no sight, and no homage, let the agony of constant failure, of continual defeat, overcome him, and cursed aloud the madness which possessed him, which drove him on for ever in this ungrateful service, and would not let him do as other men did—tell the world lies, and take its payment out in gold.

Until now she had hated all things, grieved for none, unless, indeed, it were for a galled ox toiling wounded and tortured on the field; or a trapped bird, shrieking in the still midnight woods.

But now, watching him, hearing him, a passionate sorrow for a human sorrow possessed her. And to her eyes he was so beautiful in that utter unlikeness to herself and to all men whom she had seen. She gazed at him, never weary of that cold, fair, golden beauty, like the beauty of his sun-god; of those serene deep-lidded eyes, which looked so often past her at the dark night skies; of those lithe and massive limbs, like the limbs of the gladiator that yonder on the wall strained a lion to his breast in the deadly embrace of combat.

She gazed at him until she loved him with the intense passion of a young and ignorant life, into whose gloom no love had ever entered. With this love the instinct of her womanhood arose, amid the ignorance and savagery of her nature; and she crouched perpetually under the screen of the long grass to hide her vigil, and whenever his eyes looked from his easel outward to the night she drew back, breathless and trembling, she knew not why, into the deepest shadow.

Meantime, with that rude justice which was in her, she set herself atonement for her fault—the fault through which those tender little bright-throated birds were stretched dead amongst the first violets of the year.

She laboured harder and longer than ever for her taskmaster, and denied herself the larger half of even those scanty portions which were set aside for her of the daily fare, living on almost nothing, as those learn to do who are reared under the roof of the French poor. To his revilings she was silent, and under his blows patient. By night she toiled secretly, until she had restored the value of that which she had taken.

Why did she do it? She could not have told.

She was proud of the evil origin they gave her; she had a cynical gladness in her infamous repute; she scorned women and hated men; yet all the same she kept her hands pure of thefts and her lips pure of lies.

So the weeks went on till the hardness of winter gave way to the breath of the spring, and in all the wood and orchard around the water-mill of Yprès the boughs were green with buds, and the ground was pale with primroses—a spring all the sweeter and more fertile because of the severity of the past winter.

It became mid-April. It was market-day for all the country lying round that wondrous cathedral-spire, which shot into the air far-reaching and ethereal, like some fountain whose column of water had been arrested aloft and changed to ice.

The old quiet town was busy, with a rich sunshine shed upon it, in which the first yellow butterflies of the year had begun to dance.

It was high noon, and the highest tide of the market.

Flower-girls, fruit-girls, egg-sellers, poultry-hucksters, crowds of women, old and young, had jolted in on their docile asses, throned on their sheepskin saddles; and now, chattering and chaffering, drove fast their trade. On the steps of the cathedral boys with birds'-nests, knife-grinders making their little wheels fly, cobblers hammering, with boards across their knees, travelling pedlars with knapsacks full of toys and mirrors, and holy images, and strings of beads, sat side by side in amicable competition.

Here and there a priest passed, with his black robe and broad hat, like a dusky mushroom amongst a bed of many-hued gillyflowers. Here and there a soldier, all colour and glitter, showed like a gaudy red tulip in bloom amidst tufts of thyme.

The old wrinkled leathern awnings of the market

stalls glowed like copper in the brightness of noon. The red tiles of the houses edging the great square were gilded with yellow houseleeks. The little children ran hither and thither with big bunches of primroses or sheaves of blue wood-hyacinths, singing. The red and blue serges of the young girls' bodices were like the gay hues of the anemones in their baskets. The brown faces of the old dames under the white roofing of their headgear were like the russet faces of the home-kept apples which they had garnered through all the winter.

Everywhere in the shade of the flapping leather, and the darkness of the wooden porches, there were the tender blossoms of the field and forest, of the hedge and garden. The azure of the hyacinths, the pale saffron of the primroses, the cool hues of the meadow daffodils, the ruby eyes of the cultured jonquils, gleamed amongst wet rushes, grey herbs, and freshly budded leafage. Plovers' eggs nestled in moss-lined baskets; sheaves of velvet-coated wallflowers poured fragrance on the air; great plumes of lilac nodded on the wind, and amber feathers of laburnum waved above the homelier masses of mint and marjoram, and sage and chervil.

It was high noon, but the women still found leisure time to hear the music of their own tongues, loud as the clacking of mill paddles. In one corner an eager little group was gathered round the stall of a favourite flower-seller, who wore a bright crimson gown, and a string of large silver beads about her neck, and a wide linen cap, that shaded her pretty rosy face as a great snowy mushroom may grow between the sun and a little ruddy wild strawberry.

She had brown eyes that were now brimming over with tears as she stood surrounded by all the treasures of spring. She held clasped in her arms a great pot with a young almond tree growing in it, and she was weeping as though her heart would break, because a tile had fallen from a roof above and crushed low all its pink splendour of blossom.

"I saw her look at it," she muttered. "Look at it as she passed with her wicked eyes; and a black cat on the roof mewed to her; and at that moment the tile fell. Oh, my almond tree; oh, my little darling; the only one out of three I saved through the frosts; the very one that was to have gone this night to Paris."

"Thou art not alone, Edmée," groaned an old woman, tottering from her nut-stall with a heap of ruffled, bloodstained, brown plumage held up in her hand. "Look! As she went by my poor brown hen—the best sitter I have, good for eggs with every sunrise from Lent to Noel—just cackled and shook her tail at her; and at that very instant a huge yellow dog rushed in and killed the blessed bird—killed her in her basket! A great yellow beast that no one had ever seen before, and that vanished again into the earth, like lightning."

"Not worse than she did to my precious Rémy," said a tanner's wife, who drew after her, clinging to her skirts, a little lame, mis-shapen, querulous child.

"She hath the evil eye," said an old decrepit man who had served in the days of his boyhood in the Army of Italy, as he sat washing fresh lettuces in a large brass bowl, by his grandson's herb-stall.

"You remember how we met her in the fields last Feast-night of the Three Kings?" asked a youth looking up from plucking the feathers out from a living, struggling, moaning, goose. "Coming singing through the fog, like nothing earthly; and a moment later a torch caught little Jocelin's curls and burnt him till he was so hideous that his mother could scarce have known him. You remember?"

"Surely we remember," they cried in a hearty chorus round the broken almond tree. "Was there not the good old Dax this very winter killed by her if ever any creature were killed by foul means, though the law would never listen to the Flandrins when they said so?"

"And little Bernardou," added one who had not hitherto spoken. "Little Bernardou died a month after his grand-dam, in hospital. She had cast her eye on him, and the poor little lad never rallied."

"A *jettatrice* ever brings misfortune," muttered the old soldier of Napoléon, washing his last lettuce and lighting a fresh pipe.

"Or does worse," muttered the mother of the crippled child. "She is not for nothing the devil's daughter, mark you."

"Nay, indeed," said an old woman, knitting from a ball of wool with which a kitten played amongst the strewn cabbage leaves and the crushed sweet-smelling thyme. "Nay, was it not only this very winter that my son's little youngest boy threw a stone at her, just for luck, as she went by in her boat through the town; and it struck her and drew blood from her shoulder; and that self-same night a piece of the oaken carvings in the ceiling gave way and dropped upon the little angel as he slept, and broke his arm above the elbow:—she is a witch; there is no question but she is a witch."

"If I were sure so, I would think it well to kill her," murmured the youth, as he stifled the struggling bird between his knees.

"My sister met her going through the standing corn last harvest time, and the child she brought forth a week after was born blind, and is blind now," said a hard-visaged woman, washing turnips in a brass basin of water.

"I was black-and-blue for a month when she threw me down and took from me that hawk I had trapped; and she went and fastened my wrist in the iron instead," hissed a boy of twelve, in a shrill piping treble, as he slit the tongue of a quivering starling.

"They say she dances naked by moonlight in the water with imps!" cried a bright little lad who was at play with the kitten.

"She is a witch, there is no doubt about that," said again the old woman who sat knitting on the stone bench in the sun.

"And her mother such a saint!" sighed another old dame who was grouping green herbs together for salads.

And all the while the girl Edmée clasped her almond tree and sobbed over it.

"If she were only here," swore Edmée's lover, under his breath, stealing his hand where the silver beads lay, and striving his best to console her.

At that moment the accused came towards them, erect in the full light.

She had passed through the market with a load of herbs and flowers for one of the chief hostelries in the square, and was returning with the flat broad basket balanced empty on her head.

Something of their mutterings and curses reached her, but she neither hastened nor slackened her pace; she came on straightly towards them with her firm step, and her eyes flashing hard against the sun.

She gave no sign that she had heard except that the blood darkened a little in her cheeks, and her mouth shut close with a haughtier scorn. But the sight of her answering in that instant to their hate, the sight of her with the sunshine on her scarlet sash and her slender golden limbs, added impulse to their rage.

They had talked themselves into a passionate belief in her as a thing hellborn and unclean, that brought all manner of evil fates amongst them. They knew that holy water had never reached her; that a church's door had never opened to her; they had heard their children hoot her many a time unrebuked, they had always hated her with the cruelty begotten by a timid cowardice or a selfish dread. They were ripe to let their hate take shape in speech and act. The lover of Edmée loosened his hand from the silver beads about her throat, and caught up, instead, a stone.

"Let us see if her flesh feel!" he cried, and cast it.

It fell short of her, being ill-aimed; she did not slacken her speed, nor turn out of her course; she still came towards them erect and with an even tread.

"Who lamed my Rémy?" screamed the cripple's mother.

"Who broke my grandson's arm?" cackled the old woman that sat knitting.

"Who withered my peach-tree?" the old gardener hooted.

"Who freed the devil-bird and put me on the trap?" yelled the boy with the starling.

"Who flung the tile on the almond?" shouted the flower-girl's lover.

"Who made my sister bring forth a little beast, blind as a mole?" shrieked the woman, washing in the brazen bowl.

"Who is a witch—who dances naked?—who bathes with devils at the full moon?" cried the youth who had plucked the goose bare alive; and he stooped for a pebble, and aimed better than his comrade, and flung it at her as she came.

"It is a shame to see the child of Reine Flamma so

dealt with," murmured the old creature that was grouping her salads.

But her voice found no echo. The old soldier even rebuked her. "A *jettatrice* should be killed for the good of the people," he mumbled.

Meanwhile she came nearer and nearer. The last stone had struck her upon the arm; but it had drawn no blood; she walked on with firm, slow steps into their midst; unfaltering.

The courage did not touch them; they thought it only the hardihood of a thing that was devil-begotten.

She is always mute like that; she cannot feel. "Strike, strike, strike!" cried the cripple's mother; and the little cripple himself clapped his small hands and screamed his shrill laughter. The youths, obedient and nothing loth, rained their stones on her as fast as their hands could fling them. Still she neither paused nor quailed; but came on straightly, steadily, with her face set against the light.

Their impatience and their eagerness made their aim uncertain; the stones fell fast about her on every side, but one alone struck her—a jagged flint that fell where the white linen shirt opened on her chest. It cut the skin, and the blood started; the children shrieked and danced with delight: the youths rushed at her inflamed at once with her beauty and their own savage hate.

"Stone her to death! Stone her to death!" they shouted; she only laughed, and held her head erect and stood motionless where they arrested her, without the blood once paling in her face or her eyes once losing their luminous calm scorn. The little cripple clapped his hands, climbing on his mother's back to see the sight, and his mother screamed again and again above his laughter. "Strike! strike! strike!"

One of the elder lads seized her in his arms to force her on her knees while the others stoned her. The touch of him roused all the fire slumbering in her blood. She twisted herself round in his hold with a movement so rapid that it served to free her; struck him full on the eyes with her clenched hand a blow that sent him stunned and staggering back; then, swiftly as lightning flash, drew her knife from her girdle, and striking out with it right and left, dashed through the people, who scattered from her path as sheep from the spring of a hound.

Slowly and with her face turned full upon them, she backed her way across the market-place. The knife, turned blade outward, was pressed against her chest. None of them dared to follow her; they thought her invulnerable and possessed.

She moved calmly with a firm tread backward—backward—backward; holding her foes at bay; the scarlet sash on her loins flashing bright in the sun; her level brows bent as a tiger bends his ere he leaps. They watched her, huddling together frightened and silent. Even the rabid cries of the cripple's mother had ceased. On the edge of the great square she paused a moment; the knife still held at her chest, her mouth curled in contemptuous laughter.

"Strike *now!*" she cried to them; and she dropped her weapon, and stood still.

But there was not one amongst them who dared lift his hand. There was not so much as a word that answered her.

She laughed aloud, and waited for their attack, while the bell in the tower above them tolled loudly the strokes of noon. No one amongst them stirred. Even the shrill pipe of the lame boy's rejoicing had sunk, and was still.

At that moment, through the golden haze of sunbeams and of summer dust that hung above the crowd, she saw the red gleam of the soldiers of the state; and their heavy tramp echoed on the silence as they hastened to the scene of tumult. She had no faith in any justice which these would deal her; had they not once dragged her before the tribunal of their law when she had forced asunder the iron jaws of that trap in the oak wood to give freedom to the bleeding hawk that was struggling in it whilst its callow birds screamed in hunger in their nest in the branches above?

She had no faith in them; nor in any justice of men; and she turned and went down a twisting lane shaded from the sun, and ran swiftly as a doe through all its turns, and down the steps leading to the water-side. There her boat was moored; she entered it, and pulled herself slowly down the river, which now at noontide was almost deserted, whilst the shutters of the houses that edged it on either side were all closed to keep out the sun.

A boatman stretched half asleep upon the sacks in his barge; a horse dozing in his harness on the towing-path; a homeless child who had no one to call him in to shelter from the heat, and who sat and dappled his little burning feet in the flowing water; these and their like were all there were here to look on her.

She rowed herself feebly with one oar gradually out of the ways of the town; her left arm was strained, and, for the moment, useless; her shoulders throbbed with bruises; and the wound from the stone still bled. She staunched the blood by degrees, and folded the linen over it, and went on; she was so used to pain, and so strong, that this seemed to her to be but little. She had passed through similar scenes before, though the people had rarely broken into such open violence towards her, except that winter's day in the hut of Manon Dax.

The heat was great, though the season was but mid-April.

The sky was cloudless; the air without a breeze. The white blossoms of peach-trees bloomed between the old brown walls of the wooden houses. In the galleries, between the heads of saints and the faces of fauns, there were tufts of home-bred lilies of the valley and thick flowering bushes of golden genista. The smell of mignonette was sweet upon the languid breeze, and here and there, from out the darkness of some open casement, some stove-forced crimson or purple azalea shrub glowed: for the people's merchandise was flowers, and all the silent water-streets were made lovely and fragrant by their fair abundance.

The tide of the river was flowing in, the stream was swelling over all the black piles, and the broad smooth strips of sand that were visible at low water; it floated her boat inward with it without trouble, past the last houses of the town, past the budding orchards and grey stone walls of the outskirts, past the meadows and the cornfields and the poplars of the open country. A certain faintness had stolen on her with the gliding of the vessel and the dizzy movement of the water; pain and the loss of blood filled her limbs with an unfamiliar weakness; she felt giddy, and half blind, and almost powerless to guide her course.

When she had reached the old granary where it stood amongst the waterdocks and rushes, she checked the boat almost unconsciously, and let it drift in amidst the reeds and lie there. Then she pulled herself feebly up through the shallow pools, and across the stone sill of the casement, into the chamber where she had learned to live a life that was utterly apart from the actual existence to which chance had doomed her.

It was the height of noon; at such an hour the creator of these things she loved was always absent at the toil which brought him his daily bread; she knew that he never returned until the evening, never painted except at earliest dawn.

The place was her own in the freedom of solitude; all these shapes and shadows in which imagination and tradition had taken visible shape were free to her; she had grown to love them with a great passion, to seek them as consolers and as friends.

She crept into the room; its coolness, its calm, its dimmed refreshing light seemed like balm after the noise of the busy market-place and the glare of the cloudless sunshine. A sick sense of fatigue and of feebleness had assailed her more strongly. She dropped down in the gloom of the place on the broad, cold flags of the floor, in the deepest shadow, where the light from without did not reach, and beneath the cartoon of the Gods of Oblivion.

Of all the forms with which he had peopled its loneliness, these had the most profound influence on her in their fair, passionless, majestic beauty, in which it seemed to her that the man who had begotten them had repeated his own likeness. For they were all alike, yet unlike; of the same form and feature, yet different even in their strong resemblance, like elder and younger brethren who hold a close companionship. For Hypnos was still but a boy with his blue-veined eyelids closed, and his mouth rosy and parted like that of a slumbering child, and above his golden head a star rose in the purple night. Oneiros standing next was a youth whose eyes smiled as though they beheld visions that were welcome to him; in his hand, amongst the white roses, he held a black wand of sorcery, and around his bended head there hovered a dim silvery nimbus. Thanatos alone was a man fully grown; and on his calm and colourless face there were blended an unutterable sadness, and an unspeakable peace; his eyes were fathomless, far-reaching, heavy laden with thought, as though they had seen at once the heights of heaven and the depths of hell; and he, having thus seen, and knowing all things, had learned that there was but one good possible in all the universe,—that one gift which his touch gave, and which men in their blindness shuddered from and cursed. And above him and around him there was a great darkness.

So the gods stood, and so they spoke, even to her; they seemed to her as brethren, masters, friends—these three immortals who looked down on her in their mute majesty.

They are the gods of the poor, of the wretched, of the outcast, of the proscribed,—they are the gods who respect not persons nor palaces,—who stay with the exile and flee from the king,—who leave the tyrant of a world to writhe in torment, and call a smile beautiful as the morning on the face of a beggar child,—who turn from the purple beds where wealth and lust and brutal power lie, and fill with purest visions the darkest hours of the loneliest nights, for genius and youth,—they are the gods of consolation and of compensation,—the gods of the exile, of the orphan, of the outcast, of the poet, of the prophet, of all whose bodies ache with the infinite pangs of famine, and whose hearts ache with the infinite woes of the world, of all who hunger with the body or the soul.

And looking at them, she seemed to know them as

her only friends,—as the only rulers who ever could loose the bands of her fate and lead her forth to freedom—Sleep, and Dreams, and Death.

They were above her where she sank upon the stone floor; the shadows were dark upon the ground; but the sun rays striking through the distant window against the opposite wall fell across the head of the boy Hypnos, and played before his silver sandalled feet.

She sat gazing at him, forgetful of her woe, her task, the populace that had hooted her abroad, the stripes that awaited her at home. The answering gaze of the god magnetised her; the poetic virus which had stirred dumbly in her from her birth awoke in her bewildered brain. Without knowing what she wanted, she longed for freedom, for light, for passion, for peace, for love.

Shadowy fancies passed over her in a tumultuous pageantry; the higher instincts of her nature rose and struggled to burst the bonds in which slavery and ignorance and brutish toil had bound them; she knew nothing, knew no more than the grass knew that blew in the wind, than the passion-flower knew that slept unborn in the uncurled leaf; and yet withal she felt, saw, trembled, imagined, and desired, all mutely, all blindly, all in confusion and in pain.

For the second time the weakness of tears rushed into her fearless eyes, which had never quailed before the fury of any living thing; her head fell on her chest; she wept bitterly,—not because the people had injured her,—not because her wounded flesh ached and her limbs were sore,—but because a distance so immeasurable, so unalterable, severed her from all of which these gods told her without speech.

The sun-rays still shone on the bright head of Hypnos, whilst the stones on which she sat, and her own form, were dark in shadow; as though the bright boy pitied her, as though he, the world's consoler, had compassion for this thing so lonely and accursed of her kind, the dumb violence of her weeping brought its own exhaustion with it.

The drowsy heat of noon, pain, weariness, the faintness of fasting, the fatigue of conflict, the dreamy influences of the place, had their weight on her. Crouching there half on her knees, looking up ever in the faces of the three Immortals, the gift of Hypnos descended upon her and stilled her; its languor stole through her veins; its gentle pressure closed her eyelids; gradually her rigid limbs and her bent body relaxed and unnerved; she sank forward, her head lying on her outstretched arms, and the stillness of a profound sleep encompassed her.

And Oneiros added his gift also; and a throng of dim, delirious dreams floated through her brain, and peopled her slumber with fairer things than the earth holds, and made her mouth smile while yet her lids were wet.

Thanatos alone gave nothing, but looked down on her with his dark, sad eyes, and held his finger on his close-pressed lips, as though he said:—"Not yet."

CHAPTER II.

HER sleep remained unbroken; there was no sound to disturb it. The caw of a ˙rook in the top of the poplar-tree, the rushing babble of the water, the cry of a field-mouse caught amongst the rushes by an otter, the far-off jingle of mules' bells from the great southern road that ran broad and white beyond the meadows, the gnawing of the rats in the network of timbers which formed the vaulted roof, these were all the noises that reached this solitary place, and these were both too faint and too familiar to awaken her.

Heat and pain made her slumber heavy, and the forms on which her waking eyes had gazed made her sleep full of dreams. Hour after hour went by; the shadows lengthened, the day advanced: nothing came to rouse her. At length the vesper bell rang over the pastures and the peals of the Ave Maria from the cathedral in the town were audible in the intense stillness that reigned around.

As the chimes died, Arslàn crossed the threshold of the granary and entered the desolate place where he had made his home. For once his labour had been early completed, and he had hastened to employ the rare and precious moments of the remaining light.

He had almost stepped upon her ere he saw her, lying beneath his cartoons of the sons of Nyx. He paused and looked down.

Her attitude had slightly changed, and had in it all the abandonment of youth and of sleep; her face was turned upward, with quick silent breathings parting the lips; her bare feet were lightly crossed; the linen of her loose tunic was open at the throat, and had fallen back from her right arm and shoulder; the whole supple grace and force that were mingled in her form were visible under the light folds of her simple garments. The sun still lingered on the bright bowed head of Hypnos, but all light had died from off the stone floor where she was stretched.

As she had once looked on himself, so he now looked on her.

But in him there arose little curiosity and still less pity; he recognised her as the girl whom, with a face of old Egypt, he had seen rowing her boat-load of corn down the river, and whom he had noticed for her strange unlikeness to all around her.

He supposed that mere curiosity had brought her there, and sleep overtaken her in the drowsiness of the first heat of the budding year.

He did not seek to rouse her, nor to spare her any shame or pain which, at her waking, she might feel. He merely saw in her a barbaric and yet beautiful creature; and his only desire was to use the strange charms in her for his art.

A smooth-planed panel stood on an easel near; turning it where best the light fell, he began to sketch her attitude rapidly, in black and white. It was quickly done by a hand so long accustomed to make such transcripts; and he soon went further, to that richer portraiture which colour alone can accomplish. The stone pavement; the brown and slender limbs; the breadth of scarlet given by the sash about her loins; the upturned face, whose bloom was as brilliant as that of a red carnation blooming in the twilight of some old wooden gallery; the eyelids, tear-laden still; the mouth that smiled and sighed in dreaming; on the wall above, the radiant figure of the young god which remained in full sunlight whilst all beneath was dark;—these gave a picture which required no correction from knowledge, no addition from art.

He worked on for more than an hour, until the wood began to beam with something of the hues of flesh and blood, and the whole head was thrown out in colour, although the body and the limbs still remained in their mere outline.

Once or twice she moved restlessly, and muttered a little, dully, as though the perpetual unsparing gaze bent on her with a scrutiny so cold, and yet so searching, disturbed or magnetised her even in her sleep. But she never awakened, and he had time to study and to trace out every curve and line of the half-developed loveliness before him with as little pity, with as cruel an exactitude, as that with which the vivisector tears asunder the living animal whose sinews he severs, or the botanist plucks to pieces the new-born flower whose structure he desires to examine.

The most beautiful women, who had bared their charms that he might see them live again upon his canvas, had seldom had power to make his hand tremble a moment in such translation. To the surgeon all sex is dead, all charm is gone from the female corpse that his knife ravages in search of the secrets of science; and to Arslàn the women whom he modelled and pourtrayed were nearly as sexless, nearly as powerless to create passion or emotion. They were the tools for his art: no more.

When, in the isolation of the long northern winters, he had sat beside the pine-wood that blazed on his hearth while the wolves howled down the deserted village street, and the snow drifted up and blocked from sight the last pane of the lattice and the last glimpse of the outer world, he had been more enamoured of the visions that visited him in that solitude than he had ever been since of the living creatures whose beauty he had recorded in his works.

He had little passion in him, or passion was dormant; and he had sought women, even in the hours of love, with coldness and with something of contempt for that licence which, in the days of his comparative affluence, he had not denied himself. He thought always—

>"De ces baisers puissants comme un dictame,
>De ces transports plus vifs que des rayons,
>Que reste-t-il ? C'est affreux, ô mon âme !
>Rien qu'un dessin fort pâle aux trois crayons."

And for those glowing colours of passion which burned so hotly for an instant, only so soon to fade out into the pallor of indifference or satiety, he had a contempt which almost took the place and the semblance of chastity.

He worked on and on, studying the sleeper at his feet, with the passionless keenness of a science that was as merciless in its way as the science which tortures and slaughters in order to penetrate the mysteries of sentient existence.

She was beautiful in her way, this dark strange foreign child, who looked as though her native home must have been where the Nile lily blooms, and the black brows of the Sphinx are bent against the sun.

She was beautiful, like a young leopard, like a young python, coiled there, lightly breathing, and mute and motionless and unconscious. He painted her as he would have painted the leopard or python lying asleep in the heavy hush of a noon in the tropics. And she was no more to him than these would have been.

The shadows grew longer; the sunlight died off the bright head of the boy Hypnos; the feathery reeds on the bank without got a red flush from the west; there came a sudden burst of song from a boat-load of children going home from the meadows where they had gathered the first cowslips of the season in great sheaves that sent their sweetness on the air through the open window as they went by beneath the walls.

The shouts of the joyous singing rang shrilly through the silence; they pierced her ear and startled her from her slumber; she sprang up suddenly, with a bound like a hart that scents the hounds, and stood fronting him; her eyes opened wide, her breath panting, her nerves strained to listen and striving to combat.

In the first bewildered instant of her awakening she thought that she was still in the market-place of the town, and that the shouts were from the clamour of her late tormentors.

He turned and looked at her.

"What do you fear?" he asked her, in the tongue of the country.

She started afresh at the sound of his voice, and drew her disordered dress together, and stood mute, with her hands crossed on her bosom, and the blood coming and going under her transparent skin.

"What do you fear?" he asked again.

"*I* fear?"

She echoed the cowardly word with a half-tremulous defiance; the heroism of her nature, which an hour earlier had been lashed to its fullest strength, cast back the question as an insult; but her voice was low and husky, and the blood dyed her face scarlet as she spoke. For she feared him; and for the moment she had forgotten how she had come there and all that had passed, except that some instinct of the long-hunted animal was astir in her to hide herself and fly.

But he stood between her and the passage outward, and pride and shame held her motionless. Moreover, she still listened intently: the confused voices of the children still seemed to her like those of the multitude by whom she had been chased; and she was ready to leap tiger-like upon them, rather than let them degrade her in his sight.

He looked at her with some touch of interest: she was to him only some stray beggar girl, who had trespassed into his solitude; yet there was that in her untamed regard, in her wide-open eyes, in the stag-like grace of her attitude, in the sullen strength which spoke in her reply, that warmed him to closer notice of all these.

"Why are you in this place?" he asked her, slowly. "You were asleep here when I came, more than an hour ago."

The colour burned in her face: she said nothing.

The singing of the children was waxing fainter, as the boat floated from beneath the wall on its homeward way into the town. She ceased to fancy these cries the cries of her foes, and recollection began to revive in her.

"Why did you come?" he repeated, musing how he should persuade her to return to the attitude sketched out upon his easel.

She returned his look with the bold truthfulness natural to her, joined with that apprehensiveness of chastisement which becomes second nature to every creature that is for ever censured, cursed, and beaten for every real or imagined fault.

"I came to see *those*," she answered him, with a

backward movement of her hand, which had a sort of reverence in it, up to the forms of the gods above her. The answer moved him; he had not thought to find a feeling so high as this in this ragged, lonely, sunburnt child; and, to the man for whom, throughout a youth of ambition and of disappointment, the world had never found the voice of favour, even so much appreciation as lay in this outcast's homage had its certain sweetness. For a man may be negligent of all sympathy for himself, yet never, if he be poet or artist, will he be able utterly to teach himself indifference to all sympathy for his works.

"Those!" he echoed, in surprise. "What can they be to *you?*"

She coloured at the unconcealed contempt that lay in his last word; her head drooped; she knew that they were much to her—friends, masters, teachers divine and full of pity. But she had no language in which to tell him this; and if she could have told him, she would have been ashamed. Also, the remembrance of those benefits to him, of which he was ignorant, had now come to her through the bewilderment of her thoughts, and it locked her lips to silence.

Her eyes dropped under his; the strange love she bore him made her blind and giddy and afraid; she moved restlessly, glaring round with the half-timid, half-fierce glances of a wild animal that desires to escape and cannot.

Watching her more closely, he noticed for the first time the stains of blood upon her shoulder, and the bruise on her chest, where the rent in her linen left it bare.

"You have been hurt?" he asked her, "or wounded?"

She shook her head.

"It is nothing."

"Nothing? You have fallen or been ill treated, surely?"

"The people struck me."

"Struck you? With what?"

"Stones."

"And why?"

"I am Folle-Farine."

She answered him with the quiet calm of one who offers an all-sufficient reply.

But the reply to him told nothing: he had been too shunned by the populace, who dreaded the evil genius which they attributed to him, to have been told by them of their fancies and their follies; and he had never essayed to engage either their companionship or their confidence. To be left to work, or to die, in solitude undisturbed was the uttermost that he had ever asked of any strange people amidst whom he had dwelt.

"Because you are Folle-Farine?" he repeated. "Is that a reason to hate you?"

She gave a gesture of assent.

"And you hate them in return?"

She paused a moment, glancing still hither and thither all round, as a trapped bird glances, seeking his way outward.

"I think so," she muttered; "and yet—I have had their little children in my reach many a time by the water when the woods were all quiet, and I have never killed one yet."

He looked at her more earnestly than he had done before. The repressed passion that glanced under her straight dusky brows, the unspoken scorn which curled on her mouth, the nervous meaning with which her hands clenched on the folds of linen on her breast, attracted him; there was a force in them all which aroused his attention. There were in her that conscious power for ferocity, and that contemptuous abstinence from its exercise, which lie so often in the fathomless regard of the lion; he moved nearer to her, and addressed her more gently.

"Who are you?" he asked, "and why have these people such savage violence against you?"

"I am Folle-Farine," she answered him again, unable to add anything else.

"Have you no other name?"

"No."

"But you must have a home? You live—where?"

"At the mill with Flamma."

"Does he also ill-use you?"

"He beats me."

"When you do wrong?"

She was silent.

"Wrong?" "Right?"

They were but words to her—empty and meaningless. She knew that he beat her more often because she told truth or refused to cheat. For aught that she was sure of, she might be wrong, and he right.

Arslàn looked at her musingly. All the thought he had was to induce her to return to the attitude necessary to the completion of his picture.

He put a few more questions to her; but the replies told him little. At all times silent, before him a thousand emotions held her dumb. She was afraid, besides, that at every word he might suspect the debt he owed to her, and she dreaded its avowal with as passionate a fear as though, in lieu of the highest sacrifice and service, her action had been some crime against him. She felt ashamed of it, as of some unholy thing: it seemed to her impious to have dared to give him back a life that he had wearied of, and might have wished to lose.

"He must never know: he must never know," she said to herself.

She had never imagined what fear meant until she had looked on this man's face. Now she dreaded, with an apprehension which made her start like a criminal at every sound, lest he should ever know of this gift of life which, unbidden, she had restored to him: which, being thus given, her instinct told her he would only take as the burden of an intolerable debt, of an unmeasurable shame.

Perfect love casts out fear, runs the tradition: rather, surely, does the perfect love of a woman break the courage which no other thing could ever daunt, and set foot on the neck that no other yoke would ever touch.

By slow degrees he got from her such fragments of her obscure story as she knew. That this child, so friendless, ill-treated, and abandoned, had been the saviour of his own existence, he never dreamed. A creature beaten and half starved herself could not, for an instant, look to him one likely to have possessed even such humble gifts as food and fuel.

Besides, his thoughts were less with her than with the interrupted study on his easel, and his one desire was to induce her to endure the same watch upon her, waking, which had had power to disturb her even in her unconsciousness. She was nothing to him, save a thing that he wished to turn to the purpose of his art—like a flower that he plucked on his way through the fields, for the sake of its colour, to fill in some vacant nook in a mountain foreground.

"You have come often here?" he asked her, whilst she stood before him, flushing and growing pale, irresolute and embarrassed, with her hands nervously gathering the folds of her dress across her chest, and her sad, lustrous, troubled eyes glancing from side to side in a bewildered fear.

"Often," she muttered. "You will not beat me for it? I did no harm."

"Beat you? Amongst what brutes have you lived? Tell me, why did you care to come?"

Her face drooped.

"They are beautiful, and they speak to me," she murmured, with a pathetic, apologetic timidity in her voice.

He laughed a little; bitterly.

"Do they? They have few auditors. But you are beautiful, too, in your way. Has no one ever told you so?"

"I?"

She glanced at him half-wistfully, half-despairingly; she thought that he spoke in derision of her.

"You," he answered. "Why not? Look at yourself here: all imperfect as it is, you can see something of what you are."

Her eyes fell for the first time on the broad confused waves of dull colour, out of whose depths her own face arose, like some fair drowned thing tossed upward on a murky sea. She started with a cry as if he had wounded her, and stood still trembling.

She had looked at her own limbs floating in the opaque water of the bathing pool, with a certain sense of their beauty wakening in her; she had tossed the soft, thick, gold-flecked darkness of her hair over her bare shoulder, with a certain languor and delight; she had held a knot of poppies against her breast, to see their hues contrast with her own white skin;—but she had never imagined that she had beauty.

He watched her, letting the vain passion he thus taught her creep with all its poison into her veins.

He had seen such wonder and such awed delight before in Nubian girls with limbs of bronze and eyes of night, who had never thought that they had loveliness—though they had seen their forms in the clear water of the wells every time that they had brought their pitchers thither, and who had only awakened to that sweet supreme sense of power, and of possession when first they had beheld themselves live again upon his canvas.

"You are glad?" he asked her at length.

She covered her face with her hands.

"I am frightened!"

Frightened she knew not why, and utterly ashamed to have lain thus in his sight, to have slept thus under his eyes, yet filled with ecstasy, to think that she was lovely enough to him to be raised amidst those marvellous dreams which peopled and made heaven of his solitude.

"Well then—let me paint you there," he said, after a pause. "I am too poor to offer you reward for it. I have nothing——"

"I want nothing," she interrupted him, quickly, while a dark shadow, half-wrath, half-sorrow, swept across her face.

He smiled a little.

"I cannot boast the same. But, since you care for all these hapless things that are imprisoned here, do me, their painter, this one grace. Lie there, in the shadow again, as you were when you slept, and let me go on with this study of you till the sun sets."

A glory beamed over all her face. Her mouth trembled, her whole frame shook like a reed in the wind.

"If you care!" she said, brokenly, and paused. It seemed to her impossible that this form of hers, which had been only deemed fit for the whip, for the rope, for the shower of stones, could have any grace or excellence in his sight; it seemed to her impossible that this face of hers, which nothing had ever kissed except the rough tongue of some honest dog, and which had been blown on by every stormwind, beaten on by every summer sun, could have colour, or shape, or aspect that could ever please him!

"Certainly I care. Go yonder and lie as you were lying a few moments ago—there in the shadow, under these gods."

She was used to give obedience—the dumb unquestioning obedience of the pack-horse or the sheep-dog, and she had no idea for an instant of refusal. It was a great terror to her to hear his voice and feel his eyes on her, and be so near to him; yet it was equally a joy sweeter and deeper than she had ever dreamed of as possible. He still seemed to her like a god, this man under whose hand flowers bloomed, and sun-rays smiled, and waters flowed, and human forms arose, and the gracious shapes of a thousand dreams grew into substance. And yet, in herself, this man saw beauty!

He motioned her with a careless, gentle gesture, as one motions a timid dog, to the spot over which the three brethren watched hand in hand; and she stretched herself down passively and humbly, meekly as the dog stretches himself to rest at his master's command. Over all her body the blood was leaping; her limbs shuddered; her breath came and went in broken murmurs; her bright-hued skin grew dark and white by turns; she was filled with a passionate delight that he had found anything in her to desire or deem fair; and she quivered with a tumultuous fear that made her nervous as any panting hare. Her heart beat as it had never done when the people had raged in their fury around her.

One living creature had found beauty in her; one human voice had spoken to her gently and without a curse; one man had thought her a thing to be entreated and not scorned;—a change so marvellous in her fate transfigured all the world for her, as though the gods above had touched her lips with fire. But she was mute and motionless; the habit of silence and of repression had become her second nature: no statue of marble could have been stiller, or in semblance more lifeless, than she was where she rested on the stones. Arslàn noticed nothing of this; he was intent upon his work. The sun was very near its setting, and every second of its light was precious to him. The world indeed he knew would in all likelihood never be the wiser or the richer for anything he did; in all likelihood he knew all these things that he created were destined to moulder away undisturbed save by the rats that might gnaw, and the newts that might traverse, them. He was buried here in the grave of a hopeless penury, of an endless oblivion. They were buried with him; and the world wanted neither him nor them.

Still, having the madness of genius, he was as much the slave of his art as though an universal fame had waited his lowliest and lightest effort.

With a deep breath that had half a sigh in it he threw down his brushes when the darkness fell. While he wrought, he forgot the abject bitterness of his life; when he ceased work, he remembered how hateful a thing it is to live when life means only deprivation, obscurity, and failure.

He thanked her with a few words of gratitude to her for her patience, and released her from the strain of the attitude.

She rose slowly with an odd dazzled look upon her face, like one coming out of great darkness into the full blaze of day. Her eyes sought the portrait of her own form, which was still hazy and unformed, amidst a mist of varying hues: that she should be elected to have a part with those glorious things which were the companions of his loneliness seemed to her a wonder so strange and so immeasurable that her mind still could not grasp it.

For it was greatness to her: a greatness absolute and incredible. The men had stoned, the women cursed, the children hooted her; but he selected her—and her alone—for that supreme honour which his hand could give.

Not noticing the look upon her face he placed before her on the rude bench, which served in that place for a table, some score of small studies in colour, trifles brilliant as the rainbow, birds, flowers, insects, a leaf of fern, an orchid in full bloom, a nest with a blue warbler in it, a few peasants by a wayside cross, a child at a well, a mule laden with autumn fruit—anything which in the district had caught his sight or stirred his fancy.

He bade her choose from them.

"There is nothing else here," he added. "But since you care for such things, take as many of them as you will as recompense."

Her face flushed up to the fringes of her hair; her eyes looked at the sketches in longing. Except the scarlet scarf of Marcellin, this was the only gift she had ever had offered her. And all these reproductions of the world around her were to her like so much sorcery. Owning one, she would have worshipped it, revered it, caressed it, treasured it; her life was so desolate and barren that such a gift seemed to her as handsfull of gold and silver would seem to a beggar were he bidden to take them and be rich.

She stretched her arms out in one quick longing gesture; then as suddenly withdrew them, folding them on her chest, whilst her face grew very pale. Something of its old dark proud ferocity gathered on it.

"I want no payment," she said, huskily, and she turned to the threshold and crossed it.

He stayed her with his hand.

"Wait. I did not mean to hurt you. Will you not take them as reward?"

"No."

She spoke almost suddenly; there was a certain sharpness and dullness of disappointment at her heart. She wanted, she wished, she knew not what. But not that he should offer her payment.

"Can you return to-morrow? or any other day?" he asked her, thinking of the sketch unfinished on the sheet of pinewood. He did not notice the beating of her heart under her folded arms, the quick gasp of her breath, the change of the rich colour in her face.

"If you wish," she answered him below her breath.

"I do wish, surely. The sketch is all unfinished yet."

"I will come then."

She moved away from him across the threshold as she spoke; she was not afraid of the people, but she was afraid of this strange, passionate sweetness, which seemed to fill her veins with fire and make her drunk and blind.

"Shall I go with you homeward?"

She shook her head.

"But the people who struck you?—they may attack you again?"

She laughed a little; low in her throat.

"I showed them a knife!—they are timid as hares."

"You are always by yourself?"

"Always."

She drew herself with a rapid movement from him and sprang into her boat where it rocked amidst the rushes against the steps; in another instant she had thrust it from its entanglement in the reeds, and pulled with swift, steady strokes down the stream into the falling shadows of the night.

"You will come back?" he called to her, as the first stroke parted the water.

"Yes," she answered him; and the boat shot forward into the shadow.

Night was near and the darkness soon enclosed it; the beat of the oars sounding faintly through the silence of the evening.

There was little need to exact the promise from her.

Like Persephone she had eaten of the fatal pomegranate seed, which, whether she would or no, would make her leave the innocence of youth, and the light of the sun and the blossoms of the glad green spring-time world, and draw her footsteps backward and downward to that hell which none,—once having entered it,—can ever more forsake.

She had drifted away from him into the shadows of evening as they died from the shore and the stream into the gloom of the night.

He thought no more of pursuing her than he thought of chasing the melted shadows.

Returning to his chamber he looked for some minutes

at the panel where it leaned against the wall, catching the first pallid moon-gleam of the night.

"If she should not come, it will be of little moment," he thought. "I have nearly enough for remembrance there."

And he went away from the painting, and took up charcoal and turned to those anatomical studies whose severity he never spared himself, and for whose perfecting he pursued the science of form even in the bodies of the dead.

From the moment that his hand touched the stylus he forgot her; for she was no more to him than a chance bird that he might have taken from its home amongst the ripe red autumn foliage and caged for a while to study its grace and colour, its longing eye and drooping wing; and then tossed up into the air again, when he had done with it, to find its way to freedom, or to fall into the fowler's snare;—what matter which?

END OF VOL. I.

PRINTING OFFICE OF THE PUBLISHER.

451,984

www.ingramcontent.com/pod-product-compliance
Lightning Source LLC
Chambersburg PA
CBHW030013240426
43672CB00007B/936